**LONDON BOROUGH OF ENFIELD**

**LIBRARY SERVICES**

This item should be RETURNED on or before the latest date stamped. You may obtain a renewal by personal call, telephone or post. You should quote the date due for return, the bar code number and your personal library number. Overdue items will incur charges.

# CHILDREN'S CLOTHES
1939-1970

# CHILDREN'S CLOTHES 1939-1970

## THE ADVENT OF FASHION

ALICE GUPPY

*Published in collaboration with*
THE PASOLD RESEARCH FUND LTD.

BLANDFORD PRESS
Poole Dorset

First published 1978

Blandford Press Ltd, Link House, West Street
Poole, Dorset BH15 1LL

ISBN 0 7137 0896 4

Printed in Great Britain by Biddles Ltd, Guildford, Surrey
Colour by Colourcraftsmen, Chelmsford

# Contents

# Illustrations

SKETCHES: WENDY MARTIN

# Acknowledgements

My grateful thanks are due to the following for their assistance: Beau Brummel Ltd., Cook & Pawsons, Department of Prices & Consumer Protection, Tom Etridge, Home Office, E. Jackson & Sons Ltd., Johnson & Barnes Ltd., Judy Children's Wear Ltd., Junior Age, Kinch & Lack Ltd., John Lewis Partnership, Lewis's Ltd., Lilley & Skinner, Meridian Ltd., National Children's Wear Association, Rowes of Bond Street Ltd., John Shannon & Son Ltd., Simple Garments Ltd.; and to Miss G. R. Mersh, my assistant at *Junior Age*, without whose generous help this book could never have been written.

I would especially like to place on record my gratitude to Eric W. Pasold, O.B.E., for his friendship extending over many years and his always deep interest in my work and the benefits his great abilities bestowed on the children's wear industry.

I am greatly indebted to The Pasold Research Fund Ltd. for making possible this account of the developments in children's clothing and especially to its Director, Ken Ponting, for his ever-ready help and encouragement in the preparation of this volume.

A.G.

This is an account of how children's clothing in Britain moved out of its private world into the realms of high-fashion. The momentous years were from 1939-1970, an era that witnessed the slow release from the stranglehold of 'not suitable' as the criterion for children's garments to the untrammelled brilliance of the New Young Designers; that forced the quiet trade to fight the authorities for fair shares for the youngsters during the war and battle through the criticism of the post-war years to emerge finally as international style setter; that saw the death of class-distinction in children's clothing.

# CHAPTER 1
# Post-war: the Conservative Years

In the 1930s clothing for children in Britain had settled firmly into a pattern of restraint and simplicity which conformed to rules that few dared to defy. Garments were practical in design, showed little regard for the whims of the world of adult fashion, shunned anything which savoured of 'sophistication'—that word of the times for the unconventional and ultra daring—and were conservative in the extreme. It was a static era in the history of children's clothing brought about by public opinion strongly supported by the garment manufacturers and distributors. To say that a children's styling had emerged is to put too fine a point on what was the result of a gradual paring down of irrelevant fashion details until little more than a basic shape remained yet that simplicity in itself created a characteristic form of its own. It encompassed the essentials—cloth, make, handwork, provision for letting down, protection against the elements and wrapped the children, boys and girls alike, in a cocoon which insulated them against the turbulent, often controversial, fashion scene. Happiness, not fashion, was the main theme for promoting children's clothing, the happiness wearing the garments would bring to the children and, by inference, the parents. Hard-wearing qualities came next, but fashion appeal as such was absent.

This situation had come about because of the strong forces which had influenced the clothing of children in the 20th century: in common with adults there had been a swing away from the heavy fussiness of the Victorian and Edwardian times. Women were being emancipated and had less and less time (and inclination) to spend in the home on making, laundering and caring for their children's clothes; non-repression became the slogan for rearing children and that meant, too, their clothes must permit complete freedom of movement and in no way restrict their correct development and side by side with, and because of some of, these factors mass-production had surged forward until it embraced every facet of children's clothing. There were still some things which mothers preferred to make themselves, baby garments for the first-born, particularly, jumpers and jerseys, socks, but once it was no longer a sign of a lazy mother for her children to wear 'bought' clothes then even most of the first baby's layette came from a shop.

In pre-war Britain whilst it was understood that little girls should have pretty, dainty garments, it was also agreed that these should not call too much attention to the wearer by reason of colour or shape. It was not only the parents who held this belief, the children, too, subscribed to it for at that period they wanted nothing better than to conform to the rest of their mini-society. Those parents who did stray from the path of the currently correct pattern or colour, and there were always some who did so wishing either to call attention to their own distinctive tastes or their own distinctive children, or both, caused many a heartache when their sons and daughter were seen to be markedly different from the rest of the crowd. For a boy in the 30s it was disastrous.

The pros and cons of school uniforms will be dealt with in a later chapter but they had at least one great merit from the children's point of view, they prevented parents who could afford it from indulging in any of their own peculiar ideas about the way their sons and daughters should be dressed during school hours. The parents' scope outside school was wide for even up to 18 years they had the last word in clothing purchases.

There was complete acceptance that only a modicum of current fashion should filter through to girls' and boys' wear, and then only after a decent interval. It took up to three years for extreme changes or new types of garments to percolate through to the children. The slow rate at which youngsters followed fashion was evidenced by the fact that buyers in the big stores could bring forward their stock for a second year and only reduce it, if necessary, in the sales in the third year. To later generations when a women's boutique owner could claim a turnover of a day-and-a-half for a new line or it was dead stock this would seem stagnation of the dullest unrewarding kind and so in many ways it was. The divorcing of children's wear from the frivolous atmosphere of fashion was perhaps carried too far then, and for some years to come, either because of prejudice or honest conviction that the height of achievement ought to be to make the child look 'nice'. Yet the truth remains that where high-fashion is copied for children's garments the effect is often not cute but vulgar. Is this because the real objective of adult fashion is sexual attraction and in a child's clothing it is seen to be at odds with the innocence of the wearer?

So in the late 30s children's clothing existed in its own little circle affected only remotely and belatedly by grown-up fads. Choice of materials, colours and styling was restricted by taboos which were closely observed in a manner which gave them the aspect of long tradition although this was not so.

The first results of the theory that boys and girls should be left entirely free to develop without parental discipline did not seem to be entirely happy for either parents or children: then came the second world war and pushed such ideas into the background to be revived as the permissive society evolved.

The conventions which had grown up around children's clothing were of comparatively recent origin and stemmed largely from the time when mass-production of girls' as well as boys' garments was established on a nation-wide scale. This was only after the 1914-18 war for hitherto the German industry had been the most important supplier of ready-made outer garments for girls, with Austria providing the exclusive knitted dresses and suits which were distinguished by their good design and finish. When these sources were cut off Britain had to develop its own factories and small manufacturing units making girls' wear sprang up to reinforce home dressmaking and knitting, the workrooms of the drapery shops and the machine-made knitted under and outerwear.

By far the greatest proportion of this production, both knitted and woven, was distributed through the great wholesale houses and it was the buyers for these powerful outlets together with those of the retail stores and shops who between them became the arbiters of fashion so far as children's wear was concerned and were largely responsible for the unwritten laws which all observed. Of the remaining production which was largely in the hands of one-man businesses who dealt direct with the retail it was very much the store buyer who dictated what should be made. In the women's trade the manufacturer showed his collection and the models were ordered or rejected according to their sales potential in the opinion of the buyer. With children's garments, however, the buyer would more often than not agree to place orders for certain numbers only if this or that (e.g. collar, cuffs, belt) were slightly altered. Indeed some of the prima donnas would have thought they had failed in their duty if they did not suggest improvements of this kind which would distinguish their stock from their competitors. The theory was, of course, that they had such an expert knowledge that they knew exactly what would sell but it will be seen that this could also be a way of indulging personal prejudices which then filtered through to the mass-producers. It was not only the desire to create an impression that prompted those responsible for changing the manufacturers' proferred designs. Most of the firms dealing direct with the retailer were small and the designing was almost wholly in the hands of the owner of the business, helped by his wife and supported by a faithful and knowledgeable sample hand. Only a few had a full-time designer or even considered that one was necessary so that although it was a nuisance that their samples might be regarded as in need of change and necessitated specials going through the factory it was not only accepted as customary but helpful for future collections.

Those who exerted the greatest influence on the direction which children's clothing would take were the buyers for the big wholesale houses. Practically the whole of the production on the cheaper end was distributed through the wholesale but many of the companies, particularly those specialising in, or having strong children's wear departments, had a wide price range and carried top quality garments. It was estimated at that time, and for some years after 1945, that 90 per cent of baby clothing was sold through the wholesaler and it is an extraordinary fact that it was nearly all bought by men: women buyers for any children's age group were in the minority. The managing director of one group, questioned in the 60s about the absence of women buyers in his company replied, apparently oblivious to its significance, '*We did have a woman once buying children's knitwear: she was very good but when she retired we replaced her with two men'*. There were some women whose obvious capabilities could not be ignored: one whose power was enormous because of the size of her orders kept her hat on at work to show she was a 'lady'.

The men were good at their job, despite the fact that they were dealing in anything from bibs and binders to party cloaks, were able to assess the quality of woven fabrics and the wool or cotton content of knitwear, but styling came a very poor second to getting merchandise at the right price. Added to which they were extremely conventional and because of their reactionary ideas of how little girls and boys should be dressed practically stifled any fashion changes.

Like their retail counterparts they followed the rules they had themselves created. No black for any age: never on its own, of course, or as trimming or ever introduced into a print. Even that innocuous fabric shantung with its muted floral patterns was subject to close scrutiny in case some of the colours might be too hard for juvenile dresses. One store buyer even refused to place an order for an infant's dress because in the minute eye of a duck appliqué on the pocket there was a black dot. Necklines rarely went below the base of the throat and, preferably, had a peter pan collar; puff sleeves were *de rigeur* even up to 15 years and must not be too short. These requirements were not so much for modesty although they persisted because they preserved the childish image, but because low necks and too short sleeves would 'show the vests'. (It took years for children's underwear manufacturers to appreciate that they, too, could be affected by fashion so they went on making good, cold-resisting vests with high necks and sleeves with close ribbed cuffs, thereby restricting considerably the cut of the outer garment and toddlers and young girls went without pretty necklines and sleeveless dresses). Knickers for schoolgirls must be navy. Schools were, in the middle 30s, beginning to break away from the traditional navy outfits and introducing modest grey, maroon and green and they wanted knickers, made of cotton and fleecy lined mostly, to match, but nobody could supply them. School knickers were navy and only with great reluctance were 'fancy' colours added.

Children's clothes must never, ever, be too close fitting. A four-inch tolerance was the standard, not always too reduced either on the cheapest garments which were sometimes cut with a bagginess which their more expensive counterparts avoided with their better pattern grading. The tolerance—the difference between the child's body and the garment—must serve two purposes, provide enough give for active youngsters to move about and allow room for the body to develop. Garments must be made to 'grow into' but this stipulation was a reflection of public demand. Clothes were nearly always bought one size too large and since children rarely grow in the right proportions it was only for fleeting moments in their lives that their outfits fitted them properly.

Agreement on colours was unanimous and rather like Ford's dictum on his cars *'You can have any colour you like so long as it's black'*, for children's wear it was *'so long as it's blue, white or red'*. This had proved to be what the public wanted and while one or two brave spirits tried to introduce pale green for infants or perhaps a few party frocks, and green and white stripes were recognised school wear, anything stronger such as the brilliant Irish green was shunned almost entirely due to the superstition that it was unlucky. This deeply entrenched colour preference was something that overseas producers could never understand nor accept. At the time the film-star tie-ups were being imported, principally those of Shirley Temple, and a very pretty pale apple green was included for nearly every style but nobody in Britian would buy it because it looked 'too washed-out'. The American manufacturers could not believe that one of their best selling shades could be dismissed on these grounds but they had to stop sending it to Britain.

When all the other influences had had their say, from the dyeing of the yarn through the making and selling of the product there remained one figure who had the last word on what baby at least would wear—the expectant mother's own mother. Her word was law on patterns of garments to be sewn or knitted at home and she invariably accompanied her daughter on shopping expeditions and the young wife, to whom such matters as day and nightgowns, mitts and infantees, quantities and stages of growth, were surrounded in mystic, stood shyly by while her mother, determined to perpetuate the methods by which her own offspring were reared, disregarded advances in design, material and any new ideas on clothing children. In this she played into the hands of those manufacturers and wholesalers who were quite content to continue, with little variation, their basic designs. Unlike other branches of the clothing industry they could do so for two reasons: they could use the same designs year after year because they were new to the woman having her first baby and who had probably taken very little interest in baby clothes hitherto, and they carried their own seal of approval since they were so like those purchased by their mothers when they were young.

# CHAPTER 2
# Babies' and Infants' Clothing

For the purposes of their clothing children now fell into several groups which covered the various stages of development and which overlapped here and there to provide the necessary duplication of size, but not style, where age and growth did not tally. First came baby linen (no longer linen but the name persisted even into the 70s), then toddlers', 12, 14, 16ins. (31-41cms.) in dress length and infants' wear 16, 18, 20, 22ins. (41-56cms.) in length, the 16ins. for the toddlers being cut differently from the infants' who, running about all over the place, had lost their podgy build. There was very little alteration in the styling of dresses except for the introduction of a waist definition and a tie-belt at the back. These three groups took the child up to four years.

The next section went mainly from 24-32ins. (61-81cms.) but sometimes stopped at 28 or 30ins. (71 or 76cms.) and was followed by 34-42 or 44ins. (86-106 or 111cms.) depending on the current length which would take in all girls at school. There were no teens nor junior misses, the only recognition of the older girl being the use of the term 'maids' and for boys, 'youths' but when D. H. Evans & Co. Ltd. opened their new store in Oxford Street, London, in 1936 their 'Boys' Shop' catered for all ages up to 19 years.

Baby wear had been transformed by the early 30s: now all that remained of the quantities of lavishly trimmed, tucked and pleated, heavily embroidered items that made up the layette was the christening robe, still pretty and dainty but spartan in appearance compared with past versions. The revolution which had been instigated by Miss M. B. Synge of

---

*In order to maintain a uniform comparison with the practice of two-inch size steps, conversions to the metric system throughout are indicated by rises of 5cms.*

Simple Garments, with her campaign to reduce the many layers with which babies were encompassed—and older children, too—had been so successful that for the first time babies were kicking their way to healthy growth unhampered by their clothing.

The forces at work were not confined to that vigorous crusader Miss Synge, they included worthy organisations like the National Baby Welfare Council, the Mothercraft Training Society and the Chelsea Club. Even so their combined efforts would not have achieved the success they did had it not been the era of women's emancipation for it was in 1914 that Miss Synge set out to strip off the cocoon round baby just at the time when mothers were receptive to any means of freeing themselves from the drudgery of washing, starching, ironing and mending. With the first-born it was a labour of love, with the second and third the novelty wore off. True, domestic help and nannies were not difficult to find if you had the money but it was those who could afford to pay servants to look after their babies' clothing who were among the greatest advocates of simplification both for the child's sake and the mother's. What were previously held to be evidence of a mother's loving care, for example, starched frills, were now frowned upon as harmful, as were tight bands and long hampering skirts which weighed down on tiny limbs.

The principle first put forward by Miss Synge that three even layers of clothing providing equal warmth was the ideal for babies was well established by the 30s. Light, soft materials which were porous and warm were recognised as being the most suitable. Traditional body belts and binders although still in use were dismissed as doing more harm than good. (The makers of the 'Liberty' bodice had designed a bodice, size 0, suitable for babies from six weeks old which superseded the binder and, they claimed, gave the necessary support without restraint.)

Clothing in relation to the health of the baby was being examined in greater depth than ever before and infant welfare experts were listened to with respect. Manufacturers of top quality articles, even in the mass-production field, were very much influenced by these experts, seeking their advice on new lines and keeping up to date with any fresh theories on the correct way to rear baby. There was increasing interest in the hygienic and purity properties of baby garments (in America sterilisation units were installed in some baby wear departments) and 'certificates' such as the Diploma of the Institute of Hygiene, were obtained and displayed prominently in advertisements and packing as evidence of the pristine nature of the products.

It was the experts who helped to kill the old wives' tales so inextricably associated with the rearing of babies, a formidable task when the young mother was subject to so much pressure from her seniors. The dire prophesies of what would happen if this or that were left off before the due time were gradually disregarded as more and more mothers were persuaded to dress their babies according to the temperature and not the season. They learned that it was just as dangerous for a child to be too hot as too cold and a baby could be uncomfortable in garments too large or too small. It was better to have a few clothes that fitted properly than many which baby would 'grow into'.

How basic the layette had become is illustrated by this example, advertised in 1938 by The Treasure Cot, the specialist shop in Oxford Street, London, which catered for babies of *The Times* births column. Described as an inexpensive layette and offered for £7.10s.0d. (£7.50p.) it comprised:

3 flannel binders
3 'Kumfy' vests
3 flannels (petticoats)
3 nightgowns
2 daygowns
3 long slips
1 silk/wool carrying shawl
1 wool bonnet
2 doz. Turkish squares
1 doz. 'Treasure' gauze squares
2 wool coatees
2 pairs bootees
2 fine wool head-shawls

Dominating almost all stages of the baby scene in Britain in 1939 was wool, from the finest spun Shetland yarns for soft-as-silk head-shawls to the heavier qualities for mass-produced knitted outerwear. Britain was a 'wool for babies' nation and although baby clothes made from it had to be washed and dried with great care, and even so always shrank to some extent, and the off-white appearance deepened with laundering to cream, its position in the layette was sacrosanct. Woollen garments kept baby warm and all mothers subscribed to the belief that there was no substitute for wool long before this idea was adopted for publicity purposes: their daughters and granddaughters were to take a different view once the man-made fibres were on the market and proved to have such miraculous qualities as easy-to-wash, quick drying, non-iron and, above all, to retain a dazzling whiteness.

On the woven side, although pure wool figured largely in flannels and much finer cloths such as nunsveiling, mixtures of wool and cotton were widely used and combined the best of both worlds in having the virtues of wool and the washability of cotton. There were some babies and children who were not comfortable in wool which irritated their skins and they were put into cotton underwear, for example, but these little ones were in the minority.

The search for a solution to the nappy problem was going on: baby welfare experts and designers were seeking ways of easing the washing chores of mothers, avoiding the chafing of baby's skin and reducing the bulky appearance of the terry towelling napkin. Harringtons (London) Ltd. had had great success with their gauze squares described as fitting snugly and made of 'specially absorbent thin muslin'. Other makers had brought out T-shapes of terry which they claimed gave adequate thickness of cloth and at the same time avoided an ugly bulge under the clothing but in practice some proved unable to give the protection afforded by the established terry napkin whose size was found to be essential. It was usual for a pilch or pant to be worn over the napkin. The efficacious rubber pants had fallen into disfavour because of criticism that they made the child too hot and caused chafing. Instead, oilsilk pants or pilches, just as waterproof but non-heating and soft, covered the nappy, or pants made from terry towelling. Acid-proof and free from odour were also properties which mothers expected baby pants to have. The 30s had seen the introduction of a pant from overseas made from sterilised liquid latex which rapidly gained ground. The war stopped imports of these pants and in the post-war years mothers turned to the new nylon and soft plastics as prettier, daintier ways of covering the nappy.

The first garment, important because it was worn next to the skin, was the vest. Invariably all wool this had a round neck with a crochet type edging with ribbon insertion which could be drawn up to fit snugly round the neck, and short sleeves: it was in a fine rib or knitted cloth. Full-length sleeves were recommended as being best by mothercraft specialists but most mothers chose the short sleeves which were finished with narrow ribbing. The drawstring neck design was being challenged by the wrap-over style which tied on one side with two bows of narrow ribbon, its great advantage being that it did not have to be pulled over the baby's head. Side seams of the vest were usually reinforced with tape to which the napkin could be pinned.

The petticoat had become the plainest of garments, made in a princess style with high yoke. Most popular material for this was cream flannel or flannelette and it usually had enough width so that it could still be worn when it was shortened as the baby grew. The old-fashioned barra, short for barracoat, was still worn, this 'back flannel' as it was also called, was similar to a petticoat, had no sleeves, and tied round the waist.

The daygown and nightgown were often interchangeable, cut on the same lines as the petticoat the cloth was similar. The gowns had long sleeves with the fullness caught in a narrow band at the wrists springing into a frill which was lace edged to match the neck. Because of criticism that babies often pulled ribbons into tight knots making it difficult for mothers to take off the nightgown, 'Lastex' thread began to be inserted. Beneath the yoke at the front was a flat band insertion which ran into loose ends either side, went round the baby and tied at the back. It was only in later years that the resultant bow was declared to be a needlessly uncomfortable bump for the baby to lie on and front fastening gowns were advocated, with not much success, however, mothers preferring to cross the bands at the back and tie the bow at the front. Apart from the lace edging the only other embellishment was some self-embroidery on the yoke. Both petticoat, day and nightgown were long enough, at 22-24ins. (56-61cms.), to tuck under the baby's feet but were considerably shorter than the long clothes of the earlier years although these were being sold in the late

30s. Nevertheless between the everyday gown and the christening robe was a long frock in which baby was shown off to admiring friends and relations. This might be in nuns-veiling, fine cotton or crêpe-de-chine. An immensely popular trimming for this was Valenciennes lace as a frilled edging to the neck, tiny puff sleeves and hem. Narrow vertical panels of the lace running up from the hem and down from the neck imparted an air of frothy luxury. Cheaper versions of the long frock were made in art. silk locknit with inexpensive lace sometimes going from yoke to hem to give a panelled effect all round, with posies embroidered at the hem to match others decorating the yoke.

Faggotting, drawnthread work, French knots and other fine hand or machine embroidery, most of which was in self or with the merest hint of pink and blue, broke up the long length of these gowns with panels and scallops and curves which though only a faint echo of past glories of heavily encrusted garments yet had a delicate appeal enhanced by the minuteness of the design.

No less decorative albeit for strictly utilitarian purposes was the bib. The robes and gowns all had double yokes but more protection was essential. For such a mundane article it might reasonably be supposed that the choice would be limited but one wholesaler specialising in baby linen had no less than 750 different lines of bibs and feeders. These varied from the eminently practical towelling styles with a fancy design or wording incorporated in the fabric to the exquisite imports from France and Switzerland seemingly delicate and fragile but performing their function admirably by reason of sturdy padding beneath the top finery of delicate embroidered cottons or organdies. Progression from the baby stage usually meant the adoption of more substantial protective clothing, in this case the apron feeder of terry towelling which encompassed the front, much of the sides from neck to hem and, tying at the back, almost defeated the carefree abandon of learner eaters.

Knitted bootees covered the baby's feet with ribbon insertion round the ankles so that they stayed in place. For extra warmth there was the ubiquitous matinée jacket knitted with loving care for the most part by the mother or her relations and friends. Indeed its long popularity may have been due to the fact that with the bootees it made an easy set to knit as a present for the new baby. The pattern of the jacket had become a classic: the sleeves and high yoke were in garter stitch, the neck plain and round. Opening down the front, the edges were fastened together either by two or three pearl buttons or with ribbon insertion at the neck also perhaps at the bottom of the yoke. The skirt fell away either side to allow for the fullness of the daygown beneath and it was almost invariably in a fancy, openwork stitch. It was, of course, in white. The style ran on unchallenged for decades until new light was shed on what could be done with such a simple garment. This was still to come and meanwhile the classic matinée jacket continued. Frequently there was a knitted bonnet to match the jacket and bootees. The shape most favoured was the Dutch cap, the ornamentation being confined to some embroidery or little rosette either side where the ribbon ties were attached.

Of great importance was the shawl, a popular gift for the new mother, taking a long time to knit and of such generous proportions that when the square was folded across to form a triangle it provided a double layer to wrap round the child. The knitted wool shawl was very popular but there was also the woven variety. In both instances a great deal of attention was given to the border since this part of the article was very much in evidence when the child was being carried. In the knitted shawl it was highlighted with a fancy stitch complementing the body, for the woven type the contrast was more dramatic. The white or cream material, cashmere or flannel, was bordered with a swinging fringe of silk or art. silk strands and was often further embroidered in self to match the fringe.

In a class by themselves were the hand-knitted Shetland wool shawls of cobwebby daintiness and exquisite fineness. Of equal delicacy were the small squares for covering the heads of young babies. A nestling rug fulfilled a similar function to the shawl but was more of a miniature blanket being of wool velour. It had self fringes either end and for a few pence extra its severity was broken by nursery character motifs and a touch of colourful embroidery. Tiny hands were kept warm in infantees and mitts, the former had a separate thumb, the latter was just a bag completely encasing the hand. Both were pulled into the wrist with ribbon ties.

Soft sole shoes for babies were made of crêpe-de-chine, satin, art. silk locknit or petal soft kid in white, pale pink or blue the kid being embroidered in the same spirit as the other materials or stamped with a nursery motif. Of necessity they had straps round the ankle and fastened in front with either a pearl button or more ornamental ribbon tied in a bow. The square cut of the shoes followed the shape of the baby's feet but the time was to come when this would be criticised because where the upper and sole were stitched together at the front insufficient space was provided for the chubbiness of the baby's toes, let alone allowing any room for growth. One tiny pearl button at the centre front of the upper was common to baby shoes, hard or soft sole, and few were to be seen without this modest ornament.

The christening robe whether new or handed down on its way to becoming a family heirloom, had come a long way from the old days when it was difficult to distinguish the baby from the surrounding mass of material. Something of its past lingered in the net embroidered needle-run lace in which it was made and the softly gleaming Jap silk slip retained an echo of past glories. A christening robe such as this could be purchased for 14s.11d. (75p.). The bonnet to match for about 3s.0d. (15p.). The round neck and tiny puff sleeves were bound with silk with a minute frill relieving this plain line: vertical tucks and embroidery finished the yoke, from which fell the richly embroidered full skirt to end in a scallopped hem. Sometimes there was a coat of matching material. Like the robe itself this had been watered down from a three-quarter length garment to a brief bolero jacket with a round collar and appliqués of a detail of the embroidered lace and more appliqués on either side of the cutaway front. The bonnet, too, had been reduced to a simple Puritan cap fitting close to the head but with ruched material under the front to frame the face. Rosettes of narrow satin ribbons over the ears ended in a loop to tie under the chin. If the shoes did not form part of the set they would be in silk or crêpe-de-chine or similar soft material, tying over the instep, and, like their everyday counterparts, were cut straight in front. Apart from white, ecru was liked for the christening robe as it gave the appearance of old lace treasured through the years.

Once out of the daygown the baby was 'shortened' with

dresses which only came down to the feet, the intermediate period when they wore slightly shorter gowns by now having been dispensed with. The style of the outerwear, understandably, followed very closely that of the longer garments since the limitations—in colour, texture, shape—remained the same, the short length of the dress making the skirt fullness more pronounced. The matinée jacket began to look more like a coat and to appear in a variety of cloths as well as the knitted form.

The most revolutionary garment at this point in the 20th century was the baby bag, produced and patented by Kamella Ltd., which was so simple and so practical it could only be wondered at that no one had thought of it before. Just a bag with a neck opening, shaped at the top to form short sleeves and a buttoned flap at the bottom, it was the first covering which kicking babies could not throw off. Made in a high quality pure wool velour with a waterproof lining it could be purchased for 8s.11d. (45p.) and was suitable for babies from birth to three or four years. The bag idea spread to other garments, such as sleepwear in flannelette with no buttoned flap at the bottom and slots either side for the child's hands instead of the sleeve shaping. A knitted pram set had bonnet and coat and, instead of the customary legginettes, a bag covering the baby from waist to feet, but none of these and similar adaptations achieved the success which the 'Kamella' baby bag had over the years.

As the baby grew new shapes and colours were added to its wardrobe. After the 'shortening' the next stage was the knitted pram set comprising bonnet, coat and legginettes, the latter had elastic round the waist, generous width over the seat to encompass the nappy and covered the feet as well as legs, with ties at the ankle for a snug fit. More choice of fancy knits brought greater variety to collars, bodices and skirts of the coats which had double-breasted fastening suitable for boy or girl, but now there was some recognition of the sexes with extra flare to the skirts of those intended for little girls and a straight fall without a waisted effect for little boys. For girls, too, there was a bonnet shape hat and for boys a masculine beret. Both were, however, hand-embroidered, in addition to the fancy knit, in slightly stronger shades than the earlier counterparts.

The matinée jacket was gradually being joined by the

cardigan with ribbed cuffs and waist and low buttoned front again embroidered in a similar way to the other knitted garments for all of which wool continued to predominate. At the walking stage the legginettes with feet in the knitted sets gave way to breechettes which were shaped to the ankle and had straps under the instep instead of feet. The rest of the outfit was substantially the same except that the bonnet developed into a hat with a turned back brim. There was some concession to boys in these sets for instead of the coat top with side or front fastening, they could have the newer 'lumber' style which was virtually a sweater but relieved with fancy stitching and embroidery so that it was not too old looking. Boys could now also have their first jersey suit which again was knitted, with close fitting knickers and jersey top fastened on the shoulder, and always with long sleeves, which came well down over the knickers and concealed all but the ends of the brief legs. Pastel colourings, handwork and knit were similar to all the other baby articles but the tiny flower and leaf and little posy embroideries were joined by nursery motifs, chicks, ducks and rabbits, the universal favourites with each succeeding generation, and, at a later stage, the immensely popular elephant trumpeting cheerfully.

Apart from the knitted pram sets there were woven pram jacket and dress sets which had three-quarter length coats with long sleeves and nearly all, at every price level, followed a similar pattern of V-shape panels of smocking on the yoke either side of the front fastening. These sets, of a more dressy nature than the knitted ones, were mostly in suede, crêpe-de-chine, shantung, art. silk and cotton. It was surprising that although the choice of materials was limited for baby wear because of the special requirements the cloths at that time included all wool, all silk, silk and wool, cotton and wool, rayon and wool, rayon/wool/cotton, silk/wool/cotton and cotton.

Very little change had taken place in dresses for girls at the toddler stage but an extra outfit had come on the scene for boys. This was the tunic suit which comprised a smock top—very similar to the original garment—which was short enough to show the knickers, these were not baby style with fullness gathered into elastic round the thighs but fully lined and cut on plain tailored lines which identified the masculinity of the wearer immediately (not always easy except to the mother). Many tunic suits were made in tussore and they were especially effective in off-white and cream colours which had a warmer and more expensive air than the dead whites.

Now that the baby was actively crawling and toddling—and more often than not hitting the floor with unexpected swiftness—the fullness of dresses presented a hazard as they flopped about in front of the lively explorers. The answer had been found in the romper and buster-romper made in 16-18in. (41-46cms.) sizes. The former was in one piece with high yoke, smocked and/or embroidered, with elasticated legs and buttoning under the crutch for easy nappy changing: some were caught in round the middle with self-belts. The buster-romper was a two-piece with blouse top, trimmed as the romper, on to which buttoned bloomer style knickers. Both garments had plenty of width to accommodate the nappy. Although some buster-rompers were in one colour it was customary for the knickers to be in a contrasting shade, still within the baby pastel limits, and for the collar, cuffs or sleeve edges of the top to pick up this colour which was often introduced again for the embroidery.

Once the magnificent achievement of walking was reduced to the commonplace, infant boys' and girls' clothing pursued their separate ways with the exception of some items, notably coats and breechette sets which continued to have two-way buttoning and styling until the child reached the age of about four years. It was in small boys' wear that the biggest difference began to emerge. Whilst the girls went along with their dress and knicker sets (pilch shape knickers in the early stages) boys' blouse and knicker sets (buster suits) showed greater variety of material and design. For everyday use the knicker part of the sets were in plain cloths such as cotton or lightweight wool and for the cold weather, fleck or pepper-and-salt tweeds. The legs were square cut, reaching to mid-thigh and the self fabric belt slotted through a matching loop at centre front or through a small buckle; the belts became heavier and the buckles more manly as the wearer aged.

An innovation for small boys towards the end of the 30s had been the introduction of elasticated thread at the waistbands of knitted knickers, later also those of woven cloth, which gave a neater finish when pulled over jerseys and, even more important, saved mother's time when dressing the child. The elastication was not welcomed everywhere, there was criticism that it was difficult to get an exact fit without creating a tight band which restricted the little one's tummy, and conversely that repeated washing could destroy much of the elasticity so that the knickers became too loose and virtually unusable. These difficulties were overcome and since the virtues of the pull-on knicker far outweighed its disadvantages it became established both for small boys and their older brothers. Not the least of its merits was that it was a garment which the child could manage to put on by himself and this was an added attraction now that the value of self-help clothing was being realised as an aid to growing up.

Stitched creases down the front of each knicker leg of the buster suits helped to maintain a smart appearance throughout the boisterous life of the wearer. Slit pockets at the sides replaced the babyish front patch pockets, and the knickers were lined throughout. As a concession to the tender years of the wearer the blouse was often smocked below the saddle yoke but sleeves were full-length as well as short. Turned down collars were peter pan shape or with slight points which became more pronounced as the years went by. There was a slight change, too, in the choice of materials, the cotton or art. silk cloths were replaced in the autumn and winter by wool taffeta, a particularly fine fabric which gave warmth without weight and, in plain colours and fine checks, was just the right material for tailored styles with breast-pocket and buttoned centre front to which by now the little boy had progressed. He had progressed, too, into co-ordinated outfits for he could be provided with a top coat in a similar material to the knickers; the final touch was a bow tie at the neck of his blouse or shirt top. Cotton buster suits with striped cotton or gingham blouses and linen-finish cotton knickers provided excellent outfits for summer days. These 'washing suits' as they were termed, sold at around 3s.11d. (20p.) for the up-to-fours and stood up well to concentrated play.

For parties the young man really blossomed with silk trousers, still mid-thigh length, and blouses in a lighter but toning colour with long sleeves and colourful smocking at wrists and across the front and frills round the collar, down the front, and edging the sleeves. Smooth brown velvet with cream shantung for the blouse, piped to match, was a popular party combination. The younger boy's trousers often fastened on to the blouse with large pearl buttons, the straight line of the trouser top sometimes cut into points above the front two buttons then, as for day wear, as the child grew older, this was replaced by a stiffened belt and stronger buckle.

Knitted garments continued to be important, the boy's jersey suit was now made with knickers similar to the woven article and like it had permanent creases down the fronts which were knitted-in to last the life of the garment. These 'play suits' were mostly in two colours, the stronger tone for the knicker and the pastel jersey top enlivened with embroidery or fancy stitches. Separate jerseys and woven and jersey cloth knickers were worn now that the little boy had an identity of his own.

Once out of the toddler phase knitted dresses with round, ribbed necks, long sleeves and flared skirts provided warmth in winter for girls and they all had knickers to match. Dresses in wool and cotton mixture cloths, frequently with lined bodices, likewise had long sleeves. Mini window-pane checks in white on pastel grounds were the most popular alternatives to plain cloths; stripes and the allover floral patterns were mainly reserved for summer wear.

It was in the Sunday best and party wear sphere that mothers could dress their toddlers in some of the frills and furbelows discarded by 20th century moderns. Whatever the age of the infant or its position in society, two cardinal rules had to be observed about party dresses, they must have full skirts, they must have a large pussy bow at the back. Basically the design of the dresses was simple, round neck, short puff sleeves, natural waist and full skirt. Frills came top of the trimmings; from narrow edgings of lace to relieve the plain neckline to rows in tiers on the skirts they were always in proportion to the size of the garment. Collars were not so much seen on the party frock proper except when in genuine lace they provided a delicate contrast to crisp pastel taffetas. Rouleau, ruching, embroidery, appliqués and flowers clustered at neck or waist were to a great extent hand done to achieve the often subtle effects on these pretty dresses. Materials varied from the soft falling georgettes over silks to stiff poults and included silk and art silk fabrics, net over silk, crêpe-de-chine, taffeta and even white velvet with cloaks to match (a most impractical cloth this since it could not be washed as the latter day nylon velvets but had to be cleaned, presumably after each confrontation with jellies and cream cakes).

It was at this point in a child's life that organdie came on the scene and it was to have an importance right up until the teens. The more expensive embroidered organdies from Switzerland were reserved for party dresses but the material went through the gamut of plain and printed cloths which embraced all manner of dresses from the Sunday best to the simple frocks for summer days.

There were several good reasons for its adoption as primarily a child's fabric: it had the necessary stiffness without solidity to make the skirt stand away from the body, it could be tied in a highly satisfactory bow at the back; its dainty diaphanous appearance belied its toughness; it was much easier to launder and iron than most other glamour fabrics; it dyed well in any of the pastel shades with an admirable clarity. Even the plain, cheaper organdies still had many of the qualities of the more expensive embroidered fabrics and could be made at home into pretty summer and party frocks or bought from shops at all price levels. Organdie lost ground and eventually became passé after the war as tastes changed and man-made fibres opened up new cloth possibilities for children's clothing.

In no time at all tiny mites were toddling off to real parties, their frilly dresses concealed beneath velvet party cloaks which provided warmth without crushing their full skirts. Red velvet lined with white silk was the most popular for, appropriately, the Little Red Riding Hood style with the attached hood gathered to fit round the face. Almost as popular was a cloak with a deep collar ruched to stand up at the neck. Yet another change was rung with ruching continued over the shoulders and upper arms which not only looked luxurious but kept the cloak snugly in place. The stand-up collars on this type of cloak were often faced with white fur which was also used on other designs to edge the hood, making a sweet frame for the face. Reversible cloaks, pink to blue velvet, for instance, were great favourites amongst those able to afford such fineries.

Short socks, silk and lacy if the girls were lucky, art silk or cotton if that was all that funds would allow, and black patent shoes with ankle straps or satin slippers kept on with elastic crossed over the ankles in miniature ballet form, completed the party-going outfit. It was in the latter shoes that the bronze shade first appeared. This metallic colour was so completely accepted as correct for parties and evenings that it was worn through childhood, slipper or one-bar style, to the 18-year-olds' dancing sandals.

The social life of the toddler was extended to weddings at an early age and their attire for this varied according to the brides' tastes. Generally the Society brides favoured a simple style and fabric with restrained headdress and posy whilst the low income households spent a great deal of money on ornate flashy satins and fussy headdresses, muffs, dangling Dorothy bags, baskets filled with flowers and so forth, with mauve the dominating colour. What they did have in common was that all the dresses were ankle-length and the satin shoes were dyed to match. Unfortunately for small boys not all brides left them to current outfits of Regency trousers of velvet or satin and blouses with frilled front and cuffs and Cromwell buckled shoes: a great many of them were forced into replicas of high-ranking military uniforms of bygone days and a flourishing trade was carried on in the hire of such costumes.

Apart from these highlights, outerwear for infants was very restrained in concept. The fact that many of the coats, and coat sets, were destined for wear by either boy or girl dictated an indeterminate style and cloth, the only concession to the difference in the sexes being the two-way fastening. The big cover-up for winter was the breechette set which was worn up to four or five years. It consisted of hat or cap and coat, slightly shorter than one worn on its own, with flared skirt to allow for the breechettes; these were bulky round the seat and then shaped into the legs to give a close fit. Buttons fastened either side, or the newer zips, a big help these in dressing the children. Straps under the instep kept the legs in place. Velour led the cloths for these sets with velvet, toning or contrast, on collar, cuffs, buttons or, perhaps, piping of some kind and the inevitable bows.

Winter coats not part of a set demonstrated that the little one was really moving away from the baby stage. Apart from the velours there were a surprising number of tweeds to choose from, Yorkshire, Cumberland, Harris and Irish, dogstooth and puppytooth, friezes and fancy weave woollens and there was covert, a classic, hard-wearing material much worn by children of middle and upper-class families which combined with rich brown velvet did justice to the high standard of tailoring that went into children's coats of that period.

In the spring, coats for little girls took on a daintier appearance. Instead of velvet trimmings there were shantung, crêpe-de-chine, crash and organdie overlays on collars and cuffs, embroidered with minute flowers or French knots, and face cloths, velours, baratheas, fancy lightweight wools and tweeds and fine gaberdines were in lollipop colours. Either high-waisted or simply panelled from the shoulder to the hem the line was flared with contrast details, such as piping, cording or scalloping to break up the line. The majority had a stitched half-belt at the back above a centre inverted pleat to meet the requirements of the hop, skip and a jump brigade. Spring coats were mostly single-breasted but sometimes with the fastening taken to one side and the collars were a different shape from the usual peter pan. Provision was made for the vagaries of the climate by the introduction of two-position collars which could either be fastened up close to the neck on chilly days or left open to form lapels in warmer weather. Allowance for growth was given by three-inch French hems which were customary and easy for the mother to let down.

Although at first small boys at the infant stage wore coats with peter pan collars like their sisters they very soon discarded these and went into open necks with turned down collars and lapels. The collar might still be faced with velvet to prevent skin chafing but the cut of the coat was as much like father's as possible and manly herringbone tweeds were added to the materials.

A hat, beret or cap was usually included with the winter coat and breechette sets and some spring coats had hats to match but more often girls wore straws with narrow brims and ribbon and flower trimming, the latter being hand-made in the majority of cases. There was variety in the straw itself, pedal straws, leghorns and fancy chip straws were among those used for these hats. The Sunday best in fancy straw was seen less but still around and poke brims lined with silk or organdie continued to frame little faces, as did velvet bonnets and berets. There was growing support for hatlessness but in hot weather children's heads had to be protected and sunbonnets of cotton or organdie in traditional style with a frill to cover the nape of the neck, were worn; these were purchased separately but some summer dresses were sold with matching sunbonnets. The boys had cotton or linen hats with stitched brims turned up at the back and down in the front and the younger ones, paddy hats, with bigger, stitched brims turned down all the way round. The dwarf craze, started by Walt Disney's 'Snow White and the Seven Dwarfs' had affected the younger set, at least about the head, and the characteristic dwarf's cap livened up matching coat and hat sets. At last, too, the benefits of the headgear seen on the Continent had begun to be appreciated and caps with ear flaps and chin straps were being taken up for the winter.

In wet weather rubberised cotton and oilskin weatherproof coats with sou'-westers and Wellington boots gave complete protection. The macs could be bought in all manner of cheery colours, but the most beloved of the children was the bright yellow in the true fisherman spirit. Macs were worn longer than the topcoat length so that more of the legs were covered and since so many mothers insisted on buying their children's garments one size too large the wearers were swamped more by their outfits than the rain.

British mothers, unlike the American and the French, were not disposed to spend money on providing their offspring with fancy underwear; they just could not see the point of paying out for clothing which would not be seen and, moreover, would soon be outgrown. Their own mothers may have spent many loving hours making and embroidering petticoats but so far as the 20th century ones were concerned, the advent of rayon locknit met most of their daughter's fancier underclothing needs. Toddlers and infants did quite well in petticoats and knicker sets of fine locknit in delicate pastel shades embellished with bows and lace and scalloped hems. The constant washing might change the shape a bit but rarely to any great detrimental effect, and the underwear was cheap. The woven rayons, plain or in floral prints, and again lace edged, provided slightly more expensive alternatives.

The petticoats were in a style known as 'opera top' (a grandiose name for U-shape necks) as distinct from those with straps but they were destined in the winter certainly to be worn with vests which came much higher at the neck and had sleeves. The vests were in wool Swiss rib, which had great elasticity and adapted itself to the growth of the wearer and were exceedingly comfortable and warm, or in wool or cotton interlock which was especially soft to the skin. In addition there were the fine quality wool or wool and cotton mixtures of knitted cloth, cut and sewn and finished with silk bindings. These wore so well that they were not only handed down from one child to the next but from one generation to another with periodic trips back to the makers for repair and renovation. In contrast, when vests were on sale in the chain stores at 1s.0d. (5p.) each some mothers never bothered about washing them, they bought a new one every week and threw the old one away.

For night-time winceyette, flannel and flannelette and interlock sleeping suits, with or without feet, and nightdresses all with long sleeves were generally worn. The sleeping suits had hitherto been made with trousers buttoned to the tops but in the 30s the drop-back had made its appearance: its obvious advantages at potty time had quickly been appreciated and widely adopted. Rubber buttons, too, which stood up to boiling and mangling and could be dyed to match the sleeping suit fabric were another useful innovation which helped mothers. Pyjamas for those past the drop-back stage had pull-on tops with Cossack necklines and buttoning for the boys. Cut on simple lines and made from interlock fabric the plainness was relieved by bands of contrast colour at ankles, cuffs and necks. The girls' were similar in style but the collars were narrower and they were fastened along the shoulders and had some machine embroidery.

Dressing gowns for the tinies were a luxury in many homes; in best quality velour they cost approximately 10s.6d. (53p.), with peter pan collar, pocket, silk girdle and colourful appliqués of farmyard animals and embroidered flowers. At the end of 1938 the customary motifs had been joined by famous newcomers, the characters from Walt Disney's, 'Snow White and the Seven Dwarfs'. A British manufacturer had obtained the sole rights to reproduce these on his dressing gowns. More universally worn were dressing gowns of ripple cloth, without ornamentation save for braid trimmings, lower in price but with splendid wearing and washing qualities.

Fur felt slippers in cheerful colours with rabbit or kitten

heads on the fronts and ankle straps, packed in brightly printed cartons with 'doors' which opened to reveal the contents were popular as 'granny' gifts to augment the everyday plain felt bedroom slippers, flat heeled, round toed, pull-on or with ankle-straps.

# CHAPTER 3
# The Schoolgirl: Outerwear

The dividing line in a child's life, so far as its clothing was concerned, came with the advent of school. There were new factors now to be considered, the pretty-pretty days were over and parents were no longer the sole arbiters of what should be worn. For the middle and upper-classes the decision was taken out of their hands. Kindergarten, public and private schools had rules which must be obeyed without question and the official uniform list, covering in and out of school hours in the case of boarding schools, stipulated the dress even to the last pair of socks. Occasionally in the 30s there were grumbles about school uniforms. The bone of contention was not, at that time, the principle of compulsory uniforms but the length of the official clothing lists and of boarding schools in particular which forced parents to purchase garments which, the critics said, were outgrown before half worn. Quantities and types, dresses, for example, for special occasions at boarding schools used only a few times in a term, came under fire. (One school stipulated a white coat, white gloves, straw hat, white crêpe-de-chine dress with long sleeves, long white stockings, white knickers). It was claimed, and with good reason, that old ideas should be discarded in favour of healthier modern clothing. Snobbery was often at the heart of the lengthy official clothing requirements, snobbery on both sides, the school's and the parents'.

Lower down the social scale the school uniform was not so widespread. For the majority, school wear had resolved itself into a few basic items embodying some distinctive symbol or colouring which identified the school but provided the right kind of apparel for the classroom. In central, secondary, high schools, grammar schools and technical colleges, the State-aided establishments, uniforms were worn and worn with pride as they were symbols that the child had passed or won a scholarship and they were regarded with respect. In the elementary schools no such compulsion existed as they were attended by children from a wide section of the community many of whom came from extremely poor families. Their sisters' cast-off dresses and coats and their brothers' trousers and jackets, much too big and often threadbare, were their uniform and in the big cities and Welsh valleys where unemployment was rife bare feet were commonplace. Nevertheless in most elementary schools there was an attempt, save in the 'mixed infants', to introduce an identification with the school by badges for hats, caps and jackets. The drill slip, the box-pleated common denominator which was known as the gym, tunic in higher circles, was gently promoted as being serviceable for school wear with, preferably, a white blouse which could be washed frequently. To this was added a coloured girdle following the introduction of 'houses' as in the upper crust establishments and a badge for sewing on to the yoke of the tunic. The drill slip once purchased was expected in many areas to last the whole of the school life of the wearer so it was bought at least a size too large. Children of more moneyed parents who could afford to replenish their children's wardrobes could easily be distinguished by the length of the first drill slip, it was two to three inches above the knee and not flopping two or three inches below waiting for the wearer to grow.

By the end of the 30s the average British schoolgirl's outfit was so well-known it was almost a national dress. There was the hat, hatband and badge; double-breasted navy nap coat with full or half-belt or gaberdine raincoat with all-round belt and open vent at the back of the skirt; blazer, turnback collar, high lapels, three-button, s.b. fastening, breast and hip pockets, piped or faced with petersham ribbon or cord, with breast-pocket badge; navy serge gym slip with three box pleats back and front, square yoke (more expensive versions had velvet faced yokes) self belt or braid girdle in the school or house colour; white blouse with action pleat at the back to allow for movement, long sleeves and buttoned cuffs, shirt collar and school tie; black or brown stockings and black or brown lace-up shoes. The school ties and badges of the girls were identical to those worn by the boys. Additional accessories might include a scarf in the school colours and a leather purse buttoned over the girdle, or suspended from a shoulder strap, containing the week's pocket money, a handkerchief kept in a pocket in the knickers and a shoulder slung leather satchel full of school books and probably games shoes as well. The hair was taken back from the face and kept in place by a plain slide or hair ribbon. Schools frowned upon frivolous colours and insisted on either black or brown ribbon to curb unruly locks.

Culottes, divided skirts in navy serge or grey flannel, were worn for games or the special games tunic which was shorter than the gym tunic and cut with a slight flare instead of pleats.

The tailored costume played a large part in school life, especially for the seniors up to 18 years. It was extremely severe in cut and very much a copy of a man's suit. Unlike the fashion costume it was double-breasted with four or six buttons, and the jacket pockets, one either side and a breast-pocket, were inset. The straight skirts generally had either inverted pleats or a wide box pleat front and back but these were stitched down for much of their length to prevent any unseemly swinging fullness. For the younger ones the skirts were on white cotton bodices so that they hung from the shoulders. Of course there were some schools who departed from the d.b. fastening and had more pleats to give extra movement in the skirt but for the majority the school costume meant the style described. Some changes in the appearance could be rung by the choice of cloths; these included the navy serge and grey flannel completely identified with school costumes, and also a large number of tweeds. When accompanied by school tie, panama with hatband in the school colours and lace-up shoes the result was truly a uniform stripped of all femininity but despite the chilling effect of such sobriety it must be admitted that the combination of fine tailoring and simplicity of design helped young girls to appear always neat and tidy.

Straw was only one of an incredible number of different materials from which hats for schoolgirls were made: these included panama, tweed, linen and cotton, wool and fur felt, velour and even silk. The panama was identified as the school hat for summer and the velour for winter, the former in natural and the latter in black, navy and brown. The crowns of both were quite high and rounded and the brims wide, usually turned up at the back and down in the front; both velours and panamas embodied some link with the school such as hatband in the official colours and embroidered or metal badge. More schools had been adopting the beret because they wanted a change and it had no brim nor crown to get out of shape and weatherproof models were on the market. Parents approved of the beret, it did not entail a hatband, only a badge. Destined to weather all fashion storms was that most snobbish of all school hats, the classic, hard straw boater.

Petticoats had no place at all in the school uniform and the average schoolgirl wore a vest, navy blue fleecy-lined knickers, white knicker lining and a 'Liberty' bodice, with or without suspenders attached, below her blouse and gym tunic. Even so in 1939 one school list included, under Optional Items, 'long-sleeved Shetland underbodices'.

The items in a school outfit had come to be generally accepted because they were hard-wearing, the serge gym tunic, for instance, or hygenic, as in the washable white blouse, and impervious to the onslaughts of term-time. The exception was possibly the hat which tended to emerge somewhat battered after the first few weeks of school life. The nondescript design of the outfit was an asset since it neither flattered, nor detracted from, the wearer but the very neutrality was regarded as a liability by those who wished to use the clothing of their pupils as a vehicle for publicity and in striving to introduce distinctive uniforms for their schools adopted materials, colours, styles, trimmings and embroidery which involved the parents in needless expense. In this they were aided and abetted by retailers who wanted to secure the school contract and knew that one way of doing so was to submit designs and/or colours which would not be seen elsewhere. Special materials and dyes and badges in several colours increased substantially the production costs for which in the end the parents had to pay. Not all retailers encouraged this unnecessary expense but instead endeavoured to persuade school heads to curtail expenses by using standard materials and designs which did not require so much labour but their efforts were often thwarted by the desires of the heads to have exclusive uniforms.

Alterations to the basic outfit were creeping in, the pinafore tunic, no pleats and a V-neck, began to get wider acceptance, ankle socks for summer instead of thick stockings, flesh coloured stockings instead of black or brown, blouses and skirts for the older girls and summer dresses with different styling for seniors and juniors, proof of the growing awareness that the former must be treated separately. The boarding schools maintained their rigid rules for after-class wear insisting on dark dresses with white collars and long sleeves and white silk for speech days and other special occasions.

Even in the classroom fashion began to manifest itself with the means at its disposal, the point at which the girdle was worn fluctuated from well above the waist to a dangerously insecure point just above the hem according to the current phase. The angle of the hat was affected in a similar manner: the inexpensive beret could be pulled into various shapes at the whim of the school leaders and the brims of panamas and winter beavers could be daringly swept up one side and down the other and the truly elite wore them turned down all the way round. Coat collars were similarly affected and were worn up or down as the style setters decreed. No one knows how these fads started, they had no connection with any adult fashion but were akin to childhood games, all of a sudden it was the hop scotch season throughout the land and when some school idol chose to wear something in a certain way then her admirers swiftly followed suit but this does not explain why that became right for schools in other districts.

Whether money was required for official uniforms or just for clothes to wear in the classroom once a child started school there was not much left over in many households for extra garments for out-of-school hours, nor, since they would be worn such a short time before being outgrown, were even parents with money available disposed to spend a great deal on them. This lack of demand was another factor in restricting any large development of fashion in children's clothing in Britain, unlike America where uniforms wre practically non-existent and a powerful fashion industry had been built up. Strangely enough this very conservatism resulted in British children's clothing achieving tremendous prestige overseas and particularly in the USA. Added to the workmanship, the cut, the tailoring and the smocking, and the high quality of the cloth, was the restrained good taste of the garments, a restraint which could only be attained by virtue of the experience and craftsmanship that went into them and the classic British children's wear became as desired, and readily recognisable in Royal and aristocratic circles, as the Savile Row suit.

Whilst this superb conservatism brought honour abroad at home it resulted in the maxim that children's clothes did not change much. This, broadly speaking, was true and remained so until long after the second world war. Apart from the fact that parents were spared the necessity of keeping up with any junior Jones of fashion it had the advantage that clothing could be handed down without openly proclaiming that it was several years old.

There had now become established a series of garments which provided girls and boys with protection against the elements, allowed freedom of movement, were hard-wearing (commensurate with the price paid) were free of unnecessary ornamentation and so easy to launder, and provided room for growth by reason of good hems and seam inlays; within these confines the changes were rung—a collar shape, here, a bolero added there. Already though this little world was being expanded to take in new garments.

The inconspicuous nature of boys' clothing of the period was almost equalled by the girls'. True a more feminine air was given by the prints and lighter cloths and wider range of colours but the attitude towards clothing for girls was the same, it must not draw attention to the child nor encourage her to be vain about her appearance; taking an undue interest in clothing was to be deplored. This was particularly frustrating for the 15-18-year-olds of whom the impression was given that they were in some way to blame for being too old for some things and too young for others. The transition between girl and woman was regarded as a nuisance. On no account must the adolescent be allowed to enter the adult world too quickly and whilst mother held the purse strings she certainly would not do so.

The big stores, reflecting the wishes of the age, made hardly any provision for the older girl—the 'teens' was a virtually unknown term—except for those catering for the upper classes which recognised their needs and had instigated débutante departments which stocked outfits designed for their increased social activities and reflected the styles their mothers were wearing. In the majority of retail outlets, however, the juvenile departments went up to 46ins. (116cms.) length in coats and dresses (lower calf length) from which the up-to-18-year-olds were expected to choose their garments. The latter end of the ranges, the 'maids', were only slightly altered in their styling from the younger girls'. Eventually the in-betweens were to be recognised and have separate sections of their own with articles specially designed for them but this was still a long way ahead.

There was some resistance on the part of retail managements to cater for the teen girl and allocate to her an exclusive space. It was hoped that if she felt that the tail end of the juvenile department was not suitable she would find something in the Small Ladies, an all embracing term for anyone too small for the average women's sizes and a department much frequented by little old ladies. The difficulty with maids was that they were not 'small' ladies, their measurements were often greater than their mothers' since they had not yet fined down across the back, around the waist and thighs and still had plenty of puppy fat. This was accepted in the juvenile department where the suppliers were used to clothing buxom wenches in school uniforms but for the women's wear manufacturers accustomed to small ladies' sizes such colossal and, to them, unbalanced measurements were quite outside their province and alien to their designers. They did not want the bother of devising and grading sets of patterns for a troublesome and not necessarily lucrative business. Supplies of the right kind, then, were not easy for retail buyers to obtain and in addition the managements were conscious of the dangers of introducing departments for older girls. In any department store, buying for the fashion sections was divided into clearly defined groups of garments and sizes, and this maids' business looked as if it would overlap nearly everyone's size territory—even O.S.! So the managements trod warily believing that the profits might not be worth the bitter disputes which would arise even though their counterparts in America were already operating a booming trade in teen girl clothing.

At the other end of the scale there were no problems of this kind, girls' garments were a natural development from infancy with the big break at five years when school began. There was marginally more attempt to recognise the various stages of development of the female than there was of the male, the stodgy attire of which varied only slightly from juniors through to seniors. After four years the same designs would be made for girls approximately 5, 6 and 7 years (24, 26 and 28ins. [61, 66 and 71cms.] for coats and dresses) but in many instances they went up three more sizes so that a ten-year-old girl would be wearing the identical style to that of a child of five. Sometimes there would be no break at all and the identical dress or coat would be made for a girl in her late teens. This often happened with school wear and caused bitter resentment amongst the seniors. It was certainly true of the navy nap coat, an incredibly hard-wearing garment which was common at nearly all schools. The cloth from which the coats were made furnished full protection from cold, wind and rain and was so tough it was impossible to wear out. The thickness of the material prohibited any flights of fancy into high-fashion and it probably never occurred to anyone to think that such an excursion could be possible, or desirable, but the double-breasted fastening, all-round belt, deep, storm collar and lapels were so eminently suited to school life in the winter that no deviations were considered necessary. In this very perfection were sown the seeds of its demise for it became so manifestly associated with schooldays that its place was gradually usurped by the gaberdine raincoat and supply difficulties during the war finally killed it off altogether.

Once past the fourth birthday and out of the 'infants' so far as clothing was concerned made scant difference to the styles and types of garments worn by girls. The pastel shades were slightly deeper than the baby blues and pinks for coats and there were more and bigger checks. Teddy bear and blanket cloths joined the velours and more interesting surfaces were provided by frieze and fleck cloths, but the basic patterns remained the same. Coats were knee-length, the waists were in the natural position or somewhat higher, they fell with a slight flare at the sides and inverted pleats and peter pan collars were everywhere. Open necks with revers were reserved for spring and summer, for the colder weather coats fastened high at the neck. The majority were single-breasted but instead of closing down the centre they fastened well over to the left; this had the advantage of leaving a smooth panel down the centre which might be broken at the waist with a narrow, matching belt or fancy stitching or piping but which did not spoil the simple line. There was a pleasing absence of rows of buttons, many had only one at the neck, hidden under the collar, and one, or perhaps two, at the waist. Some had no visible fastenings at all the coats being held together by hooks and eyes concealed beneath the overlap. With a side fastening of this nature an important feature was the jigger button which kept the underlap in place on the opposite side and so prevented it from sagging below the front. The cross-over collar, narrower than the peter pan, invariably in a contrast cloth or colour, was worn a great deal, linking up with the side fastening.

A striking fact about the children's coats for all ages in the 30s was the absence of fur trimming. This was in keeping with the extremely conventional attitude of the day that anything of a showy nature in children's clothing was vulgar and too 'sophisticated'. There is no doubt that the tailored lines and good quality cloths needed no fur collars nor cuffs. Velvet and velveteen was much preferred as a trimming and so was suede discreetly introduced for appliqués in toning or subtly contrasting colours.

As the girl moved out of the infant plus stages and into the 7-15 age group a modicum of fashion influence was reflected in her clothing, albeit lagging two or three years behind the adults. In coats (some were still being described as 'flapper') the style element was largely confined to the neck and the many interpretations of the scarf collar. There were the bold versions in which the neckline merged into a complete scarf looped over at the throat with the ends hanging down past the waist and held in place by an all-round belt, this type, and shorter versions, was also worn with one end slung casually over the shoulder; there were scarves in fancy shapes with insets of eye-catching stripes; scarves which crossed over high at the neck and slotted through tabs either side; and scarves in contrast check which tied in enormous pussy bows under the chin and scarves so small they were mere cravats. The changes could be rung easily with this form of neckline and they all had a jaunty, casual air which was youthful and attractive. Like those of the younger girls' coats, side fastenings predominated, waists were slightly higher than the natural position and although there were some pleats and flares the overall effect was a long, slim line.

The older the girl the longer she wore her clothes until in her teens her coats and costumes reached the top of her calf: dresses were usually an inch shorter than the top coat. Even with this recognition of her grown-up state more often than not her hat was made from matching cloth and was bought as part of a set and with its stitched, upturned brim and a bow or two here and there it differed very little from that of her young sister.

Her raincoat, bought primarily for school, was identical to the boys' except for the reverse fastening. Many were made with two-way buttoning right through to the sub-teens. This, and the navy nap coat, accounted for most wet weather protection. In addition there were waterproofs in oilskin and oilsilk with hats to match. The oilskins followed the seaman's classic outfit, the oilsilks were less masculine.

Few children were without a scarf. This accessory being long and narrow, and purely functional, it was often knitted at home in sober wools which did not show the dirt too quickly. Woven wool scarves were livelier in bright checks, overchecks and tartans with fringed ends. Where a wool scarf was decreed the colours were introduced in horizontal stripes culminating in knotted fringes at the ends. Some home knitters went further and incorporated the school colours into the gauntlet cuffs of gloves. The latter, whether home produced or bought, were worn by a high proportion of the girls. Gloves were obligatory on Sundays, in white or fawn cotton; in 'Simplex' material with semi-gauntlet cuffs finished with raised seams or ornamental stitching; in natural coloured imitation hogskin; in kid sometimes with fur lined wrists.

Costumes displayed a greater variety of design with the advent of the swagger, bolero and tunic length coats and jackets which were a welcome alternative to the severe lines of the school costume. Short, loose jackets teamed with blouses and skirts or dresses were known as 'swing' suits and were particularly good for small children who were not ready for tailored costumes. The jackets fastened high at the neck and fell open down the front with clusters of pleats either side to give swinging fullness repeated on the otherwise straight cut skirts; sleeves were full-length and sometimes had pleated effects at the cuffs. Fleck material was the first choice of fabric for these suits with brown flecks on beige the leading colour combination. The blouse which completed the suit was likely to be crêpe-de-chine. For the most part this style was worn up to the 13-14-year-olds but this was not a rigid division. The young sizes also had full-length coats and matching skirts or pinafore style dresses but this co-ordination was for the moneyed minority.

Above 14 years the jacket lengthened to three-quarters, tunic length (two or three inches above the hem of the skirt) and for spring and summer, full-length. With the graduation into the three-quarter coat and skirt—the swagger suit—came a less lighthearted approach to styling. The youthful pleats were replaced by rows of stitching; collars, pockets and buttons were bigger and any pleats in the skirt or matching dress did not disturb the general straight line. Altogether the effect was one of maturity—and heaviness—and really represented a step straight into women's designs without acknowledgment of the in-between needs of the teens. The same could be said of the tunic, or seven-eighths, coats over frocks and skirts which had an even older air. The padded shoulder was firmly established and sometimes gauntlet cuffs were added to the sleeves which repeated striped or fancy patterns on the lapels. Full-length coat and dress ensembles were worn in the spring and summer: the coat was unlined and either of lightweight wool or art. silk and went over a plain or floral patterned dress in toning art. silk. The coat was always in a darker colour than the dress, had full-length sleeves and often only a link button at the waist to achieve the edge to edge look which revealed the frock beneath. Even though the girl had achieved the dignity of being a 'maid' and reached the age for two-piece outfits the frock might have the lace edged, net collars of the kind she had worn since infancy.

Apart from these suits with their varying coat lengths there remained inviolate the tailored costume, essentially British and 'respectable' for young girls. In these costumes the jacket covered the tops of the hips and the skirt, either with narrow inverted pleat or slight flare at the hem, was close fitting and straight cut—unfortunately the girls were not. The mid-calf skirts threw the jacket out of balance making it appear too short. Cutting the jacket off in this way round the hip was unkind to teen girls whose puppy fat made a mockery of the intended slim line. Made in many materials from country tweeds to fine suitings these costumes were mainly single-breasted with turnback collars, quite long revers and two or more plain or fancy patch pockets.

Dresses worn by girls in the late 30s fell into three broad groups: the summer cottons (a loose term which also covered rayons) and winter wools for everyday; afternoon dresses (which included the 'hotel' frocks); party dresses.

Floral prints on haircords and cambrics were by far the most popular for the summer dresses, followed by check gingham, seersuckers and zephyrs and the stripes; plain cloths were seldom used for the youngest sizes but the slub effects introduced on imitation linens were worn by the middle and teen age groups. In all the materials one colour dominated all others—blue. Floral prints were of light blue flowers and where the second choice was described as green then blue appeared on the pattern somewhere, the ginghams were blue and white, saxe or powder, and only in the striped cloths was there any challenge to its superiority and this mostly for school uniforms. It would have been a courageous manufacturer indeed who omitted blue from his selection of colours and it was the first choice of home dressmakers. Retailers' catalogues invariably listed 'blue and —' when describing the colours available. It was estimated that from after the 1914-18 war until 1938 blue sold 70 per cent better for children's clothes than any other colour. Pale green and pink and an occasional yellow were the only other shades considered suitable for summer. Saxe blue was also seen a good deal for woollen dresses although in the cheaper cloths it did not always come up as a pleasing colour. Red was regarded as much better for winter wear because of its warm, cheerful appearance but 'sensible' colours like brown which did not show the dirt were considered to be more appropriate since the woollen cloths could not be washed and dry-cleaning was expensive.

The accepted attire for the summer was a frock with knickers to match for the younger ones. For the older girl there was some slight difference in styling but next to none in the floral patterned fabric and without exception collar and cuffs were white for all ages. The dress was a general purpose one worn equally for school or vacation, at home or away on holiday. In appearance such frocks could only be described as self-effacing, exactly as intended. Summer dresses had short sleeves and for little or big girls from sizes 26-46ins. (66-116cms.) they were puffed with bands or cuffs the size of which diminished with the age of the owner. There were a few attempts to introduce novelty sleeves for the 40-46ins. sizes but not to any great extent. The waistline was natural with a tie-belt of self material at the back ending in a bow the purpose of which was to get some sort of fitted line to the non-existent waist but too often drooped dispiritedly at the rear. Most girls taking up to 38ins. (96cms.) had these ties at the back but once in the 40-46ins. (101-116cms.) group they were allowed an all-round belt with an inconspicuous square buckle. Skirts of dresses for the up-to-twelve years were always full, gathered or gauged at the waist, but never with all-round pleats or godets. Above this age frocks took on a tailored line with one or two knife-pleats back and front, panels, or slight flares, or fitted over the hips with godets at the hem.

Necklines were rarely left plain; they were finished with small peter pan or pointed collars, piped, stitched or embroidered to match the print of the dress. For summer, apart from plain cotton, collars were in fine piqué and organdie. As a variation on the peter pan collar and plain bodice, there was the bib yoke which descended to just below the waist and was piped in white. The peter pan collar was, however, largely unchallenged. It was not unusual for matching knickers to be included with summer dresses for girls up to twelve years of age and a top quality set of this kind in printed cotton carrying a guarantee of being absolutely fast to sunlight and washing, with three-inch hand-felled hem, could be purchased for 10s.6d. (53p.).

The most widely adopted style feature to emerge for dresses in this period was the bolero, due to the influence of teen age film star Deanna Durbin. The bolero was interpreted as a separate jacket, with or without short sleeves, or the front pieces only stitched into the side seams of the dress but it was the custom in all three cases for it to be in a strong contrast colour, e.g. navy on white.

On the beach the dress was discarded by the younger ones or tucked into the knickers. By the end of the 30s a new idea had been born, garments especially for play, not the more serious sports, tennis, swimming or school games which were provided for, but for mucking about at the seaside or in the country. The most important of these additional garments and the most revolutionary were shorts. So much publicity had been given to the tennis stars who had adopted these practical garments that the children had seen how good they would be for their own boisterous pursuits. It was they who persuaded their parents to try and get some youthful editions for themselves although they were still controversial and regarded as unsightly and a matter for headline stories in the Press. At first the children's clothing manufacturers tried to temper the masculine appearance of the boyish cut shorts by making them with pleats all round. This was not the idea at all: divided skirts were not new, they had been part of the uniform in many private schools for years. No, girls wanted the close cut tailored style which shocked the grown-ups with its tomboy look—and they got them in all kinds of materials, from two-year-olds upwards. They challenged the dress on the tennis courts and the cotton and knicker set on the beach and in the country. They were in every conceivable style including in sharp contrast to the prevailing daisy pattern image, side lacings, slit sides and back pockets.

Once having adopted shorts, suitable tops had to be found and jumpers and shirt type blouses in knitted and woven materials (cellular cloths were particularly popular) were designed to match or contrast.

Holiday outfits began to appear to meet the growing feeling that children should not be expected to make do with dresses or suits primarily devised for everyday wear so girls started to be dressed in mini-versions of women's sun and play suits, one or two-piece, with pleated skirts, or shorts or a mixture of both. It was indicative of the vagaries of the British climate that a high proportion of these play and beach outfits were in wool; one-piece play suits had warm looking cardigan jackets to match. The tinies, of course, frequently wore jackets over their waders or halter neck bathing costumes as a guard against the sun. Linen had become a traditional material for the seaside, white with navy contrast or *vice versa* being in the forefront. Button-through and wrap-over skirts with short matching jackets were introduced for girls to wear over the swim suits. These swim suits were one-piece with two or three inches of leg, bare backs and either built-up shoulders or cords over the shoulders crossing at centre back and taken round the body to tie in front. Wool was regarded as being the best material but the suits were made in a wide price range down to the cheapest cotton locknit. Protection for the feet against Britain's pebbly beaches was given by canvas 'paddling' shoes or rubber ones, the latter in bright colours with geometric designs. Whilst separate items were bought, swim suits and waders, tops, shorts, one and two-piece play or sun suits, there was a movement as well towards complete outfits which gave a well-turned-out look, hitherto thought unnecessary for children at play. Shorts, halter neck top (the reigning fashion for women) and hat were in plain and printed fabrics in co-ordinated colours, or knitted shorts, top and jacket were completed with a knitted beret to match.

Whatever their age girls wore in winter woven wool dresses with long sleeves: the frocks were meant for cold weather and anything less than wrist-length was unthinkable. Since the cloths were in solid colours or muted checks or flecks, with occasional variations in the texture, such as wool mousse or the more expensive embroidered wools, more detail had to be introduced into the cut than was necessary or desirable in the floral printed cottons. One or two pleats appeared and stitched panelling from yoke to hem but the basic silhouette remained the same, natural waistline and full skirts with tie belts for the youngest and narrow lines for the teens. Few collars were to be seen on the older girls' dresses the trend being for mandarin necklines and button trimming, repeated on the cuffs. The younger ones had collars and cuffs of shantung in a natural shade with hand-faggotting round the edge to relieve the rather severe aspect of the plain wool cloths.

Machine-knitted wool dresses and those made from knitted cloths, cut and sewn, for autumn and winter were mainly associated with the younger girls. Nearly all had knickers to match and these were slimmer fitting than the interlock type, with good shaping into the waist and leg provided by close ribbing on the machine knits. For such utilitarian frocks they showed surprising variety in design and colour combinations. This was especially noticeable at the necks: these were not left plain nor finished with ribbing but had scalloped collars with bobbles, collars ending in artists' bows or collars which were fluted and frilled into the neck. There were bib fronts outlined with pleated frills and waists were encircled with suede, leather or self-belts except, that is, for the cut-and-sewn knitted dresses which kept the tie-belts. Added interest was given by the fancy stitches introduced for panels or complete bodices and sleeves and by machine or hand-embroidery. The colours, too, were varied, tan, brick, green, pale yellow with orange, brown and white, as well as the conventional blues and reds.

More generally worn than the dresses were machine-knitted jumper suits but both had an advantage over the woven frocks, the skirts were pleated. Whilst the cottons and woven wools relied on gathers at the waist to provide the requisite fullness, knitted skirts and dresses could have pleats which lasted the life of the garment by adjustment of the ribbing to give a firm edge down each pleat. The commonest skirt in the jumper suit was knife-pleated all round whilst the dresses usually had clusters of side pleats. By far the most popular knitted two-piece was the sailor suit in navy with pull-on middy top with sailor collar and pleated skirt which held its own for many years as a leading outfit for girls in Britain and as an export to the USA and other countries.

The drawback with knitted garments, whether factory or home made was in the washing: they needed extra care in the tub and just as much in the drying if excessive shrinkage (a calamity in children's clothes) was to be avoided. Some of the manufacturers guaranteed their products as washable and unshrinkable, others insisted that any changes in shape were due to the way the garments had been washed but behind the scenes research into the problem was continuing, even so it was not to be overcome for many years. With hand-knitting yarns the position was somewhat easier and there was already at least one children's knitting wool on the market which was guaranteed not to shrink nor stretch. It sold for 6½d. (3p.) per ounce in a choice of several colours and the manufacturers not only offered, where complaints were justified, to give credit for the yarn purchased but to recompense the knitter for her time and labour in making the garment.

Midway between the everyday and the formal party frock was the afternoon or hotel dress. This was worn for 'visiting', Sunday-best and at dinner in hotels and it was essentially pretty, soft and girlish. The collars and cuffs were replaced by narrow frills gathered or smocked into the neckline or sleeve, the latter, too, took on new shapes with bolder puffs, or intricate pleating into the armholes. The skirt fullness fell from clusters of honeycombing or smocking and whilst the tie belt remained it became part of the design, slotted through waist panels or fancy rings and in satin ribbon as it so often was, matched or contrasted with the colour of the print. Cotton voiles and sheers were chosen for their pretty prints with only slight regard for washability although the best were colour fast and uncrushable and the excellent draping qualities and exquisite colourings made pure silk an obvious choice. Another fabric in which these afternoon dresses were made was shantung particularly in the characteristic muted prints but frocks in this material often retained the collar in natural tussore with faggotting or coloured embroidery. Where the whole dress was in natural tussore the embroidery took on an unusual boldness with vivid blues, greens and reds standing out against the raw silk. Into this category, too, came the organdies, plain or embroidered. Although the girl in her teens also wore afternoon dresses for informal evening occasions she had also graduated to the full-length dinner dress with covered shoulders, fitted bodice and hips, the waist marked by a belt or sash, and a straight fall to the ankle, all of which conformed to the current dinner dress rules of the adult world.

The party dress proper was the perogative of those with parents who had money for such extras. Other little girls' dreams of fairytale finery were answered if they were lucky enough to have mothers with nimble fingers or had acted as bridesmaids, and then the ankle-length confections could be brought out again for parties. The greatest demand for party frocks was at Christmas and the New Year, the high season for the mini-crowd; later they would be worn at birthday parties throughout the year. Party dresses for the up to 12's did not change much during the 30s but, almost entirely free from adult influence, followed a familiar path which met the wishes of the wearers. First and foremost they had to be pretty; secondly they had to have full skirts; thirdly they had to be trimmed. No young girl wanted an unadorned frock to wear at a party no matter how beautiful the fabric or how becoming the colour; it had to be trimmed with ribbon, flowers, frills, ruching or embroidery; it must be as far removed as possible from everyday dresses and hopefully turn the wearer into a fairy princess.

The youngest had been wearing their party dresses above the knee, at the other end of the age scale they came to just below the knee but the ankle-length styles had been coming back for the small sizes. The shapes followed the day dresses and the difference lay in the material and trimming. Georgette, taffeta, silk, organdie and velvet in plain pastels apart from the rich reds and blues of the velvet, carried well the embellishments demanded. Fortunately these were kept in proper proportion and the result was dainty and not unduly over-ornamented. Some were marred by too much ruching. This is not a dainty trimming at the best of times and appearing as it did on bodices, sleeves and skirts as a cheap, quick way of livening up a poor taffeta, for example, it too often looked heavy and ugly.

The dreams of ugly ducklings being turned into swans by beautiful dresses were not confined to the younger girls; they were just as strong, and perhaps even stronger, in the minds of the maids, and they were fortunate in that their increased height meant greater scope for glamorous effects. In this age group women's fashions still had little influence. It was visible in such sophisticated styles as tunic dresses (knee-length tops and contrast ankle-length skirts) but these made hardly any inroad into the close fitting bodice and full skirt silhouette which represented the ideal evening wear to most adolescents. Fashion might be smart but it was rarely romantic. Layers of net with cascades of frills to the ankles swirled from modestly tight bodices, big puff sleeves and the familiar bow at the back achieved the desired floating effect. Appliqué work on net matching taffeta bodices with wings of taffeta over net sleeves—a popular treatment—and tiny peplums were pretty as icing on a cake. There were few party or evening dresses without artificial flowers at the neck or waist or dotted posy fashion over the skirt. No matter how much the style might differ it almost invariably finished in a round neck, considered appropriate and necessary to emphasise the youth of the wearer but now, at the end of this period, the sweetheart neckline was at last providing an alternative. This was a simple modification of a V-neck (never thought to be right for children and young girls because it was regarded as too hard) cut away in curves either side and across the front which gave an open neck without any unseemly décolletage. There were other breakaways from round necks, for the cold shoulder dress for evening had been on the adult scene for some time: the bodice was swept up to one shoulder, leaving the other bare, but for the teens a strap, perhaps of self or contrast colour flowers robbed the line of some of its sophistication. The Grecian drape of this style was retained, softened by a cluster of flowers at the waist which, as in all other designs, was marked in some way. The ankle length had appealed as being the most becoming to all shapes and sizes but at the end of this decade the ballerina length began to creep in. The term was not so much a description of the style but of the length although its origins were clear in the close fitting bodice and extremely full skirt ending three inches above the ankle. Such a length was attractive on slim girls with good legs but not so kind to the average puppy fat adolescent.

Materials were similar to those for the younger girls with the addition of slightly bolder floral prints for the summer, moire taffeta and heavier poults and more net. There was a great deal of white as well as pastels, yellow was seen more often and there was even some black possibly because this was considered good taste for women's evening clothes.

Cloaks and coats for evenings had no relation to the dress beneath, the cloaks were simply bigger versions of those worn by the tinies. The material was similar, velvet with a toning or contrast silk lining, and if the gauging was omitted from across the shoulders it was often included on the stand-up collar. The coats, also in velvet, either had collars of similar design or were of white fur which was repeated on the cuffs. Concealed hooks and eyes fastened the front and both cloaks and coats fell smoothly without trimming to mid-calf to reveal plenty of the dress below.

Blouses did not have a prominent place in a girl's wardrobe other than those with a simple peter pan collar, front fastening style to wear with a costume, probably because they were so strongly associated with school uniforms. It was not an article either which British manufacturers cared to produce. In a dress the major part of the making went into the top half—collar, yoke, sleeves, cuffs, fastening, trimming—whilst the skirt was comparatively simple, any complex pleating effects being sent out to specialist pleating firms to be done. It was the labour in the top half of the dress for which the customer was largely paying but although the same amount of work went into a blouse—virtually the top half of a dress—parents would not pay the price the labour justified for what in their eyes was only a small, simple garment. They were able, too, during this period, to buy at extremely low prices, which no British manufacturer could match, hand-embroidered blouses imported from Hungary which were enjoying a considerable vogue because of their colourful and distinctive embroidery and unusual peasant design.

Separate cardigans and jumpers for girls from five years to the teens were nearly all in solid shades with contrast colours introduced by striped ribbing at collars and cuffs and pom-poms at the ends of cords at the neck but interest was mainly centred on fancy stitches and needle patterning. Older girls added belts to their jumpers which like their sisters' just covered the tops of the hips. The bulk of the jumpers had set-in sleeves and were worn outside the skirt but there were some raglan sleeves on ribbed styles; all were easy fitting with a good allowance for tolerance.

The ubiquitous knitted cardigan supplemented dresses for extra warmth inside the home or outside when the weather was too warm for a topcoat, and under the coats in the winter and it was very much to the fore in classrooms which were often draughty and cold. Because it fulfilled such a strictly utilitarian purpose the cardigan was purely functional in concept with plain body, ribbed cuffs and welt which embodied the low set buttoning and, as was to be expected, there was a preponderance of navy blue and grey, relieved in the case of many school dictates by the addition of official colours in the ribbing.

Those who could afford it and wanted something different from the commonplace mass-produced garments dressed their boys and girls in the hand-knitted Shetland wool jerseys, jumpers and cardigans in natural colouring with traditional Fair Isle patterning at necks and welts adding, for the girls, matching tam-o'-shanters and gloves or mitts. The boys' jerseys had turndown collars and the girls' jumpers round necklines. The shapes hardly varied over the years and this in itself became the hallmark which proclaimed their Scottish origin but it must be acknowledged that garments produced by hosiery manufacturers which owed their inspiration to the Fair Isles, whilst lacking the authentic hand-knitted look gave a touch of the Highlands to otherwise dull jerseys and jumpers.

Knitted garments in wool were a substantial proportion of the clothing for children and there was a wide price and quality range from which to choose, from the mass-produced dresses, suits, jumpers and jerseys to the top quality Scottish classics and knitted dresses imported from Austria but comprehensive as this production was it was considerably reinforced by home knitting. Many mothers not only liked to knit as much as possible for their children but they regarded buying machine-knitted garments as a lazy way of clothing them. Apart from the pleasure it gave mothers—and assorted relatives—to work on the garments it was always cheaper than buying ready-mades.

Until they were well into their teens girls did not have skirts bought specially to wear with blouses and jumpers. They made do with their school skirt if it was part of the uniform when it would most likely be knife-pleated all round, or the skirt of any costume they possessed, woven or knitted. The word skirt was not used a great deal for children except when describing the school garment, it was referred to as a kilt and this covered everything through the authentic tartans, the all-round pleated skirts, and those with plain panels in front and pleated sides and backs, the most popular of the separate skirts. They came on bodices and straps for those too young to have waists and on waistbands for the seniors: skirts of knitted jumper suits were kept in place with wide tunnel elastic at the waist.

The sober approach to much of the children's clothing was offset to some degree by the colourful tops on their socks. (One hosiery firm had over 120 different types of children's socks and stockings in their range). Half-hose, reaching half-way up the leg, had fancy patterns, stripes and checks in gay colour combinations made possible in certain cases by hand jacquard designs. Not so colourful but elegant were the pure silk socks in white or cream for wear with party frocks. The length of the sock increased with the girl's age from short sandal socks which turned over to cover the ankle and later became known as ankle socks, to half-hose with close ribbing to keep them up or elasticated inserts or garter of elastic sewn inside. The tops did not turn over as did the boys' which should have meant a neater appearance but the truth is that after a few washings the socks dropped down towards the ankles and no amount of yanking would keep them up for long.

Socks were frowned upon at school for girls and where uniforms were enforced they were forbidden even in summer. Stockings were the rule for school, in conservative black, brown and fawn, wool or cotton plated, or the very cheapest all cotton which required frequent darning. The refinements in the best of the stockings made them the most sensible buy for they gave extra strength where it was needed at knees, heels as far as the ankles, and toes. The 'gym' stockings were of splendid length going right up the thighs and under the knicker legs. The 'ordinary' length which came to less than half way up the thigh, were subjected to frequent tugging to keep them up despite garters or suspenders and ladders and holes were the inevitable result often further aggravated by the abrasion of the suspenders themselves.

The theory that it was better for children to go bareheaded had been gaining ground for some time and its advocaters derived support from the fact that neither Princess Elizabeth nor Princess Margaret wore hats except on formal occasions. Then came the Coronation of King George VI and after that they were rarely seen without them but even this could not restore the hat to its former place as a symbol of respectability. Many were worn, primarily for visits to relations, for the belief that no one was properly dressed without a hat died hard, but the Sunday-best tradition was coming to an end. Nevertheless for school the hat was compulsory and few voices were raised in protest at this accessory being part of the official uniform. Out of school hours in winter, millinery, as already noted, was part of the coat set and this, with school headwear and hood on the raincoat met most of the needs. Outside of these during the winter months the younger girls wore velour or angora felts with stitched brims turned down all the way round and the older girls had pull-on felts with wider brims which dipped over one eye. For both age groups the trimming was similar: petersham ribbon band with a single bright feather stuck through a bow at the side or front. The beret had also been taken up strongly by girls. In complete contrast were the straws worn in the summertime by the up to 18-year-olds, the last of the Sunday-best hats to die out. It was the cornfield which inspired the floral trimmings on this millinery which became indelibly associated with children's hats. The wreaths of daisies, cornflowers, buttercups, poppies and green leaves were beautifully made and grouped with such artistry that the hats were being bought long after fashion had left them behind. The most expensive were the natural leghorns with wide, floppy brims and low, rounded crowns wreathed in velvet and silk flowers. The ribbon bands no longer ended in streamers down the back but they were long enough to trail across the brim. On fine plaited straws, petersham ribbon in several colours swirled round wide dipped brims to form intricate patterns on hats designed to complete more tailored outfits. Natural straw, whether leghorn, Italian pedal or chip, provided an excellent foil for the floral or ribbon trimming but it was also dyed blue, pink, rose, lemon and green to match dresses and summer coats.

# CHAPTER 4
# Underwear and Accessories

Underwear was no more important to the five years and over than it was to the infants. The public's attitudes towards it varied from the 'chèap as possible and then throw away' right through to 'buy the best and hand it down'. In the latter category not only were vests, etc., preserved for each succeeding child they were sent back to the manufacturers for repair and renovation for grandchildren and great grandchildren. It is easy to see why manufacturers did not consider that it was necessary to create new designs when the old seemed to suit one generation after another.

Botany wool vests and cotton and art. silk mixture lacy knits were quite pretty with either opera tops or round necks and short sleeves and ribbing at the waist for a snug fit. There were panties to match with ribbed legs and waists. White and peach or pink were the colours for these and the art. silk locknit vests and knickers for summer wear. Cotton interlock vests were similar in style to the wool but without any shaping into the waist and there were also knickers in this fabric, lace edged round the legs, particularly for the smaller girls. Mesh knits in cotton and botany wool and cellular cloths were becoming more popular. Combs had been largely superseded by vest and pants but they were still worn and there were compromise 'step-ins' for the younger ages which were made in one with a vest top and elasticated legs and an opening at the back waist.

Navy blue school knickers were cut on generous lines around the seat and had tunnel elastic at the waist and legs. It eventually dawned on the makers that it was time for some changes in the design; there was no need for all that width across the seat and the legs could be shorter and narrower. This led to the introduction of the cutaway leg which meant literally that the legs were cut off just below the gusset and were finished with close ribbing incorporating 'Lastex' so dispensing with elastic which often was too tight and bad for the circulation. It took a long time for some headmistresses to be convinced that they were warm enough—and not too brief!

It was not customary for girls to wear frilled and fancy knickers except for a modest lace appliqué or baby lace edging because such finery was not considered good taste—and it was too expensive when the wearer was going to grow out of it so quickly.

Petticoats were worn on few occasions. Diaphanous summer dresses—voiles, organdies—were usually lined or sold with their own matching slips and as cotton frocks had matching knickers petticoats were unnecessary. When they were worn they were simple princess line slips with a minimum of lacy frills and machine embroidery. It irked the teen girls that their petticoats had very little shaping and were cut with 'ample room' which meant that they did not follow the lines of the figure nor set well under dresses.

Since for the purposes of her clothing a girl could be anything up to 18 years it followed that the developing figure must be taken into account and some kind of support provided. Certainly by the time she had reached 12 years her 'Liberty' bodice would have to be replaced by a garment adapted to her changing shape. Until the beginning of the 30s there was seldom any provision for this transition from girl to woman, the former had almost no alternative but to go straight from the boneless bodice to the smallest size in women's corselettes which although they had travelled far from the restrictions of the Victorian era were in tough controlling materials with plenty of bones and underwraps. Brassières and belts looked daintier but they were designed primarily for women. A few makers of women's corsetry and one or two wholesalers with strong children's departments had realised the gap that existed and launched corselettes and bras and belts specially designed for the 12-16 years but it was a difficult section for which to cater. There had been a swing away from restriction in children's clothing and the girls had enjoyed the freedom of movement which resulted. Too soon they were to lose it by wearing corsets an idea which was abhorrent to girls who were extremely sensitive and self-conscious about their growing busts. Far from wishing to acknowledge this development by wearing different garments from their possibly less mature companions they wanted to disguise it for as long as possible and loathed the idea of going into a corsetry department. It was for these reasons that corsetry manufacturers who had introduced special designs for the teens found them unprofitable. They were in any case a great deal of trouble in the factory. It was no easy task devising foundations for growing schoolgirls whose actual measurements were much larger than many women: their abdomens were often fatter and more prominent and their backs and waists thicker yet the support embodied in the garment had to be unobtrusive and the whole appearance dainty and youthful. Amongst the few who persevered were the makers of the famous 'Liberty' bodice itself who successfully marketed slip-on corselettes and corsetry for the young girl.

The all-in-one corselette produced for girls, with light boning down the front to control the abdomen, or small boned insets at the waist, side panels of elastic or 'Lastex' yarn, was being improved by the gradual adoption of zip fasteners instead of hooks and eyes and uplift bust shaping in place of the straight line across the top which did not define the bust. Slimmer girls preferred a bra and belt which looked better than the all-in-one garment. The belts had either reinforced panels or two or three bones down the front and elasticated side panels or were simply two-way stretch roll-ons. The bras relied on the cut to give all the support required. Lighter materials, strong lace and floral voiles were frequently added to the corsetry materials such as batiste, mercerised cotton and cotton mesh for bras and belts but the colours were the same, pink and peach with any patterning in self colour.

Serviceable, comfortable, warm and cheap were the principal requirements for girls' nightwear, if it was also pleasing to look at this was an advantage but not a necessity. Within the limits variety was introduced through the styling for the fabric choice was narrow. Once over the chicks and bunnies period it was flowers all the way, the prints identical on summer and winter cloths. Locknits, flannelettes, winceyettes, interlock, mercerised cotton and cellular materials were used according to the season for both pyjamas and nightdresses with more of the older girls opting for pyjamas.

In the majority of homes pyjamas meant those made from interlock and fleecy lined fabrics with pull-on tops reaching to the tops of the thighs, round necks, half- or full-length sleeves according to the season, one or two front pockets and ankle-length trousers with wide legs, held up by a white girdle round the waist. Both tops and trousers relied on bands of contrast at the neck, sleeves, pockets, hem of top and trouser legs to break the monotony of cloth and line (or the trousers themselves might be in the contrast shade). The shape of the band round the neck might be varied and a mock rifle cuff be introduced or coloured appliqués and also some machine embroidery of largely unidentifiable flowers. Breaking away from the sameness of this treatment were the Cossack pyjamas with high stand-up collars and side fastenings on contrast bands, neat and warm in wear. Pyjamas in floral printed cloths (wool and cotton) had greater design interest with more raglan sleeves and tuck-in tops to show the bias cut waists of the trousers, and collars and fancy yokes were more in evidence. There were few striped materials, these being left to the males.

Art silk locknit pyjamas were worn in the warmer weather, again some on Cossack lines, and so were cotton mesh knits which were also made into nightdresses: these were restricted in their style interest to plain cloths and contrast trimming.

Nightdresses for the younger girls whilst not following Cossack lines were similar in material and styling to the pyjamas except that the contrast band was usually omitted from the bottom hem. The smaller child quickly left behind the peter pan collar, high yoke and frill-edged buttoned front panel so closely associated with toddlers and passed on to pointed collars, bib fronts, slight gathers at the waist pulled in with half or all-round self belts, buttoned or frill edged cuffs. Midway between child and woman the teen girl was acknowledged but without relation to adult nightwear. Floral prints were the same as those of the smaller sizes but the pull-on tops of pyjamas were replaced by jackets, not just s.b. coat styles but with rever collars, link buttoning at the neck, frog fastenings down the front instead of buttons. In interlock pyjamas and in some knitted wool cloths the pull-on shapes remained but necks were V-shape or round with perhaps rouleaux bows, there was more embroidery across the front and all-round self belts; nightdresses in interlock were similarly designed. Nightdresses in art. silk locknit for the older girl possibly owed more to women's styling with similar lace and embroidery, V-necks and short, full sleeves. A great many nightdresses were made at home, a girl's size being a simple garment for the home dressmaker at a time when serviceability and warmth was all. On the other hand it was not so easy to run up a dressing-gown at home nor did many manufacturers find it worthwhile to produce children's sizes; the view was taken that this was an article which could be dispensed with and not only in the poorest families.

The object of the garment being to provide protection against chills, wool velours, lightweight fabrics in fine wool and ripple cloths of cosy, fleecy-backed cotton, supplied this requirement but there were also dressing-gowns in printed silks and crêpes for summer wear. The length gradually shortened as the child grew, rising from the ankle to lower calf, the peter pan collar and high centre buttoning disappeared, to be largely replaced by the shawl collar, wrapover design indistinguishable from the boys' except for the reverse wrap. The cloths were lighter and the checks gayer but the solid or contrast facings were similar; not so those in some fine wool fabrics, these were younger editions of women's dressing-gowns, generously embroidered with clusters of multi-coloured flowers and correspondingly more expensive. At the other end of the scale dressing-gowns in cotton ripple cloths were devised to do the job of providing warmth and their embellishments were mainly confined to trimmings of art silk braid to match the girdle. Quilting had not yet made its mark although wadded collars and cuffs, stitched down in a series of straight lines were to be seen.

Outside of the 'children's' shoes category, i.e. sturdy lace-ups for school in black or brown, rubber Wellington boots and goloshes, girls' shoes for the five-year-old upwards in the late 30s were influenced by current women's footwear, in the composition of the uppers if not the shape. In the early years the walking shoes were predominantly one-bar with backs coming well up to the ankle bone and high U-vamps, for the 3-6½ and 7-10½ sizes the heel was practically non-existent. This type of footwear was also considered to be the most suitable for the bigger girl who needed a larger size—up to 6-7—but was only in her early teens and her shoes, too, had flat heels only a degree or two higher than her younger sister's. In addition to the prosaic tan and black box calf, girls of all ages wore these one-bar shoes in red, blue or green and shiny black patent one-bar and ankle-straps. For special occasions the smaller girls had hand-sewn bar shoes in blue or pink goat or white kid: more sophisticated for the next age group were hand-sewn fawn lizard.

Sandals for girls were surprisingly advanced in styling with design features which would not have appeared dated in the 60s. The Grecian sandal in tan leather with non-slip sole was worn from five years to the teens. It consisted of two buckled straps across the front, slotted through a centre bar which ran from a strap over the instep to the toes and a closed back with a series of cut-outs either side. Somewhat similar in style but daintier was the strip sandal consisting of three pairs of crossed loops in the front again passing through a centre strap from instep to toe, and ornamental cut-outs which left the back almost as open as the front. The open look was carried even further by toeless sandals with three straps over the front which left the toes free, the sandal being held on by the closed back and buckled strap over the instep.

The more conventional parents put their children in sandals which were virtually the same for boys and girls; the uppers were of tan leather, with a punched design in the vamp, the latter being extended up the instep to pass through a strap, the backs and sides were closed, and the soles and slight heels of crêpe. Although they had a young appearance such sandals were not confined to the tinies but were worn throughout childhood right up to the teens.

'Maids" shoes whilst following current women's footwear contrived, because of adaptations considered necessary to suit the age of the wearer, to give the impression of being heavy and more appropriate for middle-aged women. There were plenty of ghillie shapes with front lacing and built-up leather heels. Monk shoes in tan or black calf with high vamps continued over the instep and fastened with wide buckle straps looked like boys' footwear and shoes with instep ties in tan calf with punched designs were quite matronly. The one-bar and court shoes were daintier with ornamental punching, sometimes suggesting a toe cap, or with diamond shape cut-outs either side of the strap: as well as the customary tan and black box calf they were made in stone glacé, brown willow and black patent, and the covered heels were lighter in appearance. The heels for the most part were low, Cuban fashion, but there were some Louis shapes which gave a touch of elegance. The toes were elongated and pointed to follow fashion and not the feet. Similar to those worn by women were the one-bar 'golfers' in white buck with tan calf toecap and half back: the two-tone effect was also carried out in lace-up versions in tan glacé and fawn canvas.

In addition to the bar sandals already described 'maids' had other light shoes for the summer which were not so casual: these were often two-tone, popular colourings being tan and beige, and although the covered heels were flat they were higher than the sandals and the fronts were pointed.

Increased interest in horse riding indicated that in a few years it would no longer be the perogative of the upper classes who considered the habit as important as the horse, perhaps more so since a poor horse might be forgiven—though deprecated—but the wrong outfit would not. Despite the fact that price was not an undue deterrent, the made-to-measure convention was proving too costly for the widening circle of young riders and realising this outfitters were offering riding kit from stock, something which would have been inconceivable a decade or so before. The ready-made riding kit in no way represented a paring down of the number of garments which by tradition were thought to be essential to the proper enjoyment of the sport, rather the manufacturers endeavoured to produce all the articles required; it was the riders themselves who were to discard the old ideas and adopt more casual ways. So from stock parents could buy for their sons and daughters canter, cubbing and hacking jackets, jodphurs and breeches in several materials, bowlers, hard and soft caps, felt riding hats, shirts, sweaters, ties, stocks and gloves, boots and jodphur boots, worthy of any Pony Club turnout. Riding mackintoshes differed only in size and weight of cloth from those worn by adults; they had the same full skirt to cover the saddle and horse's back, storm collar fastening over the chin and windproof cuffs.

In the 7-12-year-old group there had been much interest in the clothes worn by Princess Elizabeth and Princess Margaret but they were not slavishly copied. One reason was that the two

Princesses were clad in outfits which it was customary for girls of their ages to wear, jumpers and kilts, simple cotton frocks, tailored coats and other ordinary garments so that they were conforming to current fashion and not starting any of their own. Moreover they continued to be seen in the same, or similar, styles for much of their childhood. When the Princesses were attired in original and distinctive designs created specially for them there was a demand for replicas but the Royal outfits were of such a quality that they could not be reproduced successfully in cheaper versions. Witness the guardsman coats, these, militarily inspired, had narrow stand-up collars, exaggerated lapels across the chest from armhole to armhole, double-breasted fastenings with self-covered buttons, fitted waists and back fullness. The design was not a particularly becoming one for most girls and without the immaculate tailoring and high quality cloth of the originals the mass-produced imitations which could not reproduce faithfully the permanent stand-up collars and flat lapels were disappointing.

The publication of official photographs of the Princesses always resulted in requests for facsimilies of the garments but there was no great rush to get them into the shop windows, this would have been regarded as being in poor taste. One picture of Princess Elizabeth that was especially admired and did inspire a few party dresses showed her in a white organza dress with picot edged pleated frills on the skirt, double wing sleeves similarly pleated, and a blue sash. After the Coronation of King George VI in 1937, as was to be expected, the Princesses' clothes were even more keenly studied but there was no deviation from the general principle of serviceable garments beautifully understated. Despite this conservatism Britain with such a happy asset of two Princesses whose father and mother had so unexpectedly become King and Queen had thrust upon it the role of international style leader for the young set with America its most eager follower.

# CHAPTER 5
# The Schoolboy

The 30s were the ultra-conservative years in boys' clothing. Youngsters wished to conform with their schoolmates, or, when the time came, dress as did their fathers. They were considered to be boys and youths until they were 18 or 19 and although they were divided into size groups for the purposes of their clothing three only were thought to be adequate to cope with developing bodies and tastes: these were approximately 3-8, 8-14 and 14-18 years.

The small boy's transition from the frillies of the infants' era was to a knicker (shorts) suit, single or double-breasted, in serge for formal wear, tweeds for school or the many varieties of flannel. The best of these had linings in the sleeves of the jackets and double seats, extra turnings for lengthening and mending pieces and another pair of knickers could be purchased at the same time. They were guaranteed for six months and were in the same style for 6-14 years.

British parents took a down-to-earth attitude towards boys and their clothing; it must last as long as possible, should be serviceable and befitting boys who took no interest in their apparel regarding it as an encumbrance during horse-play or as a carrier for treasured possessions unappreciated by adults. The first long trousers were permitted if the boy was in his last term at school, or for the nine-year-old whose first excursion into trousers was probably a pair of whites for the School XI.

The opening of Stowe in 1923 had slowly affected school uniforms for boys. Breaking away from the black jacket, vest (waistcoat) and striped trousers, stiff collars and top hats, and straw boaters, Stowe put the boys into grey flannel suits during the week and blue serge suits on Sundays. The success of this hitherto unheard of casual approach to clothing in a public school caused other establishments to reappraise their strict mode of dress and ease their regulations to give the boys more freedom. Added impetus to this movement came with the clothes shortages of the second world war.

Meanwhile the accepted wear for boys at most public schools was a double-breasted navy serge suit which also served for semi-formal occasions. Attempts to impose a uniform way of dressing were not so strenuous in elementary schools as they were for girls presumably since there was neither the desire nor the opportunity for deviation from conventional attire. Other state-aided schools enforced certain uniform requirements but not to the same extent as the girls. Headmasters were content if the boys were clad, as they invariably were, in grey suit, shirt, tie and three-quarter TOT hose and black shoes. A cap and blazer with badge were encouraged with due regard for the parents' pockets.

Boys' blazers were identical with the girls' save for the reverse fastening but their headgear was of vast significance. Boys grudgingly wore—or carried screwed up in their pockets—compulsory caps, the elementary schools limiting their versions to grey or another drab colour with just a modest one or two-colour embroidered badge sewn on the front, other institutions regarded the cap as a cardinal feature of the uniform. There were many ways in which official colours could be introduced, from the whole cap in one shade, contrast peak, alternating segments, number of segments, one or two stripes between each segment, segments running round the cap instead of up and down, swinging tassels, number of colours in embroidered badges, variation in the shape of the badges, metal badges, type of material used, up to the giddy heights of velvet for prefects—or merely the button on top. All of which added to the cost of the article since so much labour went into the making. The caps rarely fitted the variety of pates they were intended to cover and the fact that in some the top cloth tended to shrink in the rain showing the white cotton lining was an added disadvantage. In the summer straw boaters were favoured with hatbands in the official colours and in winter seniors had trilby hats of grey flannel felt.

The school tie had achieved fame, if not notoriety, in adult circles largely through the comedians, the Western Brothers. Supplied in miniature for prep. schools and made from all manner of fabrics from serge through to pure silk like the cap it came in unlimited stripes, embroideries and shades. In order that there should be no variation in the colour of the blazer and the tie the material for both could be woven from similar yarn. The shade, design—whether woven or embroidered—and the fabric, could be combined in such a phenomenal number of ways that the diverse requirements of headmasters all over the country could be satisfied.

The gaberdine raincoat was the all-purpose topcoat but other than this overcoats were knee-length in sturdy tweeds and herringbone cloths and usually double-breasted with long broad lapels, flap pockets and half-belts at the back above an inverted pleat. Covert was also used a great deal for the younger boys, often combined with dark brown velvet on the collar in the most expensive coats and all but the heaviest weight materials were lined with wool material in a check design.

A ubiquitous garment for boys of every age was the jersey. In grey wool with turndown collar, over a tie, the jersey had a firm place for school; colour was introduced by striping on collar, cuffs or round the waist welt, tying-up with the official shades, others had bands of tartan inspired checks. Marl mixtures were a close second to plain grey and Shetland wools and Fair Isle designs were also worn, the latter by the smaller boys for whom the necks were made round and close fitting with buttoning along one shoulder. The jerseys were long, coming well below the waist and covering some of the pocket openings but they had the merit of supplying warmth where it was needed, across the small of the back. There was practically no effort to cater for anything other than 'sensible' colours and official school shades and styles. Jerseys for out-of-school hours were simply scaled down versions of whatever men's styles were considered to be suitable which meant the most mediocre in grimly purposeful colours.

Frequently matching the grey jersey were the ribbed, three-quarter, TOT hose, the turnover tops repeating the striping or fancy check. In the mid-30s 'Lastex' yarn had been brought in by the hosiery manufacturers as a means of keeping the hose in place; its success was assured since it gave the necessary achorage without restricting circulation. The grey and fawn marls of three-quarter TOT hose worn out of school hours were cheered up by colourful hand-jacquard designs round the tops. The splicing of toes and heels, as for school hose, could be of pure linen. Mending wool was included and one manufacturer was so confident of his non-shrinkage guarantee that he attached a foot-rule to every pair so they could be measured before and after washing.

In periods of intense cold, gloves would be donned, brown or black leather, fleecy lined with one or two stud fasteners, or knitted, in grey most likely or navy, and there was the scarf, not always vital for warmth but useful in blazoning forth in wide stripes and knotted fringe the school colours. If you were very young and poor and your clothing was threadbare then mother wrapped a scarf across your chest and pinned the ends round the back. The result might lack the satorial elegance of the school scarf flung carelessly over one shoulder and present a rather bumpy appearance but it gave some comfort against biting winds.

Shoes which assisted and did not impede the natural development of children's feet were being sold by reputable manufacturers who had made a thorough study of the desirability of allowing freedom for growing toes whilst giving at the same time the requisite support allied to flexibility and lightness and protection against the weather. The overall effect had been to take children's shoes for schooldays out of the field of fashion and give them a character of their own which reflected concern primarily with meeting those requirements. It was accepted that whilst adult footwear was largely affected by high-fashion however uncomfortable in wear or bad for the feet the result might be, their children's school shoes were things apart and were not to be miniature editions of their own, nor did it occur to the children to demand that this should be so.

Shoes, then, were following much more closely the natural shape of the foot and support in the right places and corrective aids were being built in not only in walking shoes but sandals and sports footwear as well. The boys' school shoe was simply that, black or brown footwear for wearing to and from and probably at, school, laced-up, low heeled, discreet, tough, as waterproof and boyproof as possible and as for appearance the only requirement was that the shoes should be well-polished. Where circumstances permitted schools liked their pupils to change into some kind of sports or games shoe during the day and these were similar to the outdoor styles, lacing up well over the instep but with no heels and crêpe soles instead of leather. A particular effort was made to stop children wearing Wellington boots at their desks. This rubber footwear made the children's feet very hot and tender if worn continually but the boots themselves were so useful in cold and wet weather that there were few children who were without a pair of 'Wellies'. Plimsolls, canvas uppers and rubber soles, served as house shoes or for outdoors in the summer, alternating with brown sandals with punched hole patterns on the vamp and one buckled strap. Football and cricketing boots and white canvas cricket and tennis shoes supplemented a boy's footwear and for the élite there were black patent dancing pumps for the evening.

A necessary item for every boy was a belt to keep up his trousers. Not much attention had been given to the design of this article except in regard to its function. It had settled down to a strip of elastic webbing with a snake or prong and buckle fastener and in either solid or stripes could incorporate the school colours. So little thought was paid to this accessory that the standard width of 1¾ins. (4.4cms.) was never varied and the younger boys had to wear belts which were far too big for them. By the mid-30s there was increasing dissatisfaction with this type of belt with its heavy clasp. It had insufficient elasticity and quickly became too loose for its purpose. The width was reduced to 1¼ins. (3cms.) and the clasp correspondingly cut down in proportion. Artificial silk fibres had enabled a more suitable type of webbing to be obtained, lighter in weight and with greater elasticity and the result was a better belt with a longer life and much neater appearance.

Since the outer garments in which boys were dressed were so plain and serviceable it is not surprising that their underwear was on the same lines. Only the younger ones wore combs with high round necks and short sleeves finished with close ribbing as were the mid-thigh legs but they were being superseded by vests and pants. The established vest had a two- or three-button front according to size with high neck and short sleeves and reached half-way down the thighs but more and more boys were attracted to the athletic vest or singlet which had no sleeves and dashing deep armholes and neck and narrow straps over the shoulders—slightly wider for the smaller sizes where warmth came before fashion. Underpants were also being subject to change. In keeping with the buttoned-up high fitting vests were the button front pants which were scaled down versions of men's underwear. They had similar reinforced waist panels even on the smallest sizes although versions for the youngest had ribbing at the legs. Even their slightly older brothers had complete copies of their father's pants: inordinately wide they came well down the thigh—and frequently below the short trousers particularly if they were made of some types of interlock which stretched in the wash. It was not until the late 30s that a well-known hosiery firm included in their range pants with short legs which would not show below the boys' knickers. The manufacture of such mundane garments as underwear for boys was treated so indifferently that their size range stopped well before the men's began and the resultant gap could only be bridged by the youth 'growing into' the smallest men's pants which were quite a size. As in the case of vests the first stirrings of a need for a change had already begun and this was served by the incorporation of 'Lastex' thread at the waist which dispensed with the three-buttoning, lined, waist shaping and resulted in a pull-on garment, neater in wear and fitting better under the shorts or long trousers.

Notwithstanding the prosaic nature of boys' underwear, boarding schools managed to specify several weights and large quantities in their official lists.

Nightwear was as sedate and as unassuming as the rest of the boy's wardrobe. Its function was to cover the body during the night hours and not to be regarded as a means of displaying bright colours and patterns, not, of course, that any boy would have wanted to do any such thing. As soon as one- and two-piece sleeping suits had been discarded their place was taken by pyjamas. These fell into two groups, tops with high round necks buttoning on the shoulder, for the beginners or with Cossack inspired collars with side front buttoning, and a jacket style with pointed collar, buttoned front and patch pocket. Older boys had identical copies of their fathers' in the same 'pyjama' striping with open neck jackets, lapels and top and side pockets. Sleeves were full-length and the material plain or striped after their elders'. The trousers were held up by white girdles threaded through the top and tied in the front and the ankle-length trousers were straight and roomy. Fabrics were cotton or tough winceyette or flannelette whilst those for the younger boys were also in soft cotton interlock.

Dressing-gowns again were based entirely on the father's garment in cut and colour. After the bunnies came off, the peter pan collar and button front were retained for a spell but soon there was much emphasis on a tailored line. The roll collar and lapels, the patch pocket and the cuffs would be finished with two-tone silk or art. silk braiding, matching the belt, or bound in self colour silk or art. silk material in which case the belt would be of self material. Colours, naturally, were dark—red, maroon, brown and navy or checks of equally subdued tone.

The one bright spot was to be found on vacation. Racing style swimming costumes were replacing the customary boxy shape with built-up shoulders, for the older boy, and an even bigger breakaway was the advent of bathing trunks. The wide-leg flannel or drill shorts for holidays were as yet hardly touched by the brief cut, close fitting shapes worn on the Continent but the older boy was rebelling at the usual collar-attached, white or grey flannel shirts with long sleeves alternative to school wear and turning to sports shirts with short sleeves in fancy knitted, woven and cellular cloths in bright colours. Boys up to eight years were wearing shorts of heavyweight jersey with elasticated waists which were easy to pull on and off and older boys were starting to copy their fathers and have flannel trousers with the new self-supporting waistbands.

This, then, was the picture when war came in 1939. In some respects the garments barely altered through the years until the middle of the 60s. The great changes in baby wear had already taken place, only refinements were to come, but at the other end of the scale there was to be a monumental upheaval. The teens were to go out of the children's sphere altogether and become an important, if not in some ways the most important, part of the community, and the word child was to encompass an ever shrinking field from 16 to 14, from 12 to 10. Coupled with this was the demise of the parents' domination over the child in the matter of clothing purchases and with it a spurning by the child of orthodox garments and a demand for copies of adult styles, and controversy over school uniforms was to start in earnest and rumble on over the years.

# CHAPTER 6
# The Early War Years

Looking back to the war years it seems incredible that a nation wholly committed to fighting the enemy should be so sensitive to the clothing needs of the young. It was an awareness not shared at first by officialdom, not through any deliberate policy but because few outside the small circle of manufacturers and distributors understood the complexities of catering for a clientele which extended from the beginning of life, through infancy, on to childhood, through the sub-teens and on to the teens. Making children's clothes was not simple, it was not easy, it was not even very profitable—but it was very necessary as events were to prove, and long before the war ended the production of these garments moved from obscurity to top civilian priority.

The state of the children's clothing in Britain was revealed in the 'trial run period' in 1938 when the youngsters were evacuated to the country during the Munich crisis. Shopkeepers were familiar with the quick purchases of underwear and nightwear that heralded an appendix operation or some other emergency but it was not until the youngsters were sent away from their homes that it became clear how sadly in need of new clothing were many boys and girls. All available stocks of nightwear and socks and stockings were bought out when the children went from the big cities in 1938 and the pattern was repeated in 1939.

After Munich and despite the 'Peace in our time' pledge the feeling persisted that crises affecting the children might recur and by the following spring wholesalers were stocking garments suitable for children being evacuated in an emergency. Warmth was regarded as the prime requisite and the wholesale houses started stocking up with jerseys and slacks, the latter not then universally worn by children.

The prevailing spirit of 'carry on as usual' during the early days of the war prompted firms to make and sell the same type of garments as they had done in peacetime. Apart from the responsibility of ensuring that sufficient clothing was available there was a strong conviction that as far as possible children should not be deprived of their pleasures; of greater importance, the nation's future was in their hands and healthy growth and development must be safeguarded. That some things had to be sacrificed was understood but there was a determination not to drop all luxuries but rather to adapt them to the altered conditions. Thus one manufacturer put gleaming white linings in his scarlet velvet party cloaks so that for homegoing in the black-out they could be worn reversed to show up in the dark. Full-length party frocks, with double or even triple layers of poult and net, trimmed with intricate ruching and lace, and uncrushable velvets with colourful embroidery were being sold until the autumn of 1940 when production finally ceased. Even then festive frocks as such did not disappear, for knee-length taffetas and velvets suitable for parties continued to be made. There were dresses, too, for afternoon and evening, the 'hotel' frocks. Embroidered organdie dresses were not yet seen as luxuries but as traditional necessities. Despite the practical simplicity of the first hurried weddings before the men went overseas, elaborate ankle-length styles for bridesmaids, with complicated cut and trimming, were going through the factories in 1940.

The view that, apart from the requirements of protection, comfort and fit, babies' and toddlers' wear should be pretty and appealing was sacrosanct in the first year of the war. Typical was the baby coat in one manufacturer's standard range in cream pure wool velour, piped in pink crêpe-de-chine: the cream collar and cuffs, also in crêpe-de-chine, were hand-embroidered with French knots in blue and pink. On the high yoke were minute pearl buttons sewn on with alternate pink and blue silk thread. Just as commonplace was a toddlers' coat in pure wool with detachable collar of organdie embroidered with minute blue and pink hyacinths and edged with lace. The underbrim of the bonnet was lined with matching organdie. Workers were busy on traditional christening robes in high-quality materials such as crêpe-de-chine, or finest net over pure silk.

Hand-embroidery was not confined to the tiny tots; generously smocked bodices and hand-worked collars and cuffs appeared on everyday wool and cotton dresses as a matter of course. Appliqué work which called for great skill in the cutting and sewing was a feature in 1940 of every type of child's garment from nightwear bunnies and rabbits to velvet leaves in clusters on tailored coats. Fine piping, pin-tucking and stitching continued as an accepted part of outerwear. The multi-rows of stitching on self or velvet inlays on collars, a hall-mark of British coats, remained so until the 'austerity' regulations came into force in 1942. Delicate pin-tucking was a favourite form of embellishment on both coats and dresses, sometimes covering the whole top of a coat to give a lattice effect with the crown of the matching hat tucked in similar fashion. Tiny velvet buttons in the centres of the diamonds formed by the pin-tucking often completed the design. Pleats—and there were plenty in coats—retained their sprat heads stitched in silk, although these could be claimed as more useful than decorative since they gave strength at places where there was the greatest pull on the cloth.

The cut of outerwear garments was generous—skirts were gathered, flared, pleated, circular or with gores—keeping to the first requirement of girls' garments that skirts must swing out when the wearer twisted round. The customary choice of cloths for coats was offered in those war years. A style could be obtained, for example, in pure Irish friezes, Donegal tweeds, pure Shetlands, naps and velours and fancy tweeds and, of course, a variety of colours. For greater warmth instead of the art silk lining, one of pure wool fabric could be ordered if required. Even more remarkable was the fact that months after the war started coat manufacturers were running a 'specials' service and offering to send shopkeepers swatches of cloth so that customers wishing to have coats made to their children's measurements could select the fabrics they preferred. There was hardly less choice for hats: these could be supplied in velours of wool or fur felt, tweed, cotton, silk, panama straw and linen and berets were in an even greater variety of materials. Even dressing-gowns, although the main emphasis was on warmth, were being produced in tussore and shantung through 1940 and beach wear could be bought in cotton, wool, rayon, silk and linen.

Merchandise tie-ups with characters likely to appeal to children continued and increased although it should have been clear that no extra inducement was going to be needed to sell goods; getting, not selling, was to be the big problem. Most powerful of all in their sales appeal were the Disney characters. 'Pinocchio', the second full-length colour cartoon, came to London in March 1940 but before that licensing arrangements had already been made with producers of handkerchiefs, bibs and feeders, rompers, pinafores, mitts, gloves and hats. Altogether there were twelve different characters in the film which were offered to manufacturers to use under licence. Retailers, too, installed special window displays of merchandise

*A typical classic tailored coat worn by girls up to eighteen years, stitched velvet collar, guardsman front, hand-felled linings. Its first challenge came with the post-war jigger and swagger coats of the Paris collections and later that formidable rival the duffle.*

following the great success of the London première. 'Gulliver's Travels' was another film which provided label lure on kiddies' garments and accessories.

The influence of these American promotions was to wane as the war progressed but some were resuscitated when peace came. There was to be no revival of their domination in another corner of the British children's market closed to the Americans now because of the ban on imports and, as it proved, lost forever. From the late 30s American dresses, mainly cotton, had been best-sellers in the UK, stealing the trade from British firms at first because of the magic of a child's name against which no home product could compete. The boom started with that phenomenon, Shirley Temple. Mothers wanted their little girls to look like her and they lapped up the copies of the frocks she wore in her films or sponsored. Apart from the tremendous attraction of the name, the styling of the dresses themselves was quite new to Britain. For years there had been hardly any change in infants' frocks, they fell from a fairly deep yoke, were invariably smocked, and had a half-belt tying at the back. More expensive dresses had the front and back smocked from shoulder seams to waist but with the fullness of the material taken in with a half-belt to give a waisted look.

Shirley Temple styles were a complete departure from the inveterate practices of British makers. The majority of the necklines were lower and wider, with no collars, instead of straight yokes they fell from curved necklines, with no tie-belts, there might be some appliqué work, a touch of machine embroidery, certainly colour contrast, but no smocking, and they were very short. They did not have the generous seams and hems of their British counterparts nor the tolerance which was customary to allow for growth but this gave a better fit which mothers liked. They had one other important feature which was completely new to mothers in Britain, many of them unbuttoned down the front and were easier to wash, iron and put on the child. The whole effect of the American dresses was babyish, undoubtedly deliberate to make the star look even younger than she was, but this, too, appealed to mothers. (As she grew up even Shirley Temple conformed to the schoolgirl image and was dressed in puff sleeve frocks with natural waists and tie belts at the back.)

*Baby coats tailored in high-quality pure wool velour cloth with fine stitching on velvet inlays gained for Britain an international reputation before and for many years after the Second World war.*

*Like the coats the exquisite smocked dresses produced in Britain had no equal and were worn by Princesses in Royal households all over the world but the puff sleeves and peter pan collars lost favour with Britain's own little girls.*

*The war was on but in 1940 manufacturers had not given up the world of children's parties and were still making elaborate dresses like this with several layers of net covered with rows of narrow lace.*

For the older girls there was the much-loved teenager with an international following, Deanna Durbin. The design of her clothes, too, was excellent and she was responsible for the popularity, among the younger set, of the bolero (adopted, perhaps, to conceal her developing bustline?). The merchandising promotion for her contemporary, Judy Garland, enjoying as well world-wide fame, ran into some difficulties in the UK. No doubt to the astonishment of the American film company, a British firm considered that in selling Judy Garland dresses there might be some confusion in the UK with their own brand. At the end of 1938 an interlocutory injunction had been imposed in the High Court upon Canadian Trading Agencies (Fashions) Ltd. restraining them from using the name 'Judy' for dresses sold by them in connection with Judy Garland because of the trade mark owned by Simpson & Godlee Ltd. of Manchester for 'Judy' fabrics and garments distributed in Great Britain by Wm. O'Hanlon & Co. Ltd. Early in 1939 Canadian Trading Agencies (Fashions) Ltd. gave an undertaking to use 'Miss Garland frocks as worn by Miss Garland, the Metro-Goldwyn-Mayer film star' or 'Miss Garland frocks' and that such frocks would not bear or imply any reference to the name 'Judy'.

The American dresses (coats never had a chance in the UK) mainly in cotton materials, achieved a considerable hold on the market, much to the chagrin of British firms who claimed, with some justification, that when mothers were shown home-produced frocks they insisted on three-inch hems, high-quality workmanship and durability—and knickers to match. The film star garments had none of these attributes but mothers bought them simply because of the drop ticket carrying the name and photograph of the Hollywood favourite and the refreshing designs. The competition was not confined to film star tie-ups, other manufacturers in the USA looked towards this lucrative market. It was said that their sales to Britain were almost all profit: they worked out their costings on the potential orders in their own country and any remainders of the long runs they were able to turn out were sent to Britain at attractive prices. Whilst they did not have the powerful appeal of named merchandise they did have similar styling and their cloth patterns were exceptionally good. It was the latter asset that helped to put British firms at a disadvantage. Few materials specially intended for children were available from the mills and of those that were, many were the nursery rhyme, chicken and bunny patterns which had been running for years. For the rest the maker-up had to choose the most suitable of the solid colours, checks and stripes or those hardy perennials, 'Manchester florals'. Because of the small orders which the makers-up were able to put down the mills were not disposed to go to the expense involved in designing new patterns and rollers. The American companies, on the other hand, because of their purchasing power, could command whatever prints they wanted in the colour, size and type most suited to their requirements.

That the lure of the American dresses was, however, almost wholly centred on the famous names with which they were linked was proved in the post-war years when American firms tried to recapture the trade. They no longer had the Shirley Temples and the Deanna Durbins and Britain had by then moved away from the 30s way of thinking and left the USA behind: considered on their own merit the styles then appeared jaded, the materials flimsy, the make cheap. It was to the Continent that the British were to look and then after a decade, take the lead themselves. Because of the inroads these frocks had made on the pre-war market the question asked when imports were banned was how the gap they left would be filled but it came to have no significance as the war went on and wearability and value for coupons became the overriding considerations.

Those days lay ahead and meanwhile there were strong underlying reasons for the apparent desire in wartime Britain to maintain peacetime behaviour. It did not mean any lessening of a total commitment to the war effort: on the contrary it was part of the fight. One of the many things the Nazis did which sickened the British was the corruption of the children from an early age through their evil philosophy. The sight of boys and girls marching and 'heiling' with military precision was an anathema to British parents although, paradoxically, the majority of their children went to school in uniforms; patriotic influences and military motifs had little or no place in children's garments. Parents wanted their boys and girls to be reared in a carefree atmosphere. This was not their war, it was one their parents had to fight and they did not want the youngsters to be deprived of the delights of childhood. How to strike the right balance between this laudable object and the demands of the Forces became more difficult for the Government as the war years rolled on.

Although 'business as usual' typified the aim of the specialist children's wear firms in the main, there were other directions in which production was already profoundly affected. In some branches of children's clothing, such as underwear and hosiery, the major suppliers were the men's and women's houses. These, however, were soon heavily committed to clothing for the Forces in addition to civilian requirements. Children's sizes had never shown the same handsome profits as men's and women's and they were more trouble to produce, so firms whose brands were household names immediately dropped this troublesome side. Some at least were to regret this afterwards when, as the war went on, special concessions over the call-up of workers and supplies of raw material were given to manufacturers of baby and children's wear.

Despite the resolve not to be panicked out of the carry-on-as-usual routine one immediate acknowledgment of the times was the invention of the siren suit, a garment destined to remain for generations. It was assumed that full-scale air raids on the big cities would begin once war was declared. Warmth and practicability had always been important factors but now a new requisite was added, speed of dressing. Anticipating the night bombing raids when the wail of the sirens would mean a quick dash to the shelters, designers realised that something better was needed than a dressing-gown or topcoat to cover pyjamas or nightdress when a child was taken from a warm bed. The solution was the siren suit. Even before production was started in the factories, prototypes went on display in Oxford Street with an announcement that orders were being taken. The first suits were simple coveralls in wool velour with attached hood and draught-excluding fitted cuffs at wrists and ankles. When the fears were realised and the reign of aerial bombardment began the siren suit became no longer an extra but a necessity. Basically the design had immense advantages and its neat appearance and wearability quickly earned it recognition as the right garment for the exigencies of wartime.

Described variously as the ARP, alarm, air raid, and, finally, the siren suit, the first choice of material, wool velour, was followed by corduroy, which had the advantage of being washable, and fleecy lined windproof cloths: some, for the smaller sizes, were knitted in wool. Once the suit was accepted as meeting the requirements of the hour the manufacturers

*Designed for war—the 'siren suit' for night dashes to air raid shelters. Battle dress style with large pockets to carry identification card, etc., there were also narrow ones for a torch and a shoulder strap to hold the gas mask.*

began thinking of it as a garment for children which meant bringing to its design the refinements which their knowledge of youngsters prompted them to include. Drop backs, with the buttons discreetly hidden, were incorporated; for babies and toddlers, feet and mitts were built-in and an appliqué or two of the well-loved bunny or chick added to give something of a familiar feeling. The droopy bagginess of the first numbers disappeared with the inclusion of darted waists and padded shoulders but the grim purpose of the garments was never forgotten. A tab on the shoulder was included for holding the strap of the gas mask; pockets, so smart in their unusual proportions, were scaled to be large enough to accommodate the identity card, or long and slim to hold a torch.

So apt was the siren suit that it became a basic item for the small sizes and many years after the warnings ceased to wail it was still called the siren suit, the name being supplanted by 'snow' suit only later when imports from Canada of snow suits, much grander versions but basically the same coverall, gave it a more peaceful title. The old expression lingers on in some firms, its sinister connotation long since forgotten. It took a war to persuade the conservative British to put its infants into a more practical outfit than the indispensable breechette set but there was no time now for the pulling-on of ill-designed breechettes and the fastening of innumerable buttons at ankles, waists and down the fronts of coats. Not that the breechette set died immediately, it only had a powerful rival but although it hung on it was against mounting and justified criticism.

The evacuation of three-quarters of a million children from densely populated areas to what were then considered to be safe regions meant, where money was available, hasty purchases to fill in the gaps in the wardrobes: biggest of these, as already mentioned, were in underwear and nightwear. Even so, many of the children were sent away without the modest number of articles thought to be the minimum necessary in the circumstances, such as, for a girl:

Nightdress or pyjamas
Raincoat
Cardigan
Blouse
Gym tunic
1 Petticoat
1 Bodice
1 Pair Knickers
1 Vest or Combinations
2 Pairs Stockings
Handkerchiefs

In the main parents tried to provide sufficient clothing, the irresponsible ones left it to the reception areas and the foster parents. The war brought benefits to at least one group of youngsters in Britain, the hitherto barefoot boys and girls of the depressed areas such as the South Wales valleys now had shoes and socks. The war and full employment brought money into the homes and some to spare at last for footwear.

It soon became evident that for the new life which the boys and girls were leading a different type of clothing was required. Instead of pavements and concrete playgrounds, nearby schools and shops and handy buses, there were unmade-up roads to walk along and muddy fields to cross and it was tramping, not transport, that got them to the shops and schools. The wind whipped across the open spaces with increased force without the barriers of built-up streets. As the light shoes and outerwear of the old life proved too thin they were replaced by stronger shoes, sturdy dungarees, shorts, slacks, heavier jumpers and jerseys. Months later when children were being sent away from Britain to North America parents were warned that even more robust outfits were essential.

Before this happened the phoney war went on and the youngsters slipped back to the cities in their thousands, going home for Christmas and the New Year and staying on. Then Holland, Belgium and France fell and the picture changed. Along the coast the reception areas had become the front line and no longer considered safe; the evacuees there were hurried away and with them, too, went the local youngsters. It can be imagined what havoc this played with distribution at retail level: first there had been a flood of new customers to the reception areas, with a consequent run on stocks, then not only did the newcomers retreat but the regular clientele went as well. The drapery shops catering for babies and juveniles found they had no customers at all and after hanging on hopefully for months in the end had to close down. The fortunate ones were able to arrange to dispose of their stocks to retailers in the new reception areas, other outfitters whose main business was in school uniforms kept contact with the school in their changed surroundings and survived.

# CHAPTER 7
# The Battle for Supplies

The manufacturers and distributors of children's clothing had found themselves in rather a peculiar position when war came. On the one hand they were for the most part small to medium size specialist concerns whose names were unknown, yet on the other they were a body of people who had immense responsibility for the furnishing of the right type of apparel for babies and children. They had quietly and efficiently operated their businesses accordingly but they could see that they were likely to be a poor third in the battle for supplies compared with the armed forces and adult civilians. So firm was their conviction that the younger generation must be looked after that their persistence put the adults' into third place and juvenile clothing became a very sensitive area indeed.

The adequate provision of clothing for children during the war years could not have been accomplished without the severe controls imposed by the Government. True, these controls sometimes initially did more harm than good but without them all the best supplies of yarn and cloth would have been taken by the powerful women's and men's trades with their tremendous financial resources and weighty influence. There was considerable ignorance in the Civil Service and in Government circles about the types of garments worn by youngsters and their actions were often prompted by somewhat old-fashioned ideas about a child's wardrobe. Articles which had become basic and wholly necessary by 1940 were unknown or apt to be dismissed as inessential by men either too old or too young to be familiar with what was being worn and since little was known of the scope and complexities of production and the subtleties of the trade its sophisticated nature was not realised. The image held in official quarters appeared to be one of the mother making her children's clothing with a minimum of fashion and styling from fabrics which had regard only for serviceability. Realisation that clothing for children had to fulfil other requirements to meet twentieth century conditions and that babies had moved out of the swaddling bands era came after the quiet trade had found its voice.

Sufficient clothing for civilians was in general maintained despite the demands of the armed forces by control by price, clamped down early on, control of supplies and production, control of consumer purchases by coupons and the utility scheme. Prices were the first concern with every effort being made to prevent profiteering, and hoarding by those with money to spare although this could never be a really serious menace in regard to clothing for children because of the growth factor. The price range in 1939 was wide, going from the cheap, and frequently poor quality and therefore bad value, garments at the bottom of the scale, to the expensive, hand-finished articles at top prices which seemed out of proportion for children's garments but which because they could be handed down through families and often passed on to their relations as well were good investments. The cheapest garments were not inevitably bad buys, plain and dull they might be but some could take the rough-and-tumble of childhood better than their expensive counterparts.

Shoppers were able to purchase boys' jerseys made from 25 per cent wool and 75 per cent cotton and fibre (small ends of artificial silk) for 1s.11d. (10p.); boys' knitted jersey suits, 16ins. (41cms.) were 4s.11d. (25p.); babies' lambs' wool coats were 7s.11d. (40p.); floral print frocks could be bought for as little as 1s.11d. (10p.); best quality cotton frock and knicker sets, 18 and 20ins. (46 and 51cms.) were 6s.11d. (35p.); tailored coats in tweed were 8s.11d. (45p.); coats in Yorkshire Dales tweed for 4-9 years cost 19s.6d. (98p.), matching skirt 9s.9d. (49p.) and hat 5s.9d. (29p.), a similar style in Harris tweed, widely used for fashion and school wear, cost 33s.6d. (168p.), for the coat, 15s.0d. (75p.) for the skirt and the matching hat 7s.6d. (38p.).

It was in January 1940 that the Government published the first list of Price Regulated Goods under the Prices of Goods Acts, 1939 and demonstrated that it had been giving children's clothing close attention. The method adopted for these first controls appeared to be simple: against each garment listed was a retail price (the 'basic' price). This meant that any article of a similar quality and kind which retailed at this price, or less, on August 21, 1939, was price controlled. For example, the basic price laid down for a girl's coat not more than 30ins. (76cms.) in length was 17s.6d. (88p.). This was not the maximum selling price but the limit of price-controlled coats of that length. Garments costing more than the basic price on August 21 were not subject to control. The trader was allowed to add on to the basic price certain permitted increases, reasonably justified by changes in the business since the basic date.

The Central Price Regulation Committee administered the Act and Local Price Regulation Committees had been set up to hear complaints from any shoppers who felt that they had been charged an amount which was unreasonably higher than, for instance, the 17s.6d. (88p.) for a coat. It was for the shopkeeper to prove his charge was not excessive.

The freedom from control enjoyed by the 'luxury' goods, i.e. those above the prices laid down in the Act, was short-lived: in June 1940 all articles of apparel (excepting boots and shoes) were brought under the Prices of Goods Act irrespective of their selling price, together with most other commodities.

As the impact of the total war effort made ever-greater inroads on labour and materials and supplies for civilians diminished dramatically an even tighter control on prices was imposed. This Bill, the Goods & Services (Price Control) Act introduced in mid-1941, gave the Board of Trade sweeping powers to fix for any kind of goods maximum prices or maximum percentage margins of profit for manufacturers, wholesalers and retailers. At first these powers were used to deal with a comparatively restricted range of more essential goods such as certain articles of clothing and boots and shoes for which the BOT could fix maximum prices either in cash or by limiting the percentage margin of gross profit.

An important sub-section enabled the BOT to stop the repeated re-sale at the wholesale stage of goods in short supply with resulting inflation of prices and another clause gave similar authority in regard to intermediaries in connection with the Limitation of Supplies Orders. These were the go-betweens who brought together wholesalers with unused quotas and manufacturers or other wholesalers who wished to dispose of further goods. The BOT's purpose was to prevent payments of large commissions to such people which were only passed on to the public to pay in the form of increased prices.

Control of prices and profit margins was not in itself, of course, sufficient to ensure that the available supplies were equitably distributed to meet the needs of the people. Predictably, when war appeared inevitable, clothing manufacturers tried to stockpile as much fabric as they could get hold of. Those who were discriminating and bought only the right weights and colours for children's wear secured a tremendous advantage when rationing came into force later and the number of coupons allocated was related to stock on hand. Others who thought that the public would be desperate to get any type of warm clothing for their children bought all colours and any weights of cloth with the result that it stayed on their shelves. Time and again during those war years the British public dug its heels in and said 'No' to some substitute when it seemed that nothing else was obtainable. Heavy as lead cloths in deep purple and maroon were not, said mothers, going to be worn by our youngsters. The amount of capital tied up in unsaleable materials was the reason for several post-war bankruptcies. Hosiery manufacturers were fortunate in that their yarns could be dyed as required.

To some extent the trade itself introduced a quota system to deal with orders, particularly for woollen garments, so that supplies should be shared fairly and not pumped into the shops to be bought and hoarded. Reference has already been made to the fact that any such hoarding could only be of a limited amount as youngsters grow out of their clothes rapidly a point which took some time to be reflected in wartime regulations. When eventually acknowledged it gave rise in officialese to a category called 'growing children' a constant source of irritation since children are growing all the time and if any are not there is something very wrong indeed.

While Government propaganda exhorted the general public to economise in every direction, cut down purchases to a minimum and save for the war effort, the BOT spread its net of restrictions and quotas and caught in it along with the big fish the minnows of children's wear suppliers, to their, and often the Government's, mortification. If the authorities were unaware of the importance of the clothing needs of babies and children at the beginning of the war they certainly had heard more than enough about them before it ended.

The implications of the first of the control of goods orders did not sink in at first. Seemingly a fair way of apportioning commodities, the Piece Goods and Made-Up Goods (Cotton, Rayon & Linen) Order introduced in the spring of 1940 laid down that over six months manufacturers and wholesalers must supply only 75 per cent of the square yardage they had supplied during an equivalent six months period of the previous year. Although the yardage was the criterion, as its name implied, the Order embraced garments. Only woven cloth and clothing was covered by the Act; knitwear, or what became a familiar description, 'knitted, netted or crocheted', was dealt with separately. In the returns which had to be made by registered manufacturers and wholesalers, children's wear, girls' and maids' were bracketed with women's; boys' and youths' with mens' but infants' wear was a category on its own. At first sight it seemed reasonable that a 25 per cent reduction should be made in woven garments for civilians now that the country was at war but it was disastrous for the younger generation. There had never been a great deal of over-production of children's garments. Manufacturing jogged along with none of the spectacular profits reaped by the women's trade if a style swept the market. However good any children's design might be, the total sales were small in comparison with the adults'. Since the chances of big rewards were remote few were attracted to this side of the industry. In peacetime, therefore, production surplus to demand was infinitesimal and, as has already been noted, when war came a number of firms seized the opportunity to stop making for children entirely so the margin was further reduced. A cut of 25 per cent in these circumstances was a severe blow.

For adults the situation was very different. The women's trade was highly competitive with massive output in excess of the minimum requirements of the female population. A reduction of 25 per cent of the peacetime sales was no hardship. Moreover, many women were going into uniform and would not be calling on civilian supplies and although for the same reason the potential demand for men's wear could only be a fraction of its former figure the cut for this was identical at 25 per cent.

So here was a situation where babies were being born, children were growing, production barely met minimum demands yet the output was to be slashed by the same percentage as that applied to trades with surplus supplies and shrinking markets.

A few weeks later knitted, netted and crocheted garments came under the axe with the announcement of the Limitation of Supplies (Miscellaneous) Order 1940 which brought under control goods of all types considered to be non-essential. Since this Order permitted companies to supply only two-thirds of the value of a similar period in 1939 this represented about half the quantity.

As the effects of the controls began to be felt, indignation mounted at the way in which children's wear had apparently been dismissed as an insignificant appendage to the adults' without any consideration being given to its special problems, importance and role in the nation's life. No one could deny that a large part of the adult population could live for a few years on its reserves of clothing by making-do and mending, especially since the prime motive for new purchases — changing fashion — was to lie dormant until the end of the war. Clothing babies, infant boys and girls, sub-teens and teens was another matter entirely. This was not a question of fashion but of satisfying stages of development and growth which would, with proper food, ensure the health of the future generations. Strength was added to this claim by the newly-introduced purchase tax which excluded clothing for young people. One Government department understood the significance of such clothing, by another it had been overlooked. The belief grew that this was because the case had not been properly stated to the BOT by any organisation mainly concerned in its affairs. The small voice of the children's wear interests in the big trade associations representing manufacturers and distributors had been drowned by the powerful men's and women's trade figures and, as one manufacturer put it, '*When it comes to infants' and children's wear everybody goes home*'.

However good the case was, however, babies' pram sets and matinée jackets seemed trifling against the background of the times. The end of the phoney war, the fall of France, the air raids, the increasing effect of the call-up of men and women into the Forces and munitions, the loss of clothing factories and warehouses destroyed by bombs left no leeway for anything but production vital to the life of the nation. Nevertheless near to the end of the first six-month period of the Piece Goods & Made-Up Goods (Cotton, Rayon and Linen) Order it was seen that the protests which had been made had not gone unheeded: the supply of infants' woven wear for up to three years was exempted from the list of controlled goods—above this age the cuts were retained. Considerable concession though this was it did not go far enough for knitted garments of cotton and wool (coming under the Limitation of Supplies (Miscellaneous) Order, included most of the juvenile underwear, all the hosiery, a large percentage of the outerwear in terms of jumpers, jerseys, cardigans and small size dresses and vital and irreplaceable baby wear. All these had to wait until the first Limitation of Supplies Order period was ended and the quota for the next six months was announced, then it was seen that this, too, excluded infants' wear—*but* above three years the quota was slashed from 75 per cent to 50 per cent. The announcement came at the end of 1940 and it was only too evident that with Britain standing alone, by the end of the next six months' period, if not before, down it would go again.

The definition of 'infant', too, was to cause some confusion. It seems straightforward to those unfamiliar with the complex nature of children's clothing to decree that such and such an age should be exempt from this or that but putting it down in legal terms is very difficult indeed. The BOT evidently found it so for after the President had announced that infants' wear up to and including three years of age was to be exempt from quota restriction, first one schedule of maximum sizes was circulated, then when the Statutory Order was published it was found the sizes had been changed—and reduced—and after widespread criticism a few weeks later this was replaced by a third which increased the maximum sizes to put them more in line with the needs of the up-to-fours. Apart from the havoc this inconsistency caused to suppliers and distributors there was now no confidence that proper regard was being paid to the legitimate requirements of the children.

The removal of infants' wear from control was the first official acknowledgement by the BOT that this section of the population merited special treatment. It by no means satisfied those who had the interests of young people at heart and who could foresee that grave shortages would occur unless the quotas were increased for those past the infant stage. It was at this point that the belief grew that the clothing claims of children would be better put forward if they were the concern of an organisation which could concentrate on them alone, untrammelled by any commitments to other branches of the apparel industry. Such a body would only have credibility if it numbered amongst its members men and women of high repute with the expertise to prepare and present the proof on which any approach to Government circles would have to be based.

The trade was fortunate in having amongst the leading firms people of great integrity who had spent a lifetime either making or selling garments which they were fully confident would advance the well-being of the youngsters. They took their responsibilities extremely seriously, preferring the satisfaction of contributing to the correct development and happiness of the boys and girls to the greater monetary rewards to be earned elsewhere. Comfort in fit, maximum wearability at the lowest prices commensurate with good value, these were their guidelines and years of experience had taught them how best they could be observed. Men like E. J. Morgans, managing director of Daniel Neal & Sons Ltd., the young people's store group, someone whose practice of submitting samples to exhaustive abrasion and washing tests struck a chill into the heart of many a would-be supplier. A quiet, dignified man, much respected, with an eagle eye which overlooked no detail, however small. Men like M. S. Pocock, managing director of The Treasure Cot Co. Ltd., another quiet man, with the air of a placid headmaster which disguised his role of a passionate advocate of the rights of expectant mothers and babies and who pleaded their cause with tenacity and an authority acquired by a lifetime's study of their singular clothing requirements. The well-loved Mrs. M. Woodham, central buyer for children's wear for the Lewis's Ltd. stores, was another personality whose gentle smiling manner masked her shrewd business brain. It was said that she spoke so softly that salemen calling on her for the first time not only '*didn't know what she had ordered, they didn't even know if she* had *placed an order*'. Implacable in her determination only to buy what she knew to be right for the children, her wide experience and sound judgment often led her to help and back, with great success, newcomers whose advanced ideas had been rejected by others.

There were manufacturers like Ben Pickup, managing director of Robert Dewhurst Ltd., whose serious mien concealed a puckish sense of humour and who knew all about the factory problems of producing tailored coats for the tinies: Guy Webb, head of M. E. & G. Webb, whose gentlemanly courtesy and genuine kindness brought more orders into his quality baby wear company than all the hard-sellers could ever achieve.

These and many others of equally high standing, drawn together by their common interest and attitude towards their little customers believed that now was the time to make a stand. There had always been a friendly spirit of co-operation between manufacturers, wholesalers and retailers and it seemed only sensible that they should act jointly as one body rather than as two or three associations possibly, although unintentionally, working against each other. The move to unite the trade was made by the trade journal *The Children's Outfitter* (re-named *Junior Age* in 1948). From the start of the wartime controls the journal had received a stream of complaints from all sides of the industry about the regulations which impinged unfairly on the supply of essential articles and the imposition of purchase tax had brought more grievances. Many of these difficulties were aired at a meeting which the paper convened in London in November 1940 and manufacturers, wholesalers and retailers, finding the problems were for the most part identical, resolved to form an association comprising the three sections.

It was not a popular move viewed from outside the confines of this family industry. Manufacturers, in particular, in other branches of the trade did not like the idea of sitting round the table with representatives who were 'mixed up with the retail' but not only did the Association formed in such troublesome times survive, it flourished through the post-war years and became an internationally known organisation of high repute. The new body made a brisk start, decided on its name, National Children's Wear Association, appointed its Council, composed of representatives from the three sides, and by the beginning of 1941 had a healthy membership. The first President was E. J. Morgans, an ideal choice for the task ahead. (Typical of his far-sightedness was the suggestion he made in those early days that the Association might run trade fairs for children's wear after the war. In fact the NCWA started to do this in 1952 and has been staging trade fairs twice a year ever since, possibly a record which no other organisation could equal and certainly no other branch of the clothing industry.)

No time was lost in preparing a case for submission to Sir Thomas Barlow, then Director General of Civilian Clothing. It was a strong argument with several incontrovertible facts: (1) because there was very little wastage of children's clothing—it was either worn out or grown out of (if the latter it was handed down or passed on)—replacements of children's clothing should be on the same scale as in peacetime; (2) a sufficient supply of woollen garments was essential for children of all ages; (3) millions of adults were in the Forces so would not be calling on civilian supplies although the quota was the same percentage as for children's clothing; (4) up-to-fours had been exempted but no extra raw materials had been released to make the garments, and these quotas remained the same as for adults; (5) manufacturers were closing down their children's departments and concentrating on men's and women's, always more profitable, and where this happened their permitted quotas ceased, but there was no indication that such a shrinkage was occurring on the adult side.

There was every reason for the Association to act with speed. Meeting the ever-increasing demands on labour and materials for the war effort could only now be done by restricting still further supplies to civilians and it was no surprise when the new quotas were announced for the next period under the Limitation of Supplies (Woven Textiles) Order covering articles of cotton, rayon and linen, etc., to find they were drastically reduced to 20 per cent and 40 per cent of the standard period. Although soon after the Limitation of Supplies (Miscellaneous) Order made no changes in the quota levels for knitted, netted or crocheted goods, the exemption from control of infants' wear had not been extended to bigger sizes.

The misgivings expressed about future supplies were not

*Two-colour effects were a by-product of the austerity regulations, or the combination of two different fabrics, but as the war went on and good materials became harder to obtain the public tired of the all-too-familiar two-tone dresses.*

*The jigger coat, introduced despite continuing Government controls, was the first breakaway from the traditional full-length, tailored coat for girls. The velvet bow, the wide, bracelet-length sleeves would have been dismissed as highly unsuitable before the war.*

going entirely unheeded. Investigators were being sent out by the BOT to ascertain whether reports of shortages were true and, if so, to what were they due. It should not have taken them long to decide that the stories were well-founded: some manufacturers were only able to deliver one buster-suit at a time to even their biggest accounts. There were attempts to persuade women's wear firms to produce more children's sizes but most of them had enough problems to cope with and were not disposed to use their precious quotas on such difficult garments which were a nuisance going through the factory. The authorities still seemed to believe, or hope, that distribution might be the cause of the complaints since the youngsters had been shepherded from one place to another. It seemed as if no one in officialdom would accept the truth that insufficient clothing was being made to meet the minimum needs of the child population.

Then children's clothing hit the headlines for the first time. The case so ably prepared by the NCWA covering present grievances and warning of the future if the situation was allowed to continue had only resulted in a lengthy correspondence with the BOT the essence of which, however well wrapped up, amounted to a complete rebuff. The evidence put forward was not accepted, it was not believed that the situation would deteriorate in the manner predicted—and there were unlikely to be any further concessions. In view of this rejection the Association decided that at least the public should know where the blame lay. Shopkeepers had been having a rough time from customers who could not believe that, war or no war, the Government was responsible for taking little children's woollies off the market. There were suspicions that the goods were under-the-counter, making money for profiteers, and retailers were disturbed and distressed at the amount of bad feeling being engendered as a result of official policy.

The only way to tell the public what was happening and the likely consequences was through the medium of the Press and so a conference was called, a startling move by any trade in those days let alone such an insignificant part of the industry. The result was a tremendous triumph with nationwide coverage in all the leading dailies and provincial papers. Apart from the strength of the evidence put forward by the NCWA, two factors made a good Press certain; one was the use of the word 'famine' in the hand-out in reference to future supplies. The word had a good Horseman of the Apocalypse ring about it and made a powerful headline. The second was that this was a story which made a change from the gloomy battle news and since it was about children could be taken up without anyone feeling guilty. There was, after all, no agitation for any increased issue of raw materials or cloth for civilian use, only for the allocation for adults to be reduced since their clothing needs were being met on a large scale by the War Office and the saving given to the children whose requirements remained the same as pre-war.

However pleased the NCWA might feel at the publicity achieved for their assessment of the position the authorities were far from happy. Stories like this were bad for morale particularly when they conjured up pictures of little ones pinched and shivering in the cold. The Government knew that if it was a question of the children or the adults going without, the latter would want to make the sacrifices and would expect controls to be administered in a way which reflected that desire. The facts could not be disputed. The most that the BOT could do as a quick rejoinder was to say that they had asked manufacturers not to concentrate on adult clothing and wholesalers to ensure that supplies were distributed to the new reception areas—which deceived no one: it was production, not distribution, that the argument was all about.

The Board's first reaction to the unexpected publicity was followed by a more considered reply to the criticisms and that they were at last acknowledged to be fully justified was apparent when it was announced that two new Orders were to be introduced. These, covering woven and knitted garments, permitted registered persons to multiply by a factor of two-thirds their permitted quota for a given month in respect of children's clothing. This meant that one-and-a-half times the quantity or value could be supplied for sizes above infants' to the maximum tax-free measurements. A minor concession but immensely important in establishing the principle that the children merited special treatment and achieved by an organisation without funds, only a good case, well presented and punched home—and yet, too late. Behind the scenes the machinery of clothes rationing was already complete and the next month, on June 1, 1941, when details were released it was apparent that there were areas where the knowledge and experience of specialists could have produced a fairer deal for the children.

The search for children's clothing and the knowledge that only by purchasing garments which would last could the coupons go round led to a major and permanent change in shopping habits. Many mothers would never have even thought of entering the big departmental stores, notably in London, or the exclusive specialist retailers when shopping for their sons and daughters. These establishments were too 'posh' and, more to the point, traded on a price level far beyond parents' resources. The quest for goods and quality took the women over the thresholds of these hitherto forbidding premises with profitable results on both sides. Never again were mothers to be intimidated by premises and for ever after they were to recognise no boundaries to their shopping forays.

One other result of wartime shortages was a universal practice of buying well in advance of the season. This was prompted firstly by a fear that youngsters would not have enough warm clothing for the cold weather, consequently however early winter garments were sighted in the shops they were snapped up. The custom became so deeply entrenched that retailers were well into the post-war period before they realised that freedom of choice meant that the public would no longer tie-up money in garments before the time came for them to be worn.

# CHAPTER 8
# Clothes Rationing

That clothing should be rationed in wartime was inevitable and added to the Government's moral duty to see that poorer people obtained their fair share was the problem of maldistribution caused by the shifts in population due to the air raids. Only one group came outside the scheme, infants up to four years. Unfortunately for mothers with bigger-than-average offspring the exemption was not allied to age but governed by the measurements already laid down in the Limitation of Supplies Orders and this arbitrary ruling was bitterly resented by parents who saw no reason why they should be penalised because their infants were under four but over size. Above the exempted measurements the number of coupons which had to be given up was the same whether the child was four or fourteen. The provision for the infants, which was to bring a good many problems in its train, did nothing to alleviate shortages, on the contrary it led the public to assume that supplies were adequate, or should be. The reverse was the case in the hosiery trade, for example, which produced the majority of baby clothing, supplies of wool yarn were desperately short and despite responsible companies reserving it for babies and eating into their stocks, there were still not enough woollen garments to meet essential needs.

Firms, from producers to distributors, who had high stocks when rationing came into force were obviously at a tremendous advantage since this more or less determined their future trading level. The BOT had, in addition, stipulated that there would be a coupon-free period when registered suppliers could despatch goods up to one-sixth of their anticipated quota to retailers. For the children's outfitter, rationing could not have come at a worst moment. It was only a month after the Government, convinced by the NCWA of the seriousness of the stock position, had announced the quota concessions and it was too early for these to have had any great effect. Moreover it was soon after a back-to-school season when departments and shops had sold out of every available outer and underwear line suitable for term-time, although even so, few, if any, of the considerably pruned school lists were completely met. Retailers were therefore in an unfavourable state but even worse was that of some manufacturers who, like the shops, with virtually nothing in hand faced a future under the rationing scheme of ever-decreasing trade in a number of lines. This was inevitable because of the Government's wish to make allowances for children growing out of their clothes rapidly which they did by keeping as low as possible the number of coupons required for each article, consistent with the need for restriction in supplies. (The scheme had been worked out to allow households with low incomes to have slightly more clothing than they had pre-war and wage earners of £5 a week to have a quarter less.) It was here that the absence of specialist advice became apparent for in some instances the coupons the public had to surrender were insufficient to cover the amount of cloth required to make the garments. There could be only one end to this: no maker-up could entertain the idea of running out of coupons as he continually gave up more than he received, rather he would refuse to manufacture garments which resulted in a coupon loss and these would disappear from the market. Examples of such discrepancies came to light as rationing tightened its grip and makers-up realised that they were subsidising from their small stocks of cloth, coupon-uneconomic lines. The coupon rate for a coat for a 12-year-old, for example, was 11, but the number of coupons which the manufacturer needed to cover the fabric, lining, interlining, etc., was 16. During one week one maker lost an average of 30 per cent of his coupons in this way.

Much of this was brought about because only those with a long experience of clothing youngsters were familiar with the amount of material needed for normal, healthy boys and girls from the tummy bulging infants to the beefy teens. Whilst this was true of the children's side where the pointing inadvertently caused supplies to dwindle still further, in other directions it was deliberate policy on the part of the BOT to force manufacturers to stop producing articles which they considered should have no place in wartime Britain. The Board was also not unduly disturbed at first by the complaints that children could not be clothed adequately on their coupon allowance. The truth was that the system had been based on the assumption that other members of the family would use their own coupon allocations to meet the children's needs—a cunning way of tightening the belt unobtrusively.

As a consequence of statutory controls, restricting as they did the amount which manufacturers could use, production was being concentrated on making up the most expensive cloths available so that greater cash profits would be earned. To a certain extent the public had realised that paying for good clothes which would last and could be let down and out was the right policy in wartime but rationing now made this imperative.

Predictably the freedom from rationing granted to the up-to-fours (it did not at first include their shoes, even babies' soft sole sizes, or their knitted bootees but this was remedied within a month) attracted women's wear manufacturers who saw a means to compensate for restrictions on their businesses by running up 'kids' stuff'. Unluckily for them it was not quite so easy as it appeared: the sizes for a start were bewildering and rather more than just a scaling down of adult measurements. There was astonishment and disbelief that companies who had spent a lifetime perfecting their patterns were not disposed to pass them over to competitors who already had their own substantial market. Despite the difficulties of getting hold of merchandise, retail buyers were not stampeded into placing orders for dresses and coats in fabrics, styles and cut totally unsuited to small girls and boys. The children's wear manufacturers themselves also began to concentrate more on making garments from woven cloth for infants. Since they were unable to increase their overall production the result was that the bigger sizes suffered, so much so that retailers who saw what was happening began to stop buying from houses who could not show ranges for all ages.

A month after rationing was imposed an announcement came of concessions to help shopkeepers to convert 'white elephant' stocks, brought about by the public's drastically changed buying habits, into coupons. This was for a six week period only and coupons still had to be given up, for, said the BOT, 'coupon-free sales or too low pointing would encourage foolish buying'. Shopkeepers were not compelled to sell at the lower pointings if they thought they could get the full number of coupons but they must observe one or the other and not impose their own intermediate rates. Because of the shortage of children's clothing only one or two classes were downpointed, unlined mackintoshes or capes at a retail price not exceeding 7s.0d. (35p.), boys' white or cream trousers and boys' and girls' holiday sandals.

By now the public was realising that the lower pointing for children's clothing was not such a favour as it had seemed when the Consumer Rationing Order 1941 was introduced. There was no provision for the mothers who made the clothes at home—always a substantial number—for piece goods and knitting wools were pointed on yardage and weight and not according to their end-uses. Another factor was that at no time do boys and girls have excess clothing on hand as do most men and women and, further, rationing had come at a period when because of the gaps in supplies many were without even the necessities and were still waiting for these to reach the shops. Additionally, peculiar to the younger members of the population was the matter of natural growth and wear and tear and these it seemed had not been estimated correctly.

Socks were a major problem. The hard-wearing worsted yarns were reserved for the Forces and only botany was being released for civilians but this was too soft for children's socks—hosiery made from this yarn wore out too quickly despite repeated darning. Youngsters rapidly grew out of their socks and unless coupons were available there was a temptation to let them go on wearing them when they were too small and impede the correct development of the feet. Shoes, too, made heavy inroads on the ration books and were to be a constant source of complaint and to remain so for many years.

A list prepared by the NCWA of the minimum requirements based on the needs of a 12 to 13-year-old boy or girl attending a State-aided school totalled 178 coupons over a two-year period for the boy and 183 for the girl as against the 132 allocated. It assumed a modest wardrobe to start with and did not include dressing-gowns, ties and scarves. The jackets, shorts and trousers given for the boy amounted to 1½ suits over two years. Amongst other items were an overcoat or raincoat, three woollen shirts and three non-woollen and two waistcoats or jerseys. For the girl there was a gym tunic to last two years and two woollen and two non-woollen blouses. She could have a jersey and skirt, a woollen frock and two more dresses from some other material but no games tunic so they must do physical exercises in their blouses and knickers. Yet another illustration of the ignorance in official quarters of the realities of the extent of youngsters' clothing requirements was given over the handling of physical training outfits. The Board of Education issued a circular stating that as 'lending' was not regarded as 'supplying' under the terms of the Consumer Rationing Order clothing and footwear for physical training could be purchased by the local authority for the use of instructors and pupils. Three months later when confronted by the local authorities' estimates and realising the number of coupons needed to implement this decision the scheme was abandoned and instead only a limited supply of p.t. outfits were issued on loan.

Extra coupons for older children were promised when rationing was first introduced but it was not until five months later that these were issued, and then, it appeared, only after considerable prompting of the Government and comment in the national Press which reflected public opinion that clothes rationing was unfair to children. The allocation was made by date of birth, 40 or 20 coupons according to the age group, with 40 more for those born after a given date above a certain weight or height. The main burden of administering the scheme fell on the school heads and with between two and three million claimants the work involved was considerable. The coupons were issued through the schools who had to verify the date of birth and, in the case of the bigger pupils, check that their measurements entitled them to an extra 40. The terms for the latter were precise: the heights and weights were to be measured without boots or shoes, jackets, waistcoats and other outerwear and 2½lbs. was to be deducted to allow for the weight of other clothing. For children who had left school the procedure was more complicated, special forms had to be obtained, completed and returned by a certain date and those who did not possess an unemployment book had to apply for a form of a different colour and have the details witnessed by a

JP, clergyman or school head to whom they were known personally, before presenting them by the prescribed date. The allocation had to last until the end of the clothes rationing year, i.e. the following May.

The term 'growing children' was coined to cover this issue and when it was announced not unnaturally gave rise to hopes that *all* children were to benefit. Mothers looking at their young boys and girls shooting up and out of their clothes and tearing their way through the ration book needed no convincing that they were 'growing' and would qualify for help. (The point had, however, been made and children in their middle teens and certain younger children above average weight and size were to get extra coupons later as a matter of course.) So much confusion was caused by the publicity following the BOT's announcement that the NCWA issued a statement stressing that the majority of children would be unaffected by the scheme which did nothing to touch the real inadequacy of the ration. The Association drew attention to the famine which existed and urged three steps to be taken to relieve the shortage:

1. Some measure of protection should be given to children's clothing operatives
2. Preferential release of raw materials for children's wear
3. Manufacturers who had closed down their children's section should be forced to resume their proportion of production of children's wear.

The statement was timely and the Association was soon to learn that action along these lines was being considered.

The exemption of baby wear from rationing was short-lived, only for two months, in fact, then it, too, went on coupons. The reason for this speedy revocation was, the Government stated, that it was unfair on poorer people who were accustomed to making their own layettes. Whilst this was undoubtedly true it was surprising that this was not known in official quarters before the Act was introduced. Cumbersome machinery had had to be put into operation because baby wear was outside the scheme.

A promise made to one section of the community by the Government had so far not been honoured, this was that expectant mothers would receive extra coupons and the delay had occasioned considerable criticism. Much stalling went on in the House of Commons in response to Members' questions about the BOT's tardiness in implementing their pledge: 'details being worked out', 'great difficulties in administration', the extra coupons would be issued soon and then there would be some for the baby, too, so that mothers who preferred home-made clothes would have enough. The following month the secret of the 'details' and 'difficulties in administration' was out, the pregnant woman's right to coupons was acknowledged with an extra 50—and baby wear went on the ration.

There seemed to be no appreciation of the troubles of the expectant mother and this was borne out by the attitude of one BOT official who, at a meeting with trade representatives trying to get a coupon allocation granted, remarked that he did not see why they should discuss extra coupons for a winter coat—pregnant women could always walk about with their coats open if they didn't fit. '*In winter, do you?*', was the caustic reply.

The allocation of 50 coupons to the expectant mother was parsimonious since it had to suffice both for the essential purchases due to her condition before and after the event, and for preparing the layette. In this the Government quite deliberately took the line that coupons would be forthcoming from relations who would see that she did not go without anything vital to her health and happiness or the baby's. *When* she was allowed to collect her coupons was the result of a heartless ruling which caused unnecessary distress. It was the usual practice to advise women to have the layette all ready by the seventh month but the BOT ruled that the expectant mother's allowance could not be collected until after the sixth month. This meant a weary trudge round the shops to find that hard-to-get baby wear and, or, sewing or knitting in a rush to get the garments made in time, both when she would feel far less inclined for such activity as she would have done earlier in her pregnancy. It was, too, hard on the women, and this was true in a great many instances, who bought some little item each week out of the housekeeping money. In vain it was pointed out to the authorities that it would be far more humane to grant the coupons after three months but, said the Government, what of the woman who loses her baby after that? —she will have had the coupons and we might not be able to get them all back. The percentage of miscarriages between three and six months was only small, it was argued, but officialdom was unmoved. '*It cannot be stated beyond reasonable doubt that a baby will be born before pregnancy has reached the sixth month and there must be some safeguards*' was their maxim.

It was irksome to expectant mothers that so much of their coupon allocation had to be given up for napkins. The muslin or gauze type were off the ration but no one suggested that these were adequate for the purpose on their own. Terry towelling napkins were pointed at one coupon for each and since two dozen were required as a minimum this immediately swallowed up 24 of the precious coupons. The President of the Board of Trade was pressed in the House of Commons to make terry as well as gauze napkins coupon-free since they were a necessity but refused to do so.

Children and their clothes were to be the subject of many questions in the House as legislation followed legislation in an effort to conserve and ensure fair distribution of supplies and those concerned became more vocal. Notwithstanding the impression that Parliamentary questions achieved nothing of consequence as they were effectively stonewalled by a succession of Ministerial answers, they frequently resulted in rectification of injustices. MPs, too, were well aware of the advantages of putting questions when children were involved—they were sure of a good Press. Most of the in-fighting, however, took place outside Parliament and behind the great doors of the ICI building in Millbank, wartime home of the BOT. Here the big boys of the clothing trade strode into meetings exuding importance and a sense of long experience, with bulging brief cases of impeccable leather darkened with use to a nicety and all of them such powerful orators that the rest of the committee members could barely get in more than a '*Good Morning All*'. Completely overshadowed by their affluent contemporaries the children's wear representatives made up in tenacity what they lacked in size.

The meetings, tough going though they were, did depart from the cut-and-thrust: a more than honest manufacturer when asked if coats made at a suggested low price would '*fall to pieces in the rain*' retorted, '*With mine its only got to come over cloudy!*'. Against the claims of the large companies and the overriding war effort it was no wonder that children's wear was pushed into the background but even so it was difficult to account for some of the Government's actions, over the rationing of infants' wear, for example. With the first clothes rationing Order in June shopkeepers had been given three weeks in which to take deliveries without surrendering coupons (up to one-sixth of the suppliers' quota and not more than the equivalent of 10,000 coupons to any one retailer) a proper means of continuing normal trading until the coupon system came fully into effect. A similar arrangement was denied to the shopkeeper when infants' wear was rationed. It was only after the dogged persistence of NCWA representatives that the BOT relented and granted, in respect of written orders placed before rationing commenced, a coupon-free spell. The absence of a transitional period was devastating for the infants' wear specialists who had no coupon float at all, unlike the children's outfitters who dealt with all sizes and compared even more unfavourably with the large store groups who could switch their coupons from one department to another with impunity. Yet the only reason the BOT gave for treating infants' wear so harshly was that the three weeks immunity had not been a success as it had given the multiple stores an advantage over other retailers.

A further complication then arose: suppliers sent off what goods they could before the coupon-free deadline expired on August 31 but now the BOT decided that after September 8 these, and other children's wear companies, would be de-registered. They were then in a similar position to the retailers before them—having no coupons to pass back for their materials. The BOT covered this hiatus by announcing that firms who were engaged entirely, or almost entirely, on infants' wear could make applications to them for additional coupons provided they were accompanied by a declaration of the value (money or coupon) of the goods supplied during the transitional period.

Such expediency only strengthened the conviction that valuable time and labour which should be engaged on production was being spent on activities which could have been avoided had there been a greater knowledge of the peculiarities of the trade—and there was more to come. The BOT's decision that infants' and children's firms should be de-registered had other consequences. Resentment over the discrepancy between the pointing of some of the garments and the number needed to produce them had been growing and was given a new impetus with de-registration. Hitherto as registered manufacturers they could obtain cloth without surrendering coupons although they had to make accurate returns of the latter to the authorities. Now makers-up had to pass over the correct number for the yardage they required and as this was considerably in excess of the total they actually received it revealed the deficiencies which existed. Again the women had fared better: there was already in force a scheme for reimbursing makers of outsize garments for any coupon losses they sustained. This deepening disparity could not continue and as a result of strong representatives from the NCWA the BOT asked for figures to substantiate the losses; these were sent and there the matter rested.

The coupon-drain was only one aspect of a whole chain of orders which, sometimes inadvertently, had throttled supplies for children and hamstrung the very producers they were intended to assist. Once started, the legislation controlling clothing was so correlated that in attempting to remedy some part, and having the opposite effect to that intended, another sector was disturbed and set up new dilemmas.

The predictions in the spring of '41 of shortages in the coming autumn had proved correct and there was a bitter realisation that so far as the children were concerned their wants would have to be fought for every inch of the way. After the quota concession (for one month only) following the NCWA's successful appeal to the Press in May 1941, some weeks later all children's clothing was freed from quota restriction, again for a limited period, but this time the Board offered to consider individual applications for licences to supply these goods after the closing date and if there were any difficulties about getting cloths they would arrange for licences or for raw materials. Such offers were rarely fully implemented for far too often makers-up found that the mills had no materials, the dyers and spinners had no raw material and urgent appeals to honour the promises made were only bounced from one Government department to another with negative results.

Added to the problems brought about by the BOT's

manoeuvres was the escalating loss of labour, male and female. Factories whose workers were called-up were expected to manage as every other business and make the best they could of substitutes. Not unreasonably it was assumed that older women who were skilled clothing machinists could be effectively absorbed into a children's wear factory after a minimum of re-training and prophesies that they would not be suitable were disregarded as of no account at such a time. They proved to be all too accurate: employers knew from past experience that only a special type of female labour could make clothes for infants and children. It needed skilful fingers and patience to cope with tiny collars, cuffs, armholes and short seams in a garment that measured no more than 14ins. (36cms.). It came doubly hard on women used to longer seams and the less demanding requirements of men's and women's clothing which also brought in more satisfactory financial rewards.

Shopkeepers' shelves now told only too plainly the truth about stocks of apparel for the young and for adults. Whilst shop after shop had not even one child's coat on their rails the women's departments had plenty of choice to offer. The accumulation of factors which worked against the production of children's necessities was exerting pressures which could no longer be held back by piecemeal remedies. By the autumn of 1941 the BOT could not continue to ignore the persistent clamour for something to be done but not content to accept the claims made about the gravity of the position they sent out their own investigators again. That they confirmed all that had been said of the sorry state of affairs was evidenced by the reception given to the forceful representations of the NCWA to the BOT. The Association was informed that the Board fully realised the seriousness of the situation and proposed to take immediate steps to alleviate it. At last the Association was asked formally to compile a list of manufacturers of children's wear who, because of shortage of labour or materials, or for other reasons, were unable to satisfy demand. Even more positive and encouraging was the further statement that where the Board was satisfied that a manufacturer's productive capacity as being *'adversely affected' (sic)* it would (a) by means of an arrangement *already agreed (italics added)* with the Ministry of Labour, put the manufacturer's name on a special list whereby his labour would be protected, and/or (b) take steps to ensure that he received adequate supplies of materials to meet the demand for children's garments.

The arrangement for the protection of labour was a major triumph in view of the Ministry's stern enforcement of the call-up regulations. The Board's statement gave manufacturers a new status, too, and helped them to get fabrics and subsequent rations of yarn for the making of infants' knitwear which was beneficial, although it was not always easy to find spinners to fill the allocations.

# CHAPTER 9
# Purchase Tax

The shortages, coupons, quotas, call-up, bombs, all these would end eventually when peace came but one 'emergency measure' was to linger on long after the war was over, to be rescinded only in the Value Added Tax days of 1973—purchase tax—which some thought would be removed soon after hostilities ceased but the cynical recognised as a convenient way of raising money too good for an early demise. The tax encased young people's clothing in a strait jacket of unnatural definitions exasperating in their restriction and responsible later for unjustified criticism of designers and producers.

No one was really to blame for the consequences of the imposition of this tiresome Act. Its purpose was two-fold, to cut down expenditure and to raise revenue and the intention of the Government was admirable, children's clothes would be exempt from the tax. The trouble sprang from trying to define the indefinable. At first sight there appeared to be no real difficulty in distinguishing between adults' and children's clothing, the latter was only belatedly affected by fashion (which itself was stagnant) and regarded as being 'not suitable' for the younger generation. The general view was that anyone could easily recognise a child's garment and the criteria of size and style would be sufficient to prevent tax evasions. It was assumed with the first announcement that the exemption would embrace the apparel of all those at school and there was some disappointment later when the Notice appeared and it was seen that as the wording in the Act passed by Parliament was 'young children's clothing' this had been interpreted as up to 10 years. (Even this seemingly watertight classification was found to be inadequate in the years to come.) Over 10, maximum measurements and some style restrictions were laid down which gave tax-free articles up to, and including, approximately the 13-year-olds. The measurements which were to become the boundaries of the tax-free sizes were not drawn up as a result of a highly computerised survey undertaken by an expensive market research organisation; they were drafted by a small group of people sitting round a table in the old offices of the British Standard Institution in Victoria Street, London. At one point when the subject under discussion was puppy fat and what allowance should be made for it, one or two shy young girls working in the office were called in and to their embarrassment their measurements were taken (over *all* their clothes) and helped to form the cornerstone of the first tax-free measurements. The results of the meeting were submitted to the authorities who then made their amendments to suit their own ideas and purposes.

Although size had, without question, been adopted as the main means of distinguishing between adults' and children's garments it was in reality a hopeless yardstick. There can be no doubt that those responsible for imposing the demarcation line were unacquainted with the size of the average sub-teen or early teenager. It was not so much a question of accommodating the Billy Bunters—and there were plenty of those as any school outfitter could testify—but looking after the average youngsters who were at a stage in their development when their measurements were greater than those of their older brothers and sisters. Soon the puppy fat across backs, waists, hips and thighs would disappear but until it did boys and girls required clothing roomy enough to cover them adequately without bursting at the seams in the hurly-burly of school life. Garments of that size would take in a substantial proportion of the adult population thus defeating the object. On the other hand, reducing the maximum tax-free measurements would penalise the parents who were already having to spend more on their youngsters' outfits because of their sturdy stature.

Could then the size be allied to style in such a way as to ensure that men's and women's wear was excluded? One possibility was to make school uniforms tax-free but the snag here was that whilst uniforms were widely worn in public, private, grammar, secondary and central schools they were not compulsory in the elementary schools attended by the very pupils which the Act was intended to help. Gym tunics, white blouses and grey suits for the boys were encouraged in the elementary schools but not enforced and usually their only distinguishing mark was a modest badge which could be sewn on the hat, cap, tunic or jacket. There would be no way, it was argued, of preventing men and women from buying these nondescript garments free of tax or of them being purchased by children and taken home for adults to wear. The dangers of this happening on any large scale were greatly exaggerated and as it transpired over the years it was the fashion, not the school, side which presented the most formidable loopholes. The cumbersome machinery which would have had to be set up to exempt school uniforms from tax would probably have cost far more than the amount lost by evasion. In any case it would certainly not have been welcomed by the school heads who would have been responsible for its operation. Great as the difficulties were in respect of the straightforward uniforms they were as nothing compared to those encountered over out-of-school wear. It was all very well to say that some things were not suitable for children but the question was how to put this down in black and white in such a manner that it could be enforced in law? What was meant by 'not suitable' was in reality only a matter of taste. Black satin, low necklines, tight skirts, garish colours, sequins, heavy embroidery, these were taboo in the child world but there was also the matter of the dimensions and shapes of collars, sleeves, armholes and cut. How could these be put down on paper? The answer is that some of them were and their inclusion later in the regulations started a chain of acrimonious argument which grew more heated as fashion assumed an increased importance in juvenile apparel and the matter of 'taste' was the perogative of civil servants with reactionary ideas.

It having been decided to adopt size and to some extent style implementing the intentions of the Act fell to HM Customs and Excise and forever more they were to be plagued by complaints and criticism from the public, the trade, MPs and, it seemed, from every vocal group in the country. It must in all fairness be recorded that Customs and Excise throughout acted with a willingness to adapt the rules to changed conditions provided that the trade could produce formulas which incorporated the alterations without encouraging evasion.

The necessity to keep pace with the vagaries of fashion in the post-war years resulted in a continual stream of amendments which were no sooner published than they began to get out of date. This was to be troublesome enough in peacetime but any changes in the tax-free measurements were doubly so in wartime because of the significance which they had assumed. It became the practice of the Government to use the purchase tax exemption demarcation wherever it was necessary to distinguish between children's and adults' apparel so that every time an amendment was brought out a chain reaction swept along the manifold controls, creating chaos until each in turn was brought into line.

In the light of past experience it came as no surprise that when the maximum measurements were published there were some remarkable omissions and instances where articles had been unwittingly included as taxable. There was, for example, no provision for siren suits which were so practical and this meant that they were only free of tax for the up-to-tens; this also applied to lumber jackets, overalls, bathing suits and trunks and several other items which were not mentioned. Babies' bibs and feeders were actually given as taxable although infants' garments, including napkins, were exempt. A further complication had arisen where a style limitation had been laid down, e.g. jumpers, cardigans, etc., described as plain stitch or 1/1 rib. Since no maximum measurements were given for any other type of jumper, etc., here again the tax-free sizes only went up to ten years. This had happened, also, with blouses (other than the plain gym style) and stockings (except gym hose). It can be imagined how many different interpretations were put upon 'sizes up to ten years' and retailers found they were being charged with tax or not according to manufacturers' own ideas of the ages their sizes would fit.

The 'errors and omissions' apart, the maximum tax-free limits which came into operation in October 1940 were quite reasonable bearing in mind that they might take in some borderline women's wear. Older girls were wearing their clothes about knee length with progressively shorter skirts for the younger ones so the 39ins. (99cms.) maximum tax-free size for coats and dresses and 42ins. (106cms.) for raincoats was fair. For boys, coats as well as raincoats were exempt up to

42ins. (106cms.) and their shoes went up to size 5½: for girls the limit was size 3 with a stern warning that this did *not* mean 3½ and there was a restriction on the height of the heel. Any young lady over ten who wanted to have her petticoat or vest cut with an opera top would have to pay the tax and although her combinations could be 32ins. (81cms.) across the chest they must not have bust shaping. Boys, fashion being an unknown word in their vocabulary, did not have to take heed of such frivolous conditions, their list was simplicity itself and even included a nightshirt—48ins. (121cms.) long.

For so long as the Act was in force there remained the grievance over the taxing of hats—even down to new-born babies' bonnets—and mitts and gloves, again even for a new-born babe. No satisfactory explanation was ever advanced for this peculiar decision. Admittedly the public was told that it was because it was impossible to define a hat which could not be worn by a woman but there were ways in which this could have been overcome. The height of absurdity was reached over hats forming part of a set for a toddler or a very young baby. It was the custom to sell sets comprising coat, breechettes and hat, or coat and hat, made from identical cloth. It was nonsense to suppose, as was maintained, that unless the hats were taxed women might buy them and with, or without, alteration, wear them on their own heads. This fallacious argument completely overlooked the fact that such hats were never sold except as part of a set and what woman would buy the whole outfit just to save the few pence of the tax, for that is all it amounted to. It was even more ridiculous to think that women would buy knitted pram sets—legginettes, matinée jacket and bonnet, unmistakably intended for the downy head of a tiny mite—just to get the bonnet tax-free, a saving of about 9d. (4p.). Yet one Minister of HM Government actually wore such a bonnet in the House of Commons to show MPs that it might have possibilities as an adult headcovering. When, finally, concessions were made the lengths to which suppliers had to go to make sure their bonnets conformed to the maximum tax-free measurements laid down were laughable.

Meanwhile tax had to be collected on all those items and on hoods which were not permanently attached to the coats. It was common practice for school raincoats, in particular, to have detachable hoods fastened to the coats with buttons, they could then be removed when not required, leaving a neat and tidy coat without a droopy appendage dangling from the shoulders. This must not be, said officialdom, you must pay tax on the hood if it is not permanently attached. Since these raincoats were, in the main, made in navy, brown and bottle gaberdine, just how menacing could a tax evasion be here? Who were these peculiar women the authorities had in mind? Nevertheless, that was the law and must be obeyed so down the years the hoods were sewn firmly on to the coats and the critics rallied against manufacturers for not making detachable hoods on raincoats.

One year after the exempted sizes were published a revised list was issued righting the anomalies (but not in respect of hats, mitts and gloves) that had not been adjusted during the year and making changes in the measurement limits themselves. Some were increased, others decreased in the light of the working of the Act but the repercussions went far beyond the imposition of purchase tax for by now the demarcation line set by Customs and Excise had also been adopted for quotas, coupon pointing under the Consumer Rationing Order and the newly launched utility clothing scheme.

# CHAPTER 10
# Utility and Austerity

The Limitation of Supplies (Cloth and Apparel) Order 1941 which introduced utility clothing came into operation in September of that year. It was a scheme which created a social upheaval. A great leveller, with its introduction the poor moved up and the rich slid down and class distinction disappeared from children's clothing. No longer was it to be possible to tell who was the little rich girl by her silk, satin and fine wools and the poor lass by her thin cotton and threadbare 'shoddy'. Utility was the same for all classes and non-utility so scarce as to have no impact on the scene. Class distinction in clothing never returned: when freedom of choice came back it became a matter of taste, not money.

The pattern of muddle over the children's side was repeated with the arrival of utility. The scheme provided for increased quotas for utility knitwear and cloth and apparel provided that they conformed to certain specifications. Each utility cloth bore a number which identified its type, width and, where necessary, its weight, and the price per yard. Against each cloth was given the type of apparel into which it could be made and it could not be used for any other purpose. It then followed that there must be a fixed price for the finished garment but the Order became law before the prices were finalised on the woven side and once again infants' and girls' clothing were left until last with a variety of reasons being given for the delay.

Prices for children's knitwear were listed and so were boys' garments and girls' gym tunics, the latter because the serge was reserved for children. In respect of all other children's wear (defined as purchase tax free) manufacturers were allowed to make up utility cloths subject to a 50 per cent quota for a nine month period. Infants' wear was now back on quota as the

BOT estimated that under the new arrangements there would be enough production to meet demand. The knitwear prices published with the Order showed clearly the level the BOT had determined for utility. The manufacturers' maximum price for a baby boy's all wool jersey suit, with collar and three-button front and knicker with gusset for sizes 14-18ins. (36-46cms.) was 61s.6d. (308p.) per dozen; a baby's all wool matinée jacket with collar 32s.0d. (160p.) per dozen; plain or rib socks in two-fold botany wool with spliced heel and toe 9s.0d. (45p.) per dozen. In every case a minimum finished weight per dozen had to be observed. The prices were devised to fit in with the BOT's aim of procuring inexpensive clothing to protect the public against inflated prices brought about by wartime shortages. No matter what trials it carried in its wake, utility was a good plan and by enforcing rigid specifications as to quality the Government succeeded in ensuring a flow of cheap clothing which was more than adequate for the times. That utility tended to be despised as something 'cheap and nasty' was largely due to snobbery. There were plenty of good, well-made garments in utility cloth and yarn but of necessity they had a standardised, severely practical appearance and this, after all, was the intention. There was always some 'general' or non-utility apparel to be found although this was progressively harder to get.

Admirable as the scheme was it had some drawbacks so far as the children's section was concerned, giving once more the impression that this group had been tagged on at the last minute. No one had apparently thought of the consequences of adopting the purchase tax definitions and what this would mean in practice. One result was that no matching hats nor caps could be made from utility cloth as the specifications referred to goods 'not being chargeable with purchase tax'. Since headwear was taxed it could not, therefore, be made from such fabric. As this was not the intention an Amending Order was issued giving permission for utility cloth to be used for boys' and girls' hats.

The situation had become highly complex for the children's wear manufacturers. The Order introducing quotas for utility and general apparel came into force in September but they were still working on the 'short-term' policy which permitted children's wear to be supplied free of quota until October. (In the case of knitwear manufacturers this had been extended, if they had been unable to produce the goods owing to delays in yarn deliveries, to the end of that month). At the same time these firms were being allowed to make garments from utility cloth (even if it were not stamped utility) and sell them although no controlled prices had been fixed (both offences carrying heavy penalties for other clothing producers). It was

*Fashion stopped when war began, so the bolero line and exaggerated shoulders continued for dresses, designers using the pin-tucking permitted under the austerity regulations to add interest.*

assumed that it would not be long before the prices were published but it then transpired that this was not to be the policy and they might be delayed for an indefinite period. The bewildered makers-up were then placed in the position of not knowing whether to order utility materials or not: if they committed themselves the prices for the finished garments might be too low for them to work to, if they did not place orders in advance and the prices suited them they would have no cloth.

A further problem was that as children's utility apparel could be made up and sold without a price limit (subject to the Prices of Goods Act) this might put retailers in an embarrassing position where a 39ins. (99cms.) length coat (the maximum tax-free size) might be more expensive than a 40ins. (101cms.) made to a controlled price. The BOT maintained that the delay in issuing the prices was because they did not wish to restrict output but if this was so, why had they brought them out for knitted goods, in desperately short supply, and for boys' wear which was also extremely scarce?

It was futile to ask questions like this at the end of 1941 for from now on until the end of the war Statutory Orders and Instruments were to gush forth from Government departments in a seemingly never-ending stream in the effort to clothe the civilian population with the minimum of labour and raw materials. Much of the legislation affected boys' and girls' garments but at least it was established that these were important both then and for the future well-being of the nation and if on occasion the young people's special needs were overlooked the protests were treated with respect and more often than not led to some adjustment.

Of the changes brought about by wartime controls, none was to be more beneficial to British clothing design than the 'austerity' regulations: they killed the 'bits and bobs' fussiness of women's mass-produced garments. The effect on juvenile clothing was not so marked but a few of the old practices were swept away by the Making of Civilian Clothing (Restrictions) (No. 7) Order which came into force in June 1942. The frock and knicker set was one casualty. Dresses with knickers made from matching cloth, through all price levels, were the rule rather than the exception but axed under the austerity restrictions for sizes above 26ins. (66cms.) they never returned and the knickers were in future made by the underwear manufacturers.

The BOT's aim in imposing the making restrictions was to get the maximum number of garments from the minimum amount of cloth and labour but they knew that they must not pare down to such an extent that makers would seize the opportunity to produce articles so skimped or unserviceable that they would only have a short life and thus defeat the whole purpose of the Act. A question had already been asked in the House of Commons in regard to this possibility and officials, whilst determined to cut out every unnecessary decoration, were alive to the dangers of being over-zealous.

The attack on any extravagance in making garments from woven cloths was on two fronts: to decree in the closest possible detail what must not be done in the design and cut of articles and what must not be done after those articles had been cut. (Government Orders had an irritating habit of always being couched in the negative which though correct from the legal standpoint was a source of much annoyance to those who had to work to them and discover from being told what they were *not* allowed to do, what they *were* allowed to do. This was markedly so in the austerity regulations. The negative wording sometimes seemed to work, too, in favour of the wily gentlemen looking for ways to slide in one or two little dodges against the intention of the legislation.)

The BOT did not arbitrarily dictate the austerity terms. They set up panels of manufacturers for each section—heavy, light and so on—and asked them to suggest economies. One reason for this may have been that owing to the technicalities involved the rulings could only be drawn up by specialists but the Board's motive was much more likely to have been to get the trade associations on their side, for the Orders had no chance of standing up in a court of law. They were based on trade terms and lawyers could have been kept busy arguing tucks and folds, gauging and honeycombing, ornamental stitching and seaming for the remainder of the war had manufacturers been so minded. The panels which were responsible for recommending lists of restrictions for the children's wear divisions were amiable affairs and the members co-operated, albeit sadly, in suggesting methods of curtailing their traditions. On one point the heavy and light sections held opposing views as the subsequent Orders demonstrated. It was a question of the hems. Did, or did not, mothers let down their children's garments? The BOT said they did, and if not they ought to: the light clothing side said they thought they did and were willing to go along with the Board, the heavy clothing said they did not and that was that. The established practice was for garments in the lowest price bracket to have narrow hems but all others had sufficient depth for letting down. Shopkeepers said that most mothers would not even look at a child's garment unless it had a 'decent hem'. Rationing made this allowance for growth even more desirable and the BOT maintained that a minimum hem should be written into the legislation. The light clothing panel acquiesced and so appeared, for infants' and girls' dresses, etc. up to 38ins. (96cms.), *'Hem of skirt not to be less than 2ins. (5cms.) deep or more than three ins. deep'*.

It was true that there was this insistence upon a good hem but how many mothers actually let them down was another matter. There was evidence that the letting out and down and handing on era was coming to an end, so thought the heavy panel at any rate. The length of a child's dress was not all that important but with say, coats, it was different. A good length was essential for warmth and to cover up the dress beneath, but the panel would have no compulsion. The members were adamant that not enough mothers let down hems to justify a legal minimum and it should be left to the makers to decide the appropriate depth for each style. It also meant that the cheaper manufacturers would not be compelled to raise their prices by giving a better finish but that was not advanced as part of the argument.

In fairness to manufacturers it must be admitted that letting down coat hems was not altogether satisfactory. The mark of the Hoffman-pressed edge could never really be eradicated and frequently there was a difference in the colour of the cloth even if it was only the freshness of the inside turning seen against the outer material. Neither was the prevailing fashion, the princess line, suited to such alterations, the dropping of the hem made the already high waistline look as if it had flown up to the armpits.

The resistance of the heavy section was not confined to coats, some additional items within their terms of reference were affected and so no special provision was made either in regard to skirts on bodices, waist skirts, gym tunics and jackets. Hems apart, the products of the heavy side were pruned far more drastically than any others. Gone were the scalloped collars and pockets, the hallmark of the British tailored coat, the velvet, silk or rayon covered buttons and pocket flaps to match the collars, *all* the turnback cuffs whether trimmed to match the collars or not, *all* the cording, often used between the facing and strapping on collar and cuffs—a classic detail this, on an infants' navy coat the facing would be red velvet and the cording white—there were to be no more dashing shoulder cape effects or epaulettes, furry collars, or fur trimming *anywhere*, only one box-pleat or two knife-pleats, and rows of stitching were severely limited. This last was more in the nature of a concession than a restriction. It was customary for the collars, cuffs or pocket flaps of coats on the smaller sizes to be finished with rows of stitching cleverly mitred on the pointed shapes and following the curves on the scallopped styles. No other country could equal the skill of the machinists who executed these fine rows on minute areas and made the coats wherever worn immediately recognisable as British. Under the austerity regulations eight rows of stitching on collars and four on pockets were permitted, only because they reinforced the material but the restiction helped to kill the fashion, it never came back to any extent after the war and as the years went by there were no longer enough highly skilled machinists available to do the work. Velvet, velveteen, silk or rayon facing was allowed on the collars. This trimming had been introduced originally not as a fashion feature but because otherwise the coat material would rub the back of the child's neck and make it sore. The concession had the additional merit of giving designers a chance to add contrast, not an easy thing to do on the tiny sizes and now that coats were to be on such austere lines was even more welcome as a method of adding interest. Such were some of the more than 30 listed embargoes on the making of infants' and girls' coats alone.

No blazers nor jackets could be double-breasted and the latter must not have metal buttons. Skirts suffered a major slashing; there were to be no more all-round or accordion pleated styles, by far the favourites for girls of every age. The pleated models were not only to please little ones who liked to

*Utility came to have a bad name but excellent coats such as this were produced, even when the rigid austerity requirements were observed, but they were hard to find, disappearing like lightning from the shops.*

twist round and see their skirts swing out, the all-round pleating ensured longer wear by increasing the resistance to repeated rubbing against school benches, but out they went to be replaced by two inverted or box-pleats or four knife-pleats and the overlapping of each side of the pleat was not to be greater than seven inches (19cms.) when fully extended. School blouses lost their action-pleat at the back and girls' shorts shared with slacks the somewhat harsh directive that they should have 'no rubber or fabric device (other than belt loops) for maintaining slacks in position' which was rather hard as they were not permitted to have loose or detachable belts either. Because of the shortage of metal, slide fasteners were prohibited on many garments but this was not such a hardship as it would have been post-war as zips were in their early days.

It did not take long to scan the children's underwear and nightwear austerity regulations, they were simply a list under 'Not to have' of all the dainty ornamentations which gave a mini-feminine air to even the cheapest of garments and reduced them to purposeful, practical reach-me-downs.

Baby and infants' wear were least affected by the making restrictions, although this was not the view at first of the makers. Most of these firms had spent years producing attractive garments which would be pretty on the babies and please the proud mothers. To them embroidery and lace were synonymous with baby clothing and they could not imagine their gowns and coats without these touches. When the Orders were published they discovered that the outlook was not too drab for war babies. Smocking, the universal trimming on dresses, was to be allowed, two inches (5cms.) of it up to 22ins. (56cms.) sizes. This concession was not due to officials being convinced by any arguments on the score of prettiness but that smocking served a definite purpose. It was decorative, certainly, but its wide use was because of its elasticity which enabled extra material to be taken up across the yoke and round the sleeves to give ease of fit as the child grew. This point was conceded by the BOT but on more humane grounds they allowed it for another reason. Smocking was done by hand: 'mock' smocking was seen but this, being machined, lacked the elasticity of the genuine embroidery. The work was done mainly by outworkers, in convents and by old ladies in their own homes and very much dependent on the money they earned in this way. Since none were being taken from the war effort the BOT were sympathetic and allowed them to go on smocking. Nevertheless in all there were over 40 prohibitions on infants' and girls' dresses and makers had to measure pintucking and hemstitching to ensure that they did not exceed the amount allowed. In addition to these detailed requirements, designers were only permitted 15 sets of basic style templates per annum.

The Order covering boys' clothing came into force a month earlier than the girls' and delivered, in addition to the other dictates, the severe blows of forbidding long trousers for boys taking less than Leeds size six (approx. 11 years) and turn-ups on long trousers for the over 11 years. A misplaced economy was the stopping of double cuffs on shirts. Even before rationing, cuff-turning had been common as a means of prolonging the life of a boy's shirt still with plenty of wear left in it except for fraying at the cuffs and the double layer of material was in this instance a wise use of resources. Like the girls, the boys had to give up their double-breasted blazers and this caused some criticism both on the score of lack of warmth across the chest and of extra making and stock-keeping costs. The double-breasted style incorporated two-way fastening for either sex on the smaller sizes but as the blazers were to be single-breasted they had to be made and stocked to fit boys and girls. No one had the temerity to suggest that blazers should fasten on the same side, even in wartime.

Although not covered by the same Orders, knitwear, already subject to rigorous control, came under similar prohibitions, and for infants these were more stringent in that whereas makers of garments from woven cloths had obtained permission for hand-smocking hand—as well as machine—embroidery was banned on knitwear.

It took a while for designers to realise that there were to be no exceptions to the austerity rule and however much this would despoil their creations the law must be obeyed. The best of them regarded the shackles as a challenge to their ingenuity. Ornamentation of some kind, however classic or restrained, had been of paramount importance in the styling of children's wear since lacking the opportunity of introducing differences in line, of necessity the basic patterns were simple and limited in variety. Now they would be vital in ringing the changes and must be looked at afresh, and it was to contrast that designers turned as never before, contrasts of cloth, contrasts of colour, to break up the dull, somehow pathetic appearance of the garments. Checks and plains were an obvious choice but there were also velveteen yokes and pockets on wool dresses and a general trend to give a two-piece effect with printed bodices and plain skirts. Designers looked again at shapes of pockets and yokes and set about grouping the now limited number of buttons more imaginatively and, disregarding those claims about smocking, broke away from the conventional rows of horizontal embroidery and embodied their 'depth of two inches' in vertical or V-shape panels down the bodices where they were no help at all to growing chests but were attractive just the same.

Once again the interdependence of the network of Government Orders was responsible for annoying omissions and confused the manufacturers. The false boundaries of size or style devised to suit quotas and purchase tax were adopted for austerity with no prior consideration of the gaps they would leave. Time and time again after Statutory Orders appeared the children's wear trade itself drew the attention of the authorities to the shortcomings of legislation and its effects. Not infrequently the published Orders differed from the advance Press notices and amendments were a usual occurrence.

Judging by the talk of 'standard' clothing that was being bandied about, the Government would have much preferred not to have engaged in the tangle of austerity regulations but these, together with the utility scheme, did go far towards achieving a standard of sorts and probably as far as the British public would tolerate. The Government had not, however, given up their vision of mass-produced garments for children all coming off the conveyor belt with no thought of frivolous variation of style, trimming or colour that would impede the smooth flow of output. In response to a critical question in the House of Commons about the austerity s.b. blazer, Hugh Dalton, then President of the BOT, in a written reply said he was considering the introduction of a standard style of blazer for schoolchildren which would 'secure further economies in manufacture'.

A move to formulate standard sizes for children's garments had been made in 1941 when the British Standards Institution called a conference of trade associations to discuss the subject. The conference decided that the problem should be investigated and there were hopes that any recommendations would be in time to be used as a basis for the utility clothing scheme, the ceiling prices for which had still not been published, but this was misplaced optimism and no more was heard of the matter for the time being.

A bold step by the Government in 1941 was the concentration of industry whereby companies moved in with one another in order that production and labour could be concentrated in big units instead of being scattered over the country. Despite objections the plan was a success and firms remained together for the duration of the war. Of course the authorities had a big stick to wield to keep these uneasy bedfellows together, they could withdraw labour and withhold supplies of raw material from those who were unco-operative. Under concentration the intention was not that there should be financial amalgamation or that big firms should absorb the smaller ones but rather that like would move over to like. Brand names and marketing arrangements, personal contact with customers, these would be retained by the companies acting individually and special taxation provisions were put into force by the Chancellor of the Exchequer. Looking to the future, Government departments kept records of workers affected and factories closed down—owners were required to keep them ready to open up, paying rent, etc.—so that industrial expansion would follow as swiftly as possible when the war ended.

Voluntary arrangements for concentration were encouraged with a limiting date for different industries (the hosiery trade had a early deadline) if they did not move fast enough. It was a children's hosiery manufacturer which outstripped the rest, for immediately after the concentration plans were announced, Pasolds Ltd., producers of 'Ladybird' children's wear, were granted nucleus status as a firm and were joined in their factory at Langley, Berks. by Jantzen Knitting Mills Ltd. These two well-known companies were the largest knitwear manufacturers in the South of England with famous brand names which they preserved throughout the concentration period.

The many ramifications of Government Orders affecting boys' and girls' wear continued to have a stop-go influence on production. The year 1942 had started with the perennial problem of children's hats the scarcity of which had become steadily more serious, due to a large extent to the Government's persistence in linking legislation to the phrase 'infants' and young children's garments not being chargeable with purchase tax' without, apparently, foreseeing the consequences. Both winter headwear (for warmth) and summer hats (for protection from the sun) were getting more difficult to find. Amending Orders and Special Licences followed one another in an effort to cope with the problems raised by clothes rationing and its restrictions on the use of cloth for unrationed articles such as hats and the utility scheme with its equally strong prohibitions, both of which frustrated coat makers and speciality headwear producers alike.

The only really bright spot in the whole of that year was the announcement that purchase tax was to be removed from utility clothing and footwear – and coming under the umbrella of this important move, at last some infants' and children's hats would be tax-free.

In other respects the pitfalls of administering a tax which divided children from adults were becoming increasingly obvious. From time to time alterations had been made in the maximum tax-free measurements where it was found that these needed to be reduced or raised, in the garment descriptions so that any omitted from the Schedule could be covered, and new or improved methods of measuring introduced. Despite these amendments Customs and Excise believed that there were too many women's dresses and coats being sold without tax as they conformed to the maximum tax-free measurements and rejection on the score of style alone was impossible. These evasions had the added attraction of a lower coupon rating. To reduce the maximum tax-free measurement to below 39ins. (98cms.) length for coats and 38ins. (96cms.) for dresses would penalise many parents of schoolgirls for whom the top size was indispensable. Customs and Excise sought to overcome the difficulty by ruling that in future the maximum sizes would only be regarded as being suitable for young children if they were sold in a normal range from 33ins. or 34ins. (84 or 86cms.) length in the case of coats and from 34ins. (86cms.) in dresses. There was no obligation on the shopkeeper to stock the whole range but rather it was up to the manufacturer to see that they were sold over his entire outlets. This was the usual practice of children's wear houses and the established firms had no problem in conforming to the Customs' requirements but it effectively prevented women's wear businesses from evading the tax as they were not in a position to make samples down to the small sizes and sell them in sufficient quantities to justify the top ones being tax-free. Unfortunately the ruling was one of several which were to prevent designers from introducing more sophisticated styles for the older girl and earned for the trade the reputation of offering childish models for the teens. There had been a marked increase in the number of firms prepared to produce special collections for the young teens in sizes approximately 38-42ins. (96-106cms.). To do so now was out of the question for it would not only mean charging tax but also the women's coupon pointing of 18 for a 39ins. (98cms.) coat as against 11.

# CHAPTER 11
# Clothing Exchanges: Necessitous Children

Of all the shortages which had become commonplace, and to be fair, in most instances wholly justified, one of the most worrying was the paucity of footwear for children. Wellington boots were almost impossible to obtain and scant hope was held out for any improvement in the future, nor would there be any further deliveries from overseas. Shoes had been brought into the utility scheme and this, it was thought, might alleviate the situation. The grumbles continued, questions were asked in the House of Commons and the Director General of Civilian Footwear appealed to firms to increase their production of children's shoes if they could do so. It was significant that Wales was quoted as being an area in which children's shoes were desperately needed as this was one of the districts where many children were wearing shoes for the first time and it was believed that the BOT had not reckoned with this new demand when drawing up the quotas. What made it hard for people to accept the official explanations for the empty shelves in the juvenile departments was that in contrast those in the men's and women's were stacked with plenty of boxes, offering, too, an excellent choice of styles. It was vital that children should be properly shod and also that they should not continue wearing shoes which they had outgrown and which impeded the correct development of their feet.

Almost as important as shoes in ensuring that the child's feet developed properly were socks but these, too, had joined the growing list of under-the-counter goods. Although firms were no longer restricted in the amount of utility hosiery they could supply, non-utility was cut back drastically. In the autumn after the last quota period no supplies of non-utility were allowed except in exceptional cases by individual licences, or manufactured under the authority of a Production Direction. The control of the hosiery and knitwear industry was severe—it was an offence for registered firms to manufacture knitted goods other than in accordance with their Production Directions. Businesses which did not concentrate lost all their labour, even the 16-18-year-old girl learners brought in to replace older female workers of conscription age and upwards.

The last quota period did not apply only to the knitwear industry, the selling quota mechanism was being largely abolished. Once utility had been introduced the quotas had only been maintained in order to direct production into utility goods. Now the programme was being closely co-ordinated with the Raw Materials Controls procedure, selling quota restrictions were not necessary. Instead the control was being imposed on woven cloths at the production end.

Additions and amendments to the utility schedule for infants' and children's garments made from woven or knitted cloths appeared frequently but by the end of the year no 'ceiling' prices had not yet materialised. This is not to say that manufacturers and distributors were free to charge what they liked. On the contrary, prices at every stage were governed by the Prices of Goods Act but it was admitted that this was open to evasion. At the beginning of 1942 Orders were published tying-up the percentage mark-ups for those utility goods with fixed ceiling prices, such as women's and maids', and also including infants' and children's knitwear, and these stipulated manufacturers', wholesalers and retailers' margin of net profit. Some weeks passed before manufacturers' mark-ups for infants' and children's clothing made from woven utility cloths were announced, at four per cent for categories which, broadly speaking, were non-fashion, and five per cent for other apparel such as coats and dresses. Following on these yet another series of Price Control Orders embracing a wide range of utility and non-utility clothing, footwear, etc., was imposed at short notice covering wholesalers and retailers as well as manufacturers.

There were protestations on all sides that the profit margins were not high enough: retailers of baby and girls' wear said they took no account of the service they had to give as compared with other shops. Wholesalers were disgusted and certainly their mark-up was very tight. Manufacturers were not quite so vocal—some of them would have been very glad to have made even four per cent net profit before the war. Whether the complaints were justified or not, there is no doubt that unless the Government had kept this tight rein on profit margins, with the limited supplies available prices would have soared and many a child would have had to go without much-needed new clothes.

It did not take long once the effects of rationing and shortages began to be felt for the public to realise the potentialities of clothes which had been outgrown. Mothers who would have shuddered at the thought of their offspring wearing second-hand garments were quite happy to patronise 'clothing exchanges' and felt in so doing they were helping the war effort. Second-hand goods were only exempt from coupons if sold below certain prices but this was overcome by ingenious points systems which obviated the need for cash or coupons. Garments handed in were awarded so many points and exchanged then, or later, for other articles with similar ratings. Local Councils backed these clothing pools and due largely to the sustained effort of the WVS (Women's Voluntary Services) the local depot became a familiar part of urban life.

This was one side of the children's clothing picture, the well-clothed side which was suffering inconveniences because of the shortages brought about by the war and Government controls but there was another side where children in the United Kingdom went without clothes not because of an emergency but because their parents were unable to give them the bare necessities to keep them warm and protected. That there were many kiddies in England and Wales whose parents could not afford sufficient clothing had long been known to teachers in the poorer areas. The Association of Education Committees had been investigating the matter and the information obtained as a result of a careful recording over a period of the situation in a typical large city formed the basis of an approach by the Association to the President of the Board of Trade for authority to provide clothing and footwear for necessitous children out of the education fund.

During the rehearsal of the evacuation of schoolchildren from Newcastle-upon-Tyne one week before they actually left, the Association of Education Committees had taken the opportunity of assessing the state of their clothing and footwear. In the report issued later it was pointed out that it would be expected that in such circumstances the parents would provide the best clothing they could. Head teachers were asked to classify the clothing as 'good', 'an acceptable minimum' or 'insufficient'. Of the 25,000 children inspected, 13 per cent had insufficient footwear, 9 per cent had insufficient day clothing and 12 per cent had insufficient underwear or nightwear. A sad conclusion recorded by the teachers was that many more children would have reported for evacuation if the parents had been able to provide adequate clothing and footwear.

The evacuation of the children to country districts led the Ministry of Health to make arrangements for Directors of Education to provide clothing and footwear for necessitous evacuees. In Newcastle-upon-Tyne they operated a system whereby the teacher in a reception area first wrote to parents of children whose clothing had been noted as inadequate and if prompt steps were not taken to effect an improvement the matter was notified to the Education Committee. Over 18 months such applications were running at the rate of 8,000 cases per annum and 33 per cent proved to be necessitous and had to be assisted by funds supplied by the Ministry of Health or from voluntary sources. Of the parents who were considered to be in a position to pay it was noted that many were unable to put down a lump sum and this led to the purchase of inferior quality articles. This situation was aggravated when clothes rationing was introduced and the same number of coupons had to be given up irrespective of the durability of the goods.

In the view of the Association every child should be provided with necessary medical attention, sufficient suitable food and adequate clothing and footwear. Assuming that Local Education Authorities exercised correctly their statutory powers and duties the first two requirements could be met but in England and Wales they had no mandate to provide for the third, even in respect of necessitous children. The only provision was for an officer of the Assistance Board or the Relieving Officer of the Public Assistance Committee to grant 'relief' but they had to wait until either the parent made an application or the child's plight was brought to their notice by someone else. Was it right, asked the Association, that a child of tender years should come within the sphere and influence of such bodies as the Public Assistance Committee or the Assistance Board, however benevolent such bodies might be and however efficient and sympathetic their Officers? The Ministry of Health funds were only available for children evacuated to the reception area, left out of the scheme were children at home, whether in an evacuation, neutral or reception area.

A deputation from the Association to the President of the BOT asked that local authorities should be given statutory powers to provide, with the assistance of the Exchequer, clothing and footwear as well as meals for necessitous schoolchildren wherever they were. It was also submitted that the definition of cruelty to children needed widening in such a way as to include neglect of a parent to provide such adequate provision of clothing and footwear as lay within his means. The President, whilst professing sympathy with the object behind the representations regretted that he was unable to give a promise to undertake legislation of that nature at that time because of the expenditure involved, thought it should come under the much wider question of, for example, the establishment of family allowances, and that the higher wages obtaining had lessened the necessity for action.

It was all the more galling for the Association's plea to be turned down when a Bill giving Scotland such powers had been accepted by Parliament. Bitterly the Association commented: 'It is a curious administration that requires English taxpayers to contribute towards Exchequer funds providing such assistance for Scottish children when no such assistance is provided for English children, while Scottish taxpayers do not contribute towards the clothing and footwear for necessitous children in England'.

# CHAPTER 12
# Mounting Criticism of Controls

The bitter war years rolled on, destruction by air and sea ravaging the country's means of survival and the Government's grip on the production and distribution of clothing tightened. Even at such a time civil servants could, and did, bend their thoughts to defining a baby's bib or feeder so that it would be acceptable to the utility scheme, specifying the bib's permitted length (10ins. 25cms.), width (9ins. 23cms.), the colour and nature of its binding, the number of neck tapes, its material content and, of course, its price. Special Directions were issued about infants' utility gaiter overalls which reduced the crutch-to-ankle measurement for two sizes—*by a quarter of an inch*: they directed that the minimum finished weight of a boy's 24in. (61cms.) chest utility vest should be one ounce less, *per dozen*: they put an embargo on coloured tops and striped legs on kiddies' non-fashioned socks.

At one point the BOT announced its intention of banning all-wool underwear for babies and girls as well as adults (the poor boys were never allowed all-wool underwear in the utility scheme and there was little non-utility). The nation was shocked, no wool underwear for babies?—*British* babies?—this was untenable even in wartime. Protests were swift and passionate, questions were asked in the House and within a week or two the BOT relented and far from banning woollen underwear for infants said they were going to give its production priority and there would be some, too, for girls over four years, but, like the rest of the population, most of its underwear must contain other yarns to eke out precious supplies.

Although the manufacturers of adults' clothing had been working for a long time to ceiling prices for utility none had yet been issued for children's wear and it was not until more than eighteen months later that these were announced, the reason for the delay being the BOT's wish to avoid any action which might have an adverse effect on the already depleted production. The first price schedules they proposed were rejected immediately as being too low to allow for an adequate standard of make. As usual the procrastination so often occurring over children's wear created difficulties in other areas. It was the BOT's intention that when the ceiling prices were issued certain cloths widely used for infants' and girls' wear would be listed. However, as the Schedules had not appeared it was unlawful for manufacturers to use these cloths, despite the fact that 'key certificates' for their purchase had been given to them by the BOT itself. Nevertheless it was decreed that each manufacturer must write personally to the Board seeking permission to use the materials providing at the same time a mass of details as to where, when and from whom they were purchased, the exact stage of production of every garment, the price and where, when and to whom it was to be delivered. Further, the BOT had changed its mind about the end-use of several of the fabrics and suggested that cloth suppliers should be asked to switch the orders to other materials, a completely unrealistic proposition. All this was bad enough, particularly since in issuing the certificates for the purchase of the cloths the BOT, knowing the use to which they were to be put, had signified their consent, but when the Board received what it was anticipated was a mere routine application to put right the results of their own shortcomings they had the temerity to withhold licences on the grounds that the prices were not low enough. No mention of this, of course, was made when the certificates were issued, and, it will be remembered, manufacturers' profits were in any case strictly controlled in the pricing regulations. The Board's action was an indication of the rock-bottom level which they had in mind for children's utility clothing. It was understandable that the Board wished to ensure that no one took advantage of wartime shortages by profiteering and BOT President, Hugh Dalton, could record in 1943 that the price of clothing was about 70 per cent above the pre-war level, compared with 95 per cent in 1942, due to the introduction of the utility scheme.

It was, however, of no benefit to lay down prices which were too low to permit the making of durable garments, an even greater necessity in wartime, or which stopped the output altogether. As had been proved already if manufacturers found that certain types or sizes cost more to produce than the price they were allowed to charge then they stopped making them. Firms had no alternative: overheads and salaries had to be met and under the pricing and utility regulations there was no question of swings and roundabouts whereby the mark-up on other garments could carry the loss-makers. The first to suffer in such instances were those children taking the biggest sizes which were uneconomic, a shortage then followed, whereupon the BOT, faced with a desperate situation, had to try and entice other manufacturers to fill the gaps.

It was not only the manufacturers who were concerned about price levels and their effect on good make, shops, too, were becoming increasingly wary of accepting any children's clothing of poor quality. When, frantic for goods, they had bought anything to try and satisfy their customers they found that the public had quickly learned not to waste coupons on garments and footwear which had a limited life: clothes rationing had at last brought home to parents that it was cheaper in the long run to buy good quality articles.

That the BOT's efforts both to keep down the price of children's wear and ensure supplies under the utility scheme had had the reverse effect was evident in the shortage of some articles for boys. Mothers were unable to purchase such essentials as boys' suits and separate knickers, these had almost disappeared from the scene because the ceiling prices for utility were too low. Gloves for boys and girls were affected in the same way and makers had been 'directed' to maintain their production at the expense of adult sizes. Even more important and affecting youngsters of all ages was the serious position of footwear. Dire prophecies of youngsters not being able to attend school as they had no shoes had come true as the Board of Education itself admitted. There was widespread concern amongst mothers both as to the difficulties of obtaining shoes and the poor quality of some footwear. Because of the way the footwear regulations had been framed by the BOT it was better to make women's shoes at a profit than children's at a loss. Measures to affect an improvement had resulted in a flood of hastily made shoes which lasted only a few weeks. It was next to impossible to get shoes repaired and often those produced to meet the crisis could not be repaired – a good many pairs found their way to Millbank when irate mothers posted them off to the BOT. The toll on coupons, and purse, was high and added to this was resentment over the stocks of women's shoes in the shops. As usual MPs reflecting the complaints of their constituents went after the Minister responsible in the House. When the mounting criticism could no longer be ignored and MPs persisted in putting down questions, Hugh Dalton told the House, '*The U-boat is still the enemy of the child in this country*'. He was not very sanguine about a radical change in the position, rubber was almost unobtainable and most of the hides had to run the gauntlet of the U-boats, the Services must have first call on supplies which did get through. All the same production of leather footwear for children was in excess of pre-war and factories had been switched from adults' to boys' and girls' footwear even, it transpired later, some of those engaged on boots and shoes for the Forces.

This failed to satisfy the critics since it took no account of those children who for the first time in their lives were wearing shoes or the loss of imports which were a significant factor before the war. Plimsolls, for example, worn extensively by children merely trickled through until stocks were finally exhausted and were never replaced until after the war.

For once the strict utility requirements were allowed to slip a little and where manufacturers found any of their shoes did not quite come up to the specifications the output was not lost, they were allowed to sell them provided that they were marked sub-standard and sold at 80 per cent or less of the permitted price. In a further bid to identify and prevent sales of shoddy footwear manufacturers were required to put their identification mark on every pair of outdoor shoes they produced. Not so much the target for vociferous complaints but distressing nevertheless was the paucity of supplies of soft sole shoes for babies and toddlers which were becoming increasingly hard to obtain. Despite the U-boat dangers and the calls on shipping, children's shoes were being brought into the country from the Commonwealth which had responded to appeals for prompt aid. At home all production of sandals was stopped because of the labour involved.

There was encouragement to include shoes in the children's clothing exchanges but although this was done the practice was not regarded favourably by those who believed that the wearing of second-hand shoes would do more harm than good. The possibility of substitute materials was examined, wooden soles, for example, slatted to permit the feet to bend were tried out on children with predictable results, they were unsuitable, even dangerous. Of more value were soles of reclaimed rubber composition and old conveyor belts, the former also being issued in half-soles as well for repairing children's shoes.

The bitterness and anger over the neglect of one of a child's vital requirements spread to the coupon pointing of their footwear until a concession was announced, extra coupons for girls taking over size 3 and for boys, 5½. Not too generous a concession, however, it was largely to compensate for the increased coupon rating for adult footwear which had come into force.

Expectant mothers and those with young babies were having to scramble around to get proper clothing and to make their coupons last. Although the principle had been established of an extra allowance for their requirements it was inadequate and only proof that the authorities relied on coupons being sacrificed by relatives and friends. Despite continual protests, by no means exaggerating the problems which these women had to face, not a great deal was done to alleviate the situation. Baby wear from woven and knitted cloths and knitted garments was equally hard to find. The type of babies' and infants' knitwear which hosiery manufacturers were allowed to produce was rigidly controlled and whilst this appeared satisfactory on paper the smallest delay in yarn deliveries would be reflected quickly in supplies in the shops. In wartime this would have been accepted however reluctantly had it not been, as in the case of other commodities, for the seemingly greater supply of articles for adults. Knitted shawls were fast disappearing and nor could women obtain soft knitting wools in white or pastels so that they could make the shawls at home and special directions had to be issued to spinners to get this type of yarn produced.

The biggest grievance remained the number of coupons which expectant mothers had to give up for terry napkins, a minimum of 24, plus the coupon-free gauze type, was needed but here again it was clear that the BOT believed that only the first-born were involved, otherwise those bought for precious babies would be available. (Everyone now had to make their coupons last longer for by the simple device of extending the rationing period by one month the allocation was quietly reduced.)

It was the National Children's Wear Association which decided that the true position of baby wear supplies should be ascertained. To this end they circulated questionnaires to retailers throughout the country asking for their experiences over deliveries. The replies revealed that in 54 items of baby clothing no deliveries at all had been received by many shops for months, others had obtained only a quarter, some a half, some three-quarters. The information derived from the questionnaire was sent to the President of the BOT and released to the Press. The BOT's first reaction was to dismiss the results, one of their arguments being that shortages were often exaggerated by women going from shop to shop to find goods. The NCWA was swift to retort that this was an admission that severe shortages did exist and far from destroying, in fact proved their case. The BOT took up a somewhat different attitude in replies to MPs and the Press—who had lost no time in reporting that their own investigations confirmed the Association's findings—their public utterances reiterated their concern over providing clothing for the children even to protecting the labour to make it. (Following on the concentration arrangements in the clothing industry, 25 per cent of the labour force was being taken from each manufacturer with the exception of infants' wear firms.)

The forceful, repeated representations advanced for special consideration of infants and their clothing requirements (never necessary over their food as the Ministry of Food made them a No. 1 civilian priority right from the start) bore fruit in one direction which was to have lasting results. One cloth in the Utility Schedule, No. 210, had a wide definition, it had to contain more than 15 per cent of wool but there was no upper limit to the wool content. A handful of manufacturers, among them the biggest, the producers of 'Dayella', a brand in the 'Viyella' and 'Clydella' family, were putting in up to 40 per cent wool and yet selling below the permitted price. Understandably there was a big demand for such cloths and in

1943 the BOT went to the firms concerned and suggested that a new category should be introduced for these fabrics and they should be reserved exclusively for infants' and children's wear. The companies agreed, although it meant the sacrifice of their men's and women's markets, and the new cloth, No. 236 in the Schedule, had the highly satisfactory specification of a 'washable cloth, made from blended yarn of wool and cotton, containing not less than $33\frac{1}{3}$ per cent and not more than 50 per cent by weight of wool in both warp and weft, at a weight of $3\frac{1}{2}$ to 5oz. (99 to 142grams) per square yard'. It was of inestimable benefit in ensuring first class garments, especially babies' daygowns and nightgowns, and itself set a standard for the future.

A cosy leaflet sponsored by the BOT telling the expectant mother just how easy it was to provide a layette out of the 60 coupons allocated to her nevertheless emphasised that as many clothes as possible should be borrowed from friends. The list of minimum articles which would have to be purchased took all but one or two of the 60, leaving none for the expectant mother's own essential requirements or maternity bra, corsets and outerwear. Not even the BOT could make the coupons go that far. Another leaflet published by the Board as part of their make-do-and-mend drive suggested ways of turning woollen stockings into infants' jerseys and pyjama legs into vests, presumably, that is, if you didn't want the pyjamas and the woollen stockings were not already worn out.

It was ironic that at the time when helping expectant mothers, allaying their anxieties and ensuring the well-being of the babies through the provision of suitable clothing was no part of the programme of the coldly indifferent BOT, others, far-sighted politicians and population experts, were concerned about the future of Britain unless more babies were born. The birth-rate was actually running above the pre-war level but Winston Churchill himself told the nation that people must be encouraged to have large families. This became Government policy and a Royal Commission was set up to enquire into the birth-rate, one of the terms of reference being to consider what measures, if any, should be taken to influence the future trend of population. This lofty intent was at variance with the everyday world of the expectant mother counting coupons and chasing clothing.

Toddlers going to the day nurseries while mothers went off to help the war effort did not escape bureaucracy's net. A stock of little garments might be furnished free of coupons to the nurseries at the outset, but once a month the wee mites each had to give up a coupon because after all they were wearing the overalls provided and these might eventually be worn out. There was always, of course, the possibility that mother had no coupons left.

Every so often when it seemed that wartime conditions must result in a serious dearth of clothing for new-born babies the idea of a standard layette was mooted. The theory was that a set layette would be considerably simpler to mass-produce and might merit a coupon concession. The proposal did not find favour as being practical or acceptable. One of the biggest snags was that although the layette might be standard, mothers were not, and about their babies they had markedly individual preferences as shopkeepers could testify. Another objection, equally strong, was that requirements would vary so much since one mother might have no need of, say, nightgowns, as sufficient had been passed on to her, but would require other items such as napkins, and the opposite would be the case with someone else. Wisely the suggestion was never put into practice.

The spotlight turned on shoes and baby wear did not mean that other areas of children's clothing were satisfactory, or as satisfactory as it was right to expect in wartime. Far from it, these two most readily excited public indignation but there were other gaps which were equally troublesome to families. One of these was in headwear, a classic example of the mess which bureaucracy could create simply through starting off from the wrong premise: this one was to run its pitiful course until rationing ended long after the war was over.

Because they had always made hats with winter coats, because they knew that infants' and children's headwear was in short supply, because they had received a special coupon allocation from the BOT for this purpose, manufacturers of coats not unreasonably had been making matching hats, but for this heinous crime they were severely rebuked by the Board and reminded that they must keep within the quotas laid down. This was rather puzzling considering that the offenders had received coupons from the BOT to make hats in excess of these very quotas. Ah! said the Board, but you can only do this if you apply to us for a licence for the right to exceed the quota with the coupons we let you have for this purpose in the first place.

A worse fate befell makers of knitted headwear. If that were all they made they were removed from the Register of Manufacturers of Knitted Goods and relegated to another 'Class' for which they had to make immediate application to, so to speak, be taken in. Knitwear companies who made infants' sets which included tiny bonnets would also have to have special licences to cover this production.

So it went on and on with the Board clinging tenaciously to the principle that small children were not to have their head covering assured for the winter and referring to severe limitations. As usual the British public made its own decision. Despite the war, despite the difficulty of getting winter coats at all, mothers of infants and small children refused to buy coats unless there were hats to go with them, preferring to go from shop to shop until they found what they wanted: in turn retailers refused to place orders for coats only from wholesalers, who then refused to take deliveries from manufacturers and this fouled up the manufacturers' quota arrangements and ultimately surprised and shocked the BOT. Waiting lists had already been opened in shops for children's hats and the situation grew more and more ridiculous. The pressure got too hot and the BOT capitulated and agreed, prodded by repeated representations of the NCWA to allow firms to make a hat with every utility woven coat or coat and breechette set up to 22ins. (56cms.).

Was it all necessary? Would manufacturers have gone mad and carried on making infants' and children's hats to the detriment of the war effort or would they, being businessmen possessing, like others, a degree of responsibility and patriotism, have produced only sufficient to meet the just needs of the child population? Was this registering here, deregistering there, licensing here and preventing there, a rightful use of man-power at such a moment? It seemed that in some regions the BOT had blind spots and headwear was one.

# CHAPTER 13
# Spartan Policy for Children Continues

By the end of 1943 peace was in the air and so confident were the Allies that it was only a question of time before their liberating armies swept through Europe that even while trying to make a little go a long way at home their thoughts were on relief for the Occupied Countries. Committees were already at work preparing estimates of, amongst other things, quantities and types of children's wear for distribution in the wake of the Allied landings and everyone concerned knew that babies would have lacked proper clothing and their wants must be top priority. Voluntary organisations were put to work knitting thousands of baby vests. (How many pilches should be sent to Europe was the subject of a weighty discussion in one Committee room. Afterwards through whispered confessions it was revealed that only one person in the room knew what a pilch was.) The Ministry of Supply had powers to purchase stock to build up reserves for relief clothing but only if it was surplus to civilian requirements, infants' and children's underwear, for example, was restricted to cotton vests and knickers, but actual production was also authorised, including girls' frocks from wool cloths provided by the Ministry. The specifications and prices had to be agreed between the Government and trade associations, tenders invited and contracts placed. This production was over and above home civilian consumption and subject to the austerity regulations but the cloth certificates for this purpose were issued with an eye to overall output.

Once the scheme was launched, somewhat warily as can be seen lest anyone should get the impression that the British people were being deprived so that others might benefit, it furnished a wonderful means of getting rid of fabrics which the powers-that-be and some opportunists thought a public desperate and afraid of future shortages would be only too pleased to snap up. The years had proved them both wrong and these dormant materials, joined by utility fabrics failing to move because of colour, weight, construction or equally obvious defect, stayed on the shelves. The Government accepted defeat and declared that makers-up with woollen materials which they had held for some time and 'found to be unsuitable for the home market' would be given the opportunity of offering them to the Ministry of Supply for relief clothing. Subsequently they changed their minds and decided that they would deal with made-up garments from these cloths.

Hosiery and knitwear requirements for relief had come under one body. The Ministry of Supply had relinquished its responsibilities for supplies of hosiery and knitwear for relief purposes to Hosiery Control, a newly-created section under the aegis of the BOT which embraced Services, civilian and relief requirements. A similar process brought shoes under a Footwear Control. Gradually, by a series of jerky moves backwards and forwards enough clothing was collected for a considerable contribution to be earmarked for the liberated countries without any diminution of home supplies nor any criticism of the action taken.

The clothing trade itself was also turning its thoughts to the changeover from war to peace, notably how rapidly the flow of raw materials would be stepped up, when would they get their key workers back and how quickly Government controls would be removed, and there were signs that the latter were not going to be surrendered without a struggle. Standardisation of clothing, it was being said, could be advantageous for reasons of economy and consumer protection standards ought to be retained for some cloths, make and sizes of garments. It was not a view shared by those whose businesses had been 'directed' and 'controlled' since 1939.

The declared intention was to restore labour when the factory space was released, raw materials available and machinery installed. Foremost in any plans for post-war was the recognition of the rights of ex-Servicemen to return to their old positions and have first claim on machinery, premises, finance and labour. This was fully accepted but there were already misgivings about the chances of children's wear firms getting materials and equipment in competition with the powerful men's and women's wear producers. Meanwhile the makers of children's clothing had to battle on with the BOT on their backs. Ceiling prices for infants' and girls' wear made from woven utility materials had still not been agreed yet those for the rest of the civilian population, including the boys', had been in force for months and covered both knitted and woven garments. With so much talk of liberation and relief for the Occupied Countries optimists began to think that hostilities would have ceased before the Statutory Instrument was put before Parliament and the country moved over to a control-free peace.

In the interim the absence of any official Schedule for infants and girls was a continual nuisance. One moment manufacturers were told they could use any suitable utility fabric for children's wear then they were informed that licences had to be obtained for several. Within a month this policy was reversed and there would come an announcement that firms did not have to apply for the licences at all. Headgear continued to assume an importance out of all proportion to its place in a child's life. Having agreed that every infant's coat, up to the age of five, should have a hat to match it was then found that the allocation of coupons to manufacturers was insufficient to reimburse them for the cloth needed to make the hats, so again a rescue operation had to be set in motion.

It took twelve months' consultation between the BOT and the trade before the utility order for children's wear became law. Throughout this time companies were wondering which materials they would be able to use, for what, and in what sizes, but, above all, they wanted to find out how high the ceilings would be. They had received a nasty shock the year before when news leaked out that prices were going to be very, very low, so low indeed that it was said that only the makers of the cheapest garments would be able to get down to them. It was on this aspect that their representatives argued with the Board, namely that the public would be better served if a cheap-to-medium price bracket was adopted.

Nothing could have revealed so clearly the BOT's attitude towards clothing the children than the publication of Schedule

IG in 1944 (brought into force by the Utility Apparel (Infants' and Girls' Wear) (No. 2) Directions 1944 (SR & O 1944, No. 111)). Here was a Schedule which laid down the arbitary rules for practically the whole of infants' and girls' garments made from utility woven cloth and non-utility now had no significance. Someone, somewhere had decided to reject the trade's advice (always suspect as being motivated by self-interest) where it ran counter to their own preconceived notions of what girls should, or should not, wear. Throughout the long series of discussions conducted under a mandate of Fair Shares for All there was a steely determination that no child was going to be better dressed than any other and the way to achieve this was to reduce the level of their clothing to the lowest common denominator. It was never a question of *'How much can we give the children?'* as it was at the Ministry of Food but *'How little?'*. Prejudices against garments resulted in their being left out of the utility scheme altogether, warnings that prices were being set too low in several important sectors were dismissed as coming from biased sources. If the outcome was the removal of every detail which delighted the youngsters and gladdened the hearts of the mothers, the poorest children had always had to do without them so why not everyone? All very well to try and stamp out this inequality in the guise of wartime sacrifices but it came oddly from a Government department which had just removed the austerity regulations from men's clothing simply because the civilian males refused to go without their trouser turn-ups. Suddenly at the beginning of 1944 the austerity restrictions were removed from men's clothing. What a furore this caused with women raging battle on two fronts, for themselves and their children. It did seem incredible that the men *out of uniform* should have unlimited styling and the rest of the civilian population, including boys, have to submit to finnicky regulations covering the whole gamut of their apparel. Furthermore it was almost, if not wholly, woollen cloths, reputedly so scarce, which were to be involved in such niceties. To provide for this concession out came an Order increasing the ceiling prices for men's and youths' utility outerwear to allow for this style extravaganza which if not a contradiction of everything utility stood for was certainly a blatant example of sex discrimination.

The power to impose a spartan policy for the kiddies was right there in the hands of the BOT. They had complete control over supplies, labour, machinery and even location of production: they were in a position to dictate the terms and everyone had to conform, or so it seemed but it did not quite work out like that as subsequent speedy amendments proved. The biggest job the BOT had had of all the utility schemes was how Sir Thomas Barlow, Director General of Civilian Clothing, described Schedule IG, He expressed the hope that its publication would bring order out of chaos perhaps not without much conviction, however, as he admitted that it was incomplete and discussions were taking place over the inclusion of additional, higher-quality cloths which might be listed.

Naturally this Schedule was the biggest utility task the Board had had to face. Those who dismissed children's wear as being a simple matter easily dealt with had found it embraced miniature editions of the problems encountered throughout women's and men's clothing, plus the unparalleled size range from birth to teens encompassing varying stages of development, and the observance of the unique obligations associated with clothing the child. The scope of Schedule IG extended from babies' bibs and feeders, infants' wear, boys' and girls', and girls' garments to the maximum purchase-tax free measurements as laid down by Customs and Excise, going beyond these to take in additionally bigger gym tunics and blazers. It dealt with woven wool, cotton and rayon materials and locknit and circular knitted fabrics. Only the types and sizes of garments listed in the Schedule could be made-up and then only from the fabrics indicated against each one. Cloths allowed for one or two sizes were not necessarily permitted for others, larger or smaller, even if they were the same type of garment. It was illegal to make an article of child's utility clothing not listed, or in a different size from that given, or from a cloth not stipulated. For every kind of garment and size a ceiling price was fixed which the manufacturers must not exceed. (He could not charge this ceiling if it meant his margin of profit was greater than that already in force under the price control laws.) Extra regulations governing minimum measurements were included for specific outerwear and underwear in the light clothing category and if any one measurement in a garment was less than that laid down for the size then the ceiling price shown could not be charged. No minimum measurement restrictions were applied to 'heavy' clothing items, i.e., coats, blazers, etc., for all that the public would think it more important that these articles should be correctly, if not generously, cut. This exception was not evidence that the Board did not share this view but that the manufacturers of heavy clothing successfully resisted any attempt to force them to work to standard measurements set by outsiders.

It was the omissions in the Schedule which disclosed the harsh attitude of the powers-that-be and the collection made strange reading. Prohibited were costumes, lumber jackets and slacks, dressing-gowns, school blouses in colours, baby bags, knickers for small boys, matching hats for coats for the over-fours, matching jockey caps for any size coat and siren suits. None were left out by accident but by design. That baby bags should have been rejected was surprising enough but that siren suits should be given similar treatment was extraordinary. Born of necessity, under no circumstances could they be dismissed as frivolous, glamorous, non-essentials and at the very moment that Schedule IG was published the 'scalded cat' air raids had reminded mothers of the advantages of these suits and sent them hurrying into the shops to try to buy them.

The BOT's reply to protests about the ban was to dismiss the suits as 'fashion' garments which would not have a long life (anything less like a fashion garment it would have been hard to find). How wrong they were in this phrophesy. The one-piece siren suit never died, it lives with slight alteration as an outdoor coverall and it is such a simple, practical article that it is almost impossible to believe that it was unknown before the war.

Restricting school blouses in wool and cotton mixture materials (a high percentage was made in these cloths) to white was apparently a knock at official uniforms but its effect was to cut out the more serviceable pastels which were easier to launder. It was not a matter of discouraging fancy or garish shades as these were almost non-existent in school life. For some peculiar reason the BOT had developed a dislike for girls' costumes, hard to understand since they allowed women to have them in utility. The imposition got them into deep water for jackets and skirts were permitted for girls, so when did a jacket and skirt become a non-eligible costume? They were emphatically not fashion suits by that stage of the war, the austerity regulations had seen to that.

The hidden hand of prejudice was obvious in the veto on dressing-gowns, girls' slacks and baby bags—a 20th century boon to mothers and babies. The claims of tiny boys fell on deaf ears. They could not have caps in jockey style, a simple copy of those worn by riders which met the mother's desire to establish the child's masculinity without being too old, and either had to go without or, perish the thought, wear a girl's hat if, that is, they were under four, the matching hat borderline. To protests the Board replied that sufficient provision for caps was made in another Order covering older boys' utility clothing but that, said manufacturers, was no help, the permitted cloths were different and would not match the coats. Poor little boys, the impression was the BOT had an *idée fixe* that caps were really rather frivolous. Young males of the same age suffered again by the absence of separate knickers in the utility Schedule, but this may have been one occasion when the authorities forgot that they did not wear buster suits day in and day out. The official explanation was that separate knickers could be made under the boys' wear Order but the utility cloths that gave were too thick and heavy for infants.

The cloths detailed, per size, per garment, predictably came in for criticism. Some of this was accepted and put right by subsequent amendments; some was rejected and despite repeated grumblings, gradually died down, but to one thing the public would never be reconciled and that was the prevalence of flannelette for infants' and girls' nightdresses and pyjamas, they did not like the quality and they were suspicious of its flammability. The public persisted in wanting a better material and could not be persuaded that there was no alternative. They just dug in their heels and this utility nightwear stayed on the shop shelves.

If the choice of garments and cloths for the Utility Schedule displeased knowledgeable people, what then of the ceiling prices so important to mothers and to those who would have to make and distribute the clothing? The rumours preceding the publication of the Schedule proved ill-founded in some respects: a number were not as low as predicted but those that were hit rock bottom killing a fair proportion of production in the process. There was a strange inconsistency about the fixing of the prices. The avowed object of the utility scheme was to ensure a flow of hard-wearing, sensible garments at pegged prices as cheap as possible compatible with a decent standard of make. Despite the wide variety of clothing covered by the Schedule this aim should have been visible throughout, exemplified by a regular pattern of pricing. Instead the figures went up or down according, presumably, to the strength of the trade representatives or the determination of BOT officials inspired with a desire to keep prices down. What then happened, of course, was that production and distribution followed the ups and downs of the ceilings with fateful constancy and coupled with the coupon losses incurred in certain sizes sent a number of articles straight off the market.

What the austerity regulations had begun Schedule IG finished. Smocking rarely reached the maximum permitted and not infrequently disappeared altogether, replaced by the cheaper machine gauging on the top infants' sizes. Styling and detail were forced down to vanishing point in dresses for the 13-16 year olds the ceiling prices for which were considerably lower than those in the corresponding fabrics for the smallest sizes in the women's utility Schedule although just as much labour and frequently more cloth went into the girls' garments.

The heavy side had been successful in persuading the Board to be more generous over older girls' coats but by comparison infants' coats were on a much lower scale. The prices were not, however, enough to entice makers to bear the heavy coupon wastage on the top child's size of 38ins. (96cms.) and too many decided to stop at 36ins. (91cms.). The ubiquitous blazer dropped out of sight once the Schedule was examined in detail. To all but one or two firms nightwear became one of the untouchables. Makers-up under no obligation to incur a loss to suit the theories of civil servants switched from cut-price things like infants' sleeping suits to women's nightdresses where the profits were healthier.

It was not only the manufacturers who began to realise the implications of Schedule IG, shopkeepers perusing the prices saw that they represented a quality of production in which the public had no interest. It was coupons, not price, that dictated purchases. Mothers were quick to spot poor material, skimped widths and narrow seams and hems, the sure signs of a short life and too many of the cheaper dresses, especially, were staying on retailers' shelves. There was no quarrelling with the evidence that the public would not buy cheap blouses and gym tunics despite the powerful lure of a reduced coupon rate which had been put into operation.

Schedule IG had come into force on July 1, 1944, no less than one month later a revised version, Schedule IG2 was published. Two reasons had led to this swift amendment, (1) extra cloths for certain categories; (2) alterations in ceiling prices. The latter represented no galloping inflation, the increase for a 22ins. (56cms.) gym tunic being 1d. (old pence), an infant's robe on sale to the retailer ½d. (old currency). However, one or two prices were raised sufficiently for manufacturers to reconsider their decision to drop garments, or sizes, for example blazers for which the maker could get another 1s.7d. (8p.) on a 35ins. (87cms.) in a better quality cloth and additional materials from which the public itself was demanding the blazers should be made. The Board moved quickly to allow matching hats to be made with coats in sizes 24-28ins. (61-71cms.) but this relaxation did not extend to boys' jockey caps.

If there was any optimism that the publication of the Utility Schedules would create an upsurge in supplies it was soon dispelled and the consequences of certain of their features were not long to take effect. The shortages of infants' and children's wear were at this point so widespread that they received the supreme accolade accorded only to matters of national interest, they became the subject of cartoons in the national Press, the target being Hugh Dalton himself, President of the Board of Trade. The House of Commons rang again with questions put by MPs full of righteous indignation over the suffering children. Newspapers went after the BOT President and that the stories were true was proved when the BOT was forced to issue a Press Notice (not lightly done for such a reason in those days) denying that the shortages were 'acute'. Mr. Dalton put his faith in figures which showed that stocks were naturally below the peacetime levels but there was no reason for the fears which had been expressed. Statistics have a nasty way of rebounding and it was recognised immediately that if stocks were below peacetime levels there was certainly a dire shortage and one likely to get worse for 64,000 more babies had been born in 1943. The highest birth-rate for 15 years had been recorded in that year, the September quarter had the highest total of live births for that period since 1926 and the infant mortality rate was the lowest quarterly figure ever at 40 per 1,000. Where were these extra babies going to get their clothing from *and* the three to four-year-olds, 100,000 stronger than pre-war? Certainly not from the shops for it was not unusual to hear of a departmental store where not one child's vest had been delivered throughout the winter months and women went from shop to shop seeking infants' and babies' wool knitwear from pram sets to bonnets.

Mr. Dalton reiterated that he was giving special priority to supplies of children's wear and he implemented this by ensuring that experienced workers released from munitions (except in certain areas) were sent to companies with vacancies within their approved labour force and simultaneously he raised the figure of the approved labour foce for infants' wear specialists. Despite these efforts it became evident that where the Government, to help the general public, sought to keep down ceiling prices below a realistic figure a point was reached where garments were priced out of existence and far from assisting added to parents' burdens. One solution put into operation by the BOT was a system of rebates applied to utility woven cloths and paid to cloth manufacturers and merchants. In this way the cost of the material was pegged to makers-up and made the ceiling prices for finished garments a more reasonable proposition.

Not that all clothing manufacturers found the going tough. When the war was at its height in 1944 and, it might be supposed, coat firms were fully occupied trying to get labour, materials, coupons, keep machinery in working order and observe all the regulations emanating almost daily from Whitehall, one company found time (but surely not the necessity?) to enter into an agreement with Walt Disney to put his cartoon characters on their outerwear for small boys and girls—and managed to have labels specially woven depicting Mickey Mouse and his friends to support this advertising gimmick.

The mother's desire to show the world that her daughter was different was no less in war than in peacetime and it led to some ingenious ways of breaking away from the dreary monotony of utility. Non-utility being almost impossible to track down, mothers who were not clever enough, or too busy on war work, bought non-utility materials and asked shops to make-up dresses for them in the workrooms where normally alterations were carried out. Only a lucky few could satisfy their urge for distinction of this kind for the Government limited the making-up of non-utility garments on retailers' premises. Often mothers tried to extend the arrangement by asking the shopkeeper to include more smocking than the law allowed so keen were they to see their daughters in frocks with bodices embroidered with their beloved smocking, but it was a risk retailers were not prepared to take.

Not that fashion was in the forefront of mothers' minds in the summer of 1944 for the children who had drifted back to London were sent packing once more when the flying bombs and rockets descended on the city. Mothers who had exhausted their coupons and were eagerly awaiting the first of August when they would be able to start on the new issue had to let their youngsters go without the warm garments they would soon be requiring. The Government rejected pleas to bring forward the coupon release date so that clothing could be purchased from London stores and shops stocked, so far as they were able, in anticipation of a rush to spend the next coupon allocation. Instead the BOT sent clothing and footwear to local authorities in the reception areas to avoid a run on the shops thus admitting the problem but spurning the remedy. To some extent mothers furnished their own solution, telephoning and writing for supplies to London retailers who regarded this as rather a mixed blessing as deliveries by whatever means were severely curtailed. How to make the coupons go round was an ever present worry to mothers of young babies and their cries for help were answered by a minute drop in the pointing for napkins, reduced by one-quarter to three-quarters of a coupon for each terry square. The essentials for a girl at a boarding school, on the other hand, involved an outlay of at least 150 coupons at the beginning of term, achieved by contributions from other members of the family.

There had been a noticeable increase in home dressmaking of children's frocks and other simple garments, precious coupons being saved for tailored articles such as coats which were beyond the prowess of the amateur needlewoman.

Coupon anomalies puzzled and enraged parents, the unfortunate shopkeeper bearing the brunt of the complaints. What retailer could hope to convince a woman that she had to surrender 18 coupons for her daughter's costume but only 12 for her own although women's garments were supposed to be at a higher rate? This unsatisfactory state of affairs had arisen because women's costumes were tailored to fit the figure with just enough tolerance to allow for freedom of movement whereas girls' were loose fitting in keeping with the age—and shape—of the wearers. Consequently the measurements exceeded those of the women's suits and the maximum permitted for the children's pointing. The woman should not, of course, have been allowed to get their suits for 12 coupons even if the sizes were below the borderline but as it was almost impossible to distinguish between the two in general terms they could not be blamed for taking advantage of the loophole but it was hard on mothers of teenage daughters.

The boys, too, were faring badly. Not only did the men have their turn-ups, they were stealing the boys' socks. In the bigger sizes boys' three-quarter hose provided men with a good, warm longer leg so much so that the older boys could hardly find a pair for themselves in the shops. Even Hosiery Control was moved by the lads' plight and instituted a plan whereby companies who could guarantee that they were engaged in a school trade and their hose would be sold only to schoolboys were permitted to manufacture three-quarter hose.

The heart of Hosiery Control also softened towards dressing-gowns for children and by the end of 1944 it was licensing them in non-utility knitted material. Yet another absentee was restored to the children's list, at long last permission was given for non-utility swim suits and later on these were allowed in utility.

Another breakthrough was the return of Wellington boots for children, just a small quantity was all that was allowed but a heartening sign that protective footwear was on the way. Regrettably there was as yet no indication that the plimsoll position was getting any easier. On the contrary the country was concerned at reports that in PT classes pupils were barefoot and school floors in those days were exceedingly dirty and rough with a propensity for imparting splinters. Rubber was so short that the most the authorities could do was to issue permits to schools for small reserves to be held for gym instruction, yet there were stories of firms holding stocks which the BOT would not allow them to release. Indicative of the times was the issuing of supplementary coupons for rubber boots and clothing for boys and girls helping with the harvest and potato picking as the amount of adequate clothing available was dwindling.

In the autumn of 1944 de-concentration of hosiery factories had commenced in Scotland (it was just nearing completion in clothing factories in parts of London from which more labour was being withdrawn). The news from Scotland augured well for the future, but there was no lessening of control in other directions, on the contrary the grip tightened; under an Order granting permission to firms to make-up waterproofs, including children's, from utility cloths, the BOT required them to, amongst other things, include in the exact position on the garment as laid down:

the manufacturer's name or registered trade mark;
the month and year of making-up;
the serial number or other symbol used by the maker-up;
to identify the proofer or wholesaler of each piece of cloth.

Even so there was already a hopeful feeling in the air that the stockade of controls would soon be breached, an impression heightened when the Board made it known that it wanted to get rid of the austerity Orders on women's and children's clothing and was seeking advice as to how this could best be implemented. The old spectre of chain reaction was the stumbling block, touch the austerity rules and regulations and utility prices had to be raised, and so on and so on. Hosiery Control was swifter to acknowledge the changing conditions and announced that a wider range of goods would be permitted under a new utility Schedule for knitted goods and that this would probably mean the dropping of some of the austerity regulations.

Meanwhile the authorities policed the regulations most religiously and discovered what they considered to be a nasty evasion. A minute amount of smocking had continued to be worked on daygowns and robes because they were designed to be worn solely by wee babies, but, said the BOT, smocking is not allowed on garments over 22ins. (56cms.) long and these gowns and robes are well over that. The actual length is, manufacturers conceded, but the other measurements make it impossible for them to fit anyone else but tiny mites a few weeks or months old and smocking is permitted for infants up to four years. The BOT was adamant, more than 22ins. (56cms.) long, no smocking.

# CHAPTER 14
# Awakening of Interest in Fashion

In the autumn of 1944 news of the Paris *haute couture* began to come through and with it came the first stirrings of an interest in fashion, as distinct from clothing, that British women had felt since September 1939. It would be many years before children's clothing would be affected but the seeds were sown before the war with the Nazis was over. Envious eyes had been turned during the war years to America, apparently a land of plenty brimful of every kind of slick, advanced ideas on design, for children no less than adults. Pictures in the Press of evacuees returning to Britain from America showed them dressed in sophisticated outfits which left the resident population way behind the times. There was a tremendous yearning for possession of many of the things enjoyed in the USA and anything American had great attraction but it proved to be a short-lived boom.

It was too early for Britain under controls to pay anything but an academic interest in fashion. A slight improvement had crept into cloth patterns, not influenced by fashion but of assistance to designers taxing their ingenuity in trying to create new styles. Conditions had forced fabric manufacturers to look for means of speeding up production and they turned to simple spots and stripes on white grounds involving less colour runs than intricate floral patterns. Fortunately this was welcomed by mothers as a break from the perpetual 'Manchester florals' and dress designers were able to relieve the stark lines of austerity with yokes, pockets and sleeves, etc., in diagonal striping which at least gave some impression of detail and cut. In another direction, too, the tedium of velveteen as a trimming for coats was broken when this fabric was hard to find and colourful check contrast on collars livened up the spring of 1945. A combination much in demand for children's tailored coats for five years upwards was light grey and scarlet strapping or piping on the collars or insets of cheerful red and white gingham.

Princess Elizabeth at 18 had left behind her influence on the younger set, the interest swinging to her sister Margaret who was making public appearances on her own for the first time. As befitting these formal occasions her outfits had progressed from the peter pan collars, puff sleeves and roomy fit of her earlier years and she always wore a hat but the fashion element was so played down that copying on any scale was not worthwhile.

Headmistresses were aware of the tell-tale signs that fashion competition was going to assert itself amongst the older girls and were already exploring the possibilities of reverting to stringent rules about uniforms.

# CHAPTER 15
# Peace and a Desire for Change

It was only natural that when the war ended people would expect things to get back to normal. Not overnight, of course, but soon and at all events there would be a relaxation of controls which could be noticed. Instead of that the reverse happened. The black-out went, immediately, but black-out material, hitherto coupon-free, went on the ration at two coupons per square yard. Four months after the war ended the public were told that the clothes ration was to be reduced to the lowest rate ever, an issue of 24 coupons to last for eight months. Earlier in 1945, while the war was still on, the Easter holidays had seen shops and stores besieged by mothers looking for clothing for their offspring and, hopefully, trying to track down some non-utility. The crush was so great that barriers had to be installed in children's departments of large stores to keep the queues in order. After peace was declared the pattern was repeated: on August 1, ten coupons were released for children in advance of the general allocation so that their garments could be purchased during the school holidays. There was a mad scramble to get what was available and queues formed outside shops before they were open and later when the people were allowed in it was pandemonium all day. When the main coupon allocation was released a month after retailers were raided again and mothers stood patiently waiting for hours even to get into the departments. Many threw caution to the wind and spent the whole 24 coupons, eight months ration, at one go. No more concrete evidence of the position of clothing supplies at the consumer level could be given than this. Boys and girls had worn out, or grown out of, their clothes and mothers knew that the desperately needed replenishments went to the first in the queue.

Fathers released from the Forces had quickly become

acquainted with the situation. Their 'demob' coupons, which could be exchanged for any type of civilian clothing, were being passed on to their sons and daughters.

A not altogether surprising announcement from such an austere man as Sir Stafford Cripps, now President of the BOT, informed the nation in the autumn of 1945 that the austerity restrictions were to remain in force for some time as it was not the moment to introduce frills and furbelows. Notwithstanding this gloomy pronouncement Hosiery Control determined not to be caught napping and with great foresight introduced a revised utility Hosiery Schedule which provided for new knitted garments such as cotton interlock nightwear and woollen combs, bathing suits and TOT hose and specified embroidery for a number of garments. No Production Directions were to be issued for all this until the raw material position had improved and the austerity restrictions lifted but when that happened there would be no waiting for fresh Schedules to be printed as had happened over additional utility cloths for children's dresses. No agreement having been reached over the ceiling prices, manufacturers were getting permission individually, making-up the frocks, and despatching them to the shops. There, unhappily, they stayed in the stockrooms as no Order had been published allowing their sale.

The public was sick of austerity particularly for the children. '*We won the war*', was the general attitude, '*and it's about time we had some brighter clothing*'. Children had been promised 'real' party frocks '*when the war is over*' and mothers were not to be persuaded that it was right that they should break their word. (One dress house helped those promises to be kept to a certain degree. The company had saved a stock of taffeta from the early days of the war so they could make it into party dresses once peace was declared—and they did, more to the embarrassment than pleasure of the retail recipients no doubt.)

Manufacturers of woven clothing were not altogether on the side of those who wanted austerity to go. They feared they would not be able to get the trimmings essential to pretty-up designs, nor the extra labour required, so production would suffer and, possibly of greatest importance, they were not prepared to commit themselves to putting extra work into garments unless their permitted prices were increased accordingly.

There were hopeful signs that things would improve. Better cloths and correspondingly higher prices were to be included in Schedule IG2 which would allow for a better make and ultimately more coats for bigger girls. Similarly the ceiling prices for boys' utility blazers and velveteen knickers were increased and additional materials listed for these and other garments. The same Directions revealed yet another reason for the non-appearance of boys' overcoats and suits, no lining materials. These had been getting scarcer and scarcer until at last the BOT had to give a wider freedom of choice of utility fabrics for this purpose and publish a plea to everyone, traders and public alike, not to insist on proper matching colours but to accept any serviceable fabric. Children's gloves in utility were extended to include leather and fabric styles and makers were required to continue to produce a percentage of baby sizes to the teens in an endeavour to meet the clamour for warm gloves.

Another interesting development in the utility scheme was the bringing in of waterproof pants for babies. Prices for these articles, regarded as essential by mothers but not apparently by the authorities, had been soaring and the quality had deteriorated so the BOT had no alternative but to permit these in utility with the proofing and pricing strictly controlled and subject to stringent licensing. Cotton cloths produced for the Services were gradually being released for infants and children. The procedure of having to apply for special licences for utility headwear was dropped, matching hats could now be supplied without restriction and quota-free. So far there was no relenting of the Board's prohibition on jockey caps in utility and a stern warning was issued that the 'BOT wish to make it clear that industrial protective caps do not include "pixie hoods" which are still subject to quota'. This was no doubt intended for naughty hat makers who had discovered that the specifications for industrial protective caps were identical to those of a child's pixie hood but it conjured up an entertaining picture of the foundry worker with a fashion flair.

The more generous attitude towards headwear had no marked impact. A despondent store buyer totalled the number of children's hats for which she had been waiting three years and it came to 2,860. Her allowance from one of the biggest makers at the end of 1945 was 140 hats. Nevertheless there was hope that little heads might soon be covered but for their feet prospects were bleak. Small size socks and shoes became even harder to find. Out of five warehouses not one had any socks for infants and could offer only 18 pairs of shoes. The by now familiar excuses were trotted out and to them was added a new one, demobilisation was under way and women were going back to their homes (but surely to be replaced in the factories by men?). Whatever the reason supplies of infants' socks and shoes were coming through at a rate of less than half that of 1943.

Workers could be released from munitions if they wished to go back to certain factories, making infants' wear, for example, but because of the better pay and conditions in munitions many chose not to do so, at one stage an estimated 80 per cent refused to return to the clothing industry. With fine disregard for such mundane matters school heads lost no time in making it plain that uniform rules would be enforced with rigour. Some were so misguided as to institute a system of awarding marks based on the number of correct items of the uniform the pupils were wearing.

The outlook was drab and the light at the end of the tunnel not much more than an intermittent flicker but fashion was beginning to move again and it paralleled a desire for change, an urge to throw away anything connected with the dark days of war and making do and mending and this was expressed by a sudden spurt of fashion parades which did more to demonstrate the enthusiasm of the sponsors than any advance in design. First off the mark a month or so after the war in Europe was over was a children's dress manufacturer whose three-day show won him an unexpected publicity bonus through his choice of one teenage mannequin, as they were then called. Despite her typical teenage figure the audience recognised in this girl a special quality before the news broke that young Jean Simmons had at that very moment landed a film contract and a part in 'The Way to the Stars'. It was not, however, on her that the interest centred, it was on the styles which she and the other girls from tots to teens were wearing. As was only to be expected they were not all that thrilling. The main feature for the teens was the bib front, crisp white oblong or curved inset coming from the neckline emphasised with buttons or bows down the centre and outlined with self-frills to match the cuffed sleeve edging. Skirts were full, coming below the knee, and gathered into the natural waist. Sleeves were short, ending an inch or two above the elbow. Shoes for the teens were heavy looking wedges, copies of women's sizes, with high vamps or plain court shapes.

The tiny tots displayed the inevitable loose fitting smocks with puff sleeves, the embroidery beautifully worked but sadly confined to a narrow strip under the high yokes by the austerity regulations. Ankle socks and one-bar shoes were as 1939. Out of the infant stage the waist became marked by belts or gathers but stayed high, up to the sub-teens. The latter, the in-betweens, fared worst (and were going to do so for a good many years to come) with some desperate attempts to liven up the otherwise uninspired designs with colour or cloth contrast. There was no evidence that the makers of children's wear for any size were sensitive to the trends which were developing in adult fashion nor that they had any wish to become so. This might have been thought to be due to the continuing Government controls but it was to become clear that legislation was not wholly to blame.

Following soon on this pioneer post-war parade came the revival of *The Children's Outfitter* show which, since it comprised fifty firms located in different parts of Britain covering knitted and woven outerwear and nightwear, presented a more representative picture of the country as a whole. The main emphasis continued to be on contrast of colour and cloth, notably around the shoulders, and it was on these that designers concentrated their efforts assisted by the exaggerated width which had stayed at the 1939 level. In coats insets of contrast cloth started at the shoulders and tapered to fine points either side of the waist. The high yokes of three-pieces had reverse colouring, navy on pale blue for the jacket, pale blue on navy for the hip-length jumper beneath, worn over a pale blue straight skirt. Since epaulettes and capes were forbidden coats had piping to convey these effects. The basic outline of coats was unchanged, fitted to the waist and falling with slight fullness in the skirt and with the open revers and d.b. fastening characteristic of spring and summer collections. The line hardly varied from one age group to another apart from the addition of all-round tie-belts for eight years upwards.

There was as yet no move towards the loose, boxy style of coat currently popular in America that abode of fancy-free fashion, almost another world—the world of the bobby sox, the outsize short socks initially borrowed from father which were rolled over and over and flopped on clumpy low-heeled shoes and gave the name to the youngsters of that period. With the bobby sox went larger, long, loose sweaters for boys and girls utterly unlike the classic close knit jumpers and jerseys in Britain and the neat ankle socks worn by all girls up to the teens at which point, contrary to their American counterparts, they switched to stockings.

In dresses frills over the shoulders, back and front, replaced the cloth insets of the coats but gave the same impression of shoulder width and narrow waists. Loose cape sleeves were not left to drape softly but were padded underneath to conform to the accepted shoulder width. There was much talk of the corselette waist but all it really amounted to was a new name for an old style. More imaginative and prettier was the treatment of pockets on the older girls' dresses. Often in white in keeping with the yokes they were large oblong patches starting at the waist and running well down the skirt, with self frilled edges and a centre vertical slit. These pockets served two purposes, breaking the otherwise hackneyed austerity line and introducing a feminine touch.

For the same age group there was the jumper suit silhouette, one-piece dresses, figure fitting to the hips then with a gathered skirt, toning and contrasting, plain and patterned, anything which gave a two-piece look. Pinafore dresses were coming to the fore with tartan the strong favourite. (In the spring of 1945 BOT President Hugh Dalton had assured the House of Commons that there was no truth in the stories that there was no tartan available for children's kilts as it was reserved for export. Tartan could be supplied in many utility specifications and non-utility and he would examine any details of shortages submitted to him. Mr. Dalton knew better than to raise the wrath of Scotland by keeping quiet over ugly rumours like these).

Tartan was to enjoy a tremendous vogue, from day to

evening wear, for pinafore dresses, skirts, frocks to match tartan lined coats, hats and caps, skirts and on and on through to full-length party dresses and its success lasted so long it almost became impossible to envisage any other pattern for the young.

Giving some variety but clinging to the faithful navy, white and red, were sunsuits with gathered skirts, modest halter neck tops and shorts. The long-awaited utility linen made its appearance for girls' dresses but sadly it proved disappointing. The colours and patterns were good, clean and tasteful, but the weight proved too much for small bodies and the weave so characteristic of excellent linen had a roughness to which mothers were unaccustomed in their daughters' clothing. It was hardly more successful for boys' buster suits for which it was also allowed, the less expensive slub finish cottons being preferred.

The parade idea caught on, due not so much to a feeling of fashion as that the cost could be included in the advertising and promotion figure for cost-plus prices, and the catwalk provided the first steps to fame for some of the young models. Joining them in later years was Jean Marsh (later to achieve international fame on television), a pale, thin, lovely sub-teen with a wide mouth, a straight back and a strange air of tranquillity.

There might not be much movement in styling as yet but every effort was being put into making it appear as though there were. The public wanted to see fabrics that were out of the ordinary, they were tired of candy stripes and plain cottons and moss crêpes for their daughters and already grumblings were beginning in earnest about the neglected sub-teens and teens. Such precepts as short sleeves for summer, long for winter, were being challenged by mothers who disliked winter dresses with long sleeves made in the same old way with buttoned cuffs which were anything but attractive and they were asking for warm frocks with short sleeves. Retail buyers disapproved when they saw these in the collections and dismissed them with a '*mothers will only insist on the children wearing woollies over them*'.

Strangely enough, considering all the vicissitudes which had beset headwear during the war years it was this accessory that suddenly altered its image and followed Paris whose overpowering millinery had burst upon the scene. Children's felt hats began to take on a modish appearance with deeper crowns, a copy of the women's, and wide, off-the-face brims held to the head by narrow bands of self material or contrast such as velvet, repeated in the streamers falling from bows at the back. The brims, which swept up at the front to reveal the face, came well down on the nape of the neck. The tinies were not immune to a change of style and for a while infants' bonnets lost their poke shape and instead had brims narrow at the ears, then shooting up wide and high off the face to accommodate Shirley Temple curls on the forehead. The ties under the chin remained, a necessity if the hats were to stay on the heads of lively young ones. Such forays into the world of fashion, though, left the matching hats of coat sets entirely unmoved, they continued their poke bonnet way for decades.

The shortages went on with the public becoming more vocal and the Government more on the defensive and reproving in its attitude but controls could not keep pace with the changing scene. The issuing of key certificates for wool cloths was dropped because of the wide gap existing between the placing of the certificates and deliveries. Coupon downpointing was resorted to as an inducement to the public to take goods which in its wisdom it had decided were not worth the coupons. In its train came the machinery of reimbursing makers to cover the coupons they were getting and the amount they required to buy the cloth but to mothers who knew nothing of such matters the chief concern was that the same number of coupons was required for their six-year-old sons' and daughters' clothes as for their own, worse, they had to give up two more for the sons' coats than for their 14-year-old daughters'. Utterly illogical it may have been to parents but the BOT had no alternative, stocks of women's wear were building up and not moving but for the younger generation there was more and more of less and less. Shops had been forced to operate systems which allocated seats to the firstcomers, standing room at the back for the next and a line outside the doors of the departments for latecomers, with a '*come back tomorrow*' notice for putting up when closing time arrived.

Freedom from austerity came first to most knitwear, then a few weeks after, in the spring of 1946, it was extended to garments from woven cloths, bringing with it the promise of embroidery on pram sets and sprat heads on coat pleats, hand-faggotted collars on dresses and deep smocking and velvet appliqués, but more often than not any garments with these delights were accompanied by the words 'export only' which had begun to have a dread significance for British people condemned to their spartan existence and it was doubly so insofar as the babies and children were concerned. The position of boys' clothing did not improve, ties and braces were unobtainable and small sons were having to suffer the indignity of keeping up their shorts with tape. With knitted garments the cause was the general lack of suitable yarns but even so manufacturers did not want to bother with unprofitable lines for kiddies when they could satisfy the clamour for bigger sizes.

There were waiting lists for toddlers' dropback sleeping suits and departmental store heads reported that their buyers had been unable to buy a single first-size infant's nightdress so essential to new-born babies and this was due solely to the low prices in the Utility Schedule which had been under discussion for revision at the BOT for 18 months. Yet there was a call for more legislation in an unexpected quarter. As the war ended there had come a great demand for genuine Shetland knitwear for boys and girls, jumpers, jerseys and berets in the traditional Fair Isle patterns. Quick to appreciate the possibilities of this situation, some enterprising gentlemen offered cash prizes to hand-knitters for the biggest parcels of garments. Not surprisingly the scarcity value plus the money prizes paid out resulted in sky-high prices, a swinging 3½gns. (368p.), for example, for a little girl's jumper. This was bad enough but the quality deteriorated as the knitters strove to make up the biggest parcels. The old-established firms trying to retain their standards and fair charges were having a hard time keeping their businesses going and wanted a price ceiling but eventually their worries abated as a wider choice of knitwear became available and the spivs turned to more lucrative merchandise.

Irritating measures which the BOT was finding it increasingly difficult to justify were at last rescinded, the ban on jockey caps in infants' sets in utility cloth was lifted for the 1946 winter season and firms could apply to make girls' costumes in utility. Knitted berets, useful and good-natured head coverings for all ages, were also allowed again.

# CHAPTER 16
# Price and Appearance Begin to Matter

Two words were having an increasing significance on the domestic front—nylon and plastics. The former had an unfortunate start for the quality perfected for wartime purposes, such as parachutes, was tried in dark colours as lining for boys' and girls' utility coats, hardly anything else being available, but it was cold to the touch and non-absorbent. Baby dresses in nylon had a better reception, they took the smocking extremely well and had a silky feel which did not suffer in the wash. Developments over the years were to see the man-made fibres overcome the preliminary problems but that was in the future. In common with the first nylon materials, plastics had a shaky beginning neither the handle nor the appearance being widely accepted by the public who saw them chiefly as mediums for capes and baby pants, but their coming was to change the clothing scene for children. Neither of these newcomers had as yet much influence on fashion which, in the summer of 1946, was beginning to liven up for young people. Most noticeable was the alteration in skirts for older girls which percolated through to the younger ones as well. Going swiftly were the straight, prim and proper, inverted or box-pleated skirts for the dirndl had arrived with its stiffened, deep curved waistband that hugged the figure, and carefree, all-round gathers that swished about with a dashing femininity for which the girls were yearning. Pockets had taken on an ice cream cornet shape which fitted well into the dirndl line, a happy choice for girls except the waistless tinies who had to have their gathered 'dirndls' suspended from braces.

Interest continued to be centred on the shoulders for coats

and dresses the width now extended on the latter to form wings either side which gave a sleeveless impression without actually leaving the tops of the arms bare, considered to be inappropriate for the young. Cap sleeves for the older girl made inroads on the puff sleeves, and turnback white cuffs at

*The dirndl was a godsend for girls, its trim, stiffened waist and full gathered skirt flattered all puppy fat figures.*

the shoulders, split at the top and narrowing as they followed the line of the armhole offered another alternative. Longer length sleeves were making their debut. These came just below the elbow and ended in a close fitting buttoned cuff. Chopping off the sleeve in this manner was something quite different and over the years set a pattern which progressed from below the elbow, through three-quarter to bracelet-length before, after a considerable period, returning once more to full-length.

The call for party wear, especially ankle-length dresses for the tinies, was met in part by knee-length poults trimmed with ruching for the up to early teens but even in those immediate post-war years unhappily inappropriate and childish on girls with developing bustlines whose figures were ill-suited to the plain bodices and loops of ruching on the skirts. The older teens were more fortunate—when they could find evening dresses—for them the sweetheart line was in with tight fitting gauged bodice, corselette waistband and full skirt with stiffened underskirt of remarkably stiff and prickly net but which was to become an indispensable accessory for many years for day frocks no less than party and evening wear.

The British girls' wish to have pretty things again was the opposite of their American cousins'. Further information had percolated through from the other side of the Atlantic of the ultra casual bobby soxers with their rolled-up sleeves, shirts (not blouses!) flapping about over pedal-pushers (calf-length trousers just right for cycling), glorified white canvas editions of men's golf shoes with strappings of brown leather and, of course, the inescapable bobby sox. The Americans bought six pairs of socks to one pair purchased by girls in the UK. Nothing could have been farther from the footwear worn by girls in Britain where the search for the shoe design which followed the natural development of the foot was, so far as was possible, continued during the war. It led the makers, ironically enough, to the USA where lasts had been devised which conformed to the changing shapes of growing feet. Quality of leather as well as fitting was studied by the British firms but strength was the prime object, not styling. Almost the sole concession to appearance, apart from that inherent in well-made footwear, was the introduction of colours such as poppy red and gentian blue. Typical of the vagaries of the general public now that it could, if fortunate, get shoes for toddlers in several shades all it wanted was white and that was impossible to find. It was because of gaps in supplies that the authorities were retaining their close watch on footwear companies, making certain that they did not reduce their output of children's sizes and continuing to enforce the 75 per cent utility rule.

Troubles like this were only regarded as being obstacles to overcome by brides of the day, white weddings came swinging back into their own, bringing with them appeals for bridesmaids' dresses and Society paraded again the cluster of beautiful girls and mostly resentful pageboys in velvet trousers and white frilly blouses escorting nymphs in ankle-length dresses with velvet sashes and chaplets on shining curls, brides and grooms seemingly having coupons to spare for this momentous occasion.

Pageboys apart small sons were accorded a modicum of masculinity. At long last the breechette set was being reviewed and its deficiencies acknowledged by a few good designers. The first to benefit were infant boys, for them the baggy bloomer cut, tight legs and strapping over the instep were replaced by neat trousers cut on dungaree lines with bib and brace tops far smarter than the breechettes and much easier for the mother to put on. Instead of having to manoeuvre wriggling legs into narrow breechettes and button or zip up either side (and frequently either side of the waist as well) all she had to do was to pull on easy fitting trousers and button the braces on to the elasticated back of the waist. Once the initial breakaway from the old design was made it became the custom for infant boys to have trousers but there were those who were opposed to this idea believing that it marked the beginning of apeing the Americans who dressed their young sons in miniature editions of their fathers' suits and, regrettably, their felt hats.

Of a more functional character, results of endeavours to improve the design of the simple terry napkin square were coming to light, or re-appearing, with the object of cutting down both the bulky layers and the washing chores. The thinking was along the lines of a T-shape with extra material, such as muslin, where the greatest absorbency was essential.

In other directions babies were faring badly. The country had, after all, as Sir Stafford Cripps said, been '*rather swamped with babies recently*' for the birth-rate had gone up by about a quarter-of-a-million in a year and there was just not enough clothing to go round. '*Grave situation*', '*Almost a national crisis*', was the summing up. MPs tackled the BOT President in the House, deputations went to see his officials, and were assured that the Board was 'making every effort', 'taking all possible steps' but this did nothing to help expectant mothers who could find no wrap-over vests and whose maternity homes refused to allow them to take in the pull-on type, or the women who desperately wanted nightgowns, daygowns, knitted pram sets and underwear for their babies. The deficiencies had been aggravated by the fuel cuts and three-week shut-down of industry in the winter of '47 but though this was a contributory factor it disguised the truth that the planners had failed. The outcome of their determination to direct channels of production had, notwithstanding their years of experience since 1939 and the absolute control they wielded, been the damming of the flow of vital equipment for infants and the bringing about of a flood of other garments, notably children's coats, so that shops were clamouring for coupon downpointing. The public's mood had changed; money was not so easy to come by and must not be squandered because '*You never know what might happen to-morrow*'. There was the future to be considered and many calls on the pocket in a peacetime society. There was no point in denying that babies were not getting their fair share and this was acknowledged, on paper at least, when it was announced that infants' and children's knitwear ranked as high as export for yarn allocation.

Yet at the very moment when supplies were so unevenly distributed there was a steady growth in the number of specialist shops catering for young people. Springing up in every locality they were proof that children's wear (and this included boys' to a lesser degree) was established as a separate entity. At the other end of the scale shops and departments were being opened for the teen girl, thrust into prominence in those immediate post-war years. She was no longer going to be tacked condescendingly on the end of the children's sizes or contemptously at the bottom of the women's. Emerging as a person in her own right, the teen girl was moving out of the children's field and into the orbit of adult fashion, encouraged by the national Press and the infant television and courted, not without trepidation by the store buyers who were wary of the tempermental, spoilt adolescent whose immature taste was hard to understand and still more difficult to interpret. Everyone agreed that the teen girl's preference must be channelled into the right direction otherwise she would choose the wrong things, styles that were too old for her years or colours that clashed instead of harmonising. Little did the pundits know that a future generation would set world fashion circles ablaze by doing just that very thing.

Seeping through was a scattering of pre-war revivals, the beloved organdies, lace frocks for infants, authentic tu-tus sadly with bodices of cotton instead of satin but there was a certain amount of this about for babies' robes. Baby bags became more frivolous with jolly appliqués and scalloped edges and less ornamental but infinitely valuable, copious rubber linings. Better for baby than the impractical matinée jackets were tiny knitted cardigans with shawl collars and welted waists fastened across with two buttons but there was a long way to go before the matinée jacket was to encounter any serious competition.

No doubt well aware of the present and future challenge of man-made fibres the International Wool Secretariat proceeded with its propaganda on the improvements in wool yarns, the mothproof and water-repellent finishes and others which lessened the irritation caused to sensitive skins. It was to sound like a despairing cry as man-made fibres took over in baby wear.

There were the first hints of Scandinavian patterns in jumpers, sparkling with snowflakes and reindeer heads. In headgear the round sailor or Wren shapes had made a hit with the 10-14 year olds. A prettier note had crept into rainwear with the advent of proofed nylon, appearance and handle reminiscent of the oiled silks, and oiled voiles and cottons but these were stiffer and lacked the suppleness of nylon. Co-relation, a word to be bandied about with much emphasis in the future, was modestly introduced with girls' dresses, or small boys' buster suits, and their shoes, the latter picking up a colour in the print but it brought too many problems to the stockists for it to have any impact.

One way had been found to relieve the plain cloths which constituted the bulk of the fabric available for children without the time-consuming hand-work entailed in embroidery. This was the dropping of plastic particles on to the material to form patterns. When the plastic hardened it could not come off, nor be washed off, and perhaps an even greater virtue could not be picked off however persistent the exploring fingers. The process was effective and broke the monotony when first tried but was used by so many for so long it became associated with cheap garments. A like fate was in store for flocking. This was a similar process insofar as a pattern was permanently affixed to the cloth but in this case primarily on organdies for party frocks, the flocking being either contrast or self colours, but here again it was repeated *ad nauseum* and the perverse public wanted to go back to the recognisable hand-work which distinguished their children's dresses.

Through it all children's clothing continued to be clamped down by the Government. It was not until the end of 1947 that dressing-gowns and costumes in woven materials broke through the barriers of officialdom and appeared as duly authorised utility garments, lagging considerably behind children's fur backed gloves which had been approved months before.

# CHAPTER 17
# Legislation Chases Events

A smooth flow of clothing from manufacturer to consumer, not too little, not too much, and especially nothing to encourage frivolous cravings for non-essentials, this was the goal of the BOT in the early, and not so early, post-war years. A laudible target, no doubt, and utterly unattainable in peacetime Britain. In their conviction that they knew best in the teeth of growing evidence to the contrary, officials did stupid things, and stuck to them.

The signs were all too clear, the Government was losing its grip on the situation but the bureaucrats hung on to the bitter end giving scant heed to the swiftly changing conditions. Significantly, manufacturers began refusing to provide further costings when asked to do so, snubbing the BOT by telling them they had enough figures already, a sure indication that traders were no longer afraid of the Board's powers. Closer home shopkeepers began to take coupons out of ration books before they became valid which in law-abiding Britain was incontrovertible proof that the public was taking matters into its own hands. People had only to look around to see the effects of authoritarianism. There was a glut of goods in the shops which the public did not want and there it stayed for retailers, unable to get coupons to pass back to the manufacturers, could not obtain the lines when they were available which mothers desperately wanted for their children, orders could not be despatched from the factories so the normal channels of trade were clogged and the dreaded word 'slump' was applied to such unlikely things as children's coats.

Moves to clear the accumulated stocks by the ploy of reducing the coupon values of unwanted garments hardly dented the pile. Coupon-conditioned officials had not accepted what the general public had already grasped, coupons were mere scraps of paper compared with pound notes and it was the latter that prompted purchases not the ups and downs of 'pointing'. Discontent over the continuance of rationing was growing on every side. Children's footwear, running at about 50 per cent above pre-war production was taken off the ration, so were gloves and mittens, including infantees without finger or thumb division; no fingers, one thumb, was yet another problem for the Hosiery Controller and Customs and Excise. Also coupon-free were knitted bathing suits, certain grades of wool mixture hand-knitting yarn and clothing made from pvc, but not babies' bibs and feeders. It was noticeable that infants' wear was carefully omitted from any concessions even though manufactured from cloths which had been down-pointed for other children's sizes and although shoes and infants' footwear were coupon-free, babies' knitted bootees were not. These exceptions were admissions that planning had been unable to safeguard the rights of the newcomers to the population. Babies had a new enemy—the export drive—and British knitwear being in world-wide demand the home market had to make sacrifices. Unfortunately these as always fell heaviest on the tinies. Merino yarns so suitable for infants' clothing were earmarked for export and the garments into which they were made withdrawn from the Utility Schedule. The official theory that narrowing the choice would increase the production of lower quality articles was regarded with cynicism in the light of past experience. Yarn allocations for knitwear were in proportion to a firm's export orders and many sought to fill the gap by importing yarns from war-torn France and Italy.

Export was really biting but the wrong people. Supplies of wool gaberdine raincoats, invaluable for schoolchildren, were worse than during the war. They were all going overseas to dollar-paying countries and the Government refused to interfere. The BOT might point to substitutes in the shape of cotton gaberdines but mothers had shown what they thought of them for winter wear by leaving them unsold in the shops and the strategm of taking them off the ration had not changed their opinion. On the other hand the BOT was forced to retreat over children's TOT socks and announce that since they were so scarce exports were being reduced and more made available to meet home requirements. This deficiency may have gone unnoticed but in another direction the authorities managed to find time to keep an eagle eye on children's clothing, determined that none should escape the net of officialdom. Relaxation of controls on miscellaneous goods gave a measure of freedom to boys' and girls' outfits regarded as toy apparel but whilst it was accepted that cowboys and Indians get-up was not exactly everyday wear the BOT issued grave warnings that this did not extend to sailor suits and nurses' uniforms which the children might (*just*?) wear when not actually playing at ships or nursing sick dolls.

The legislation chasing events continued with prices running second to export as the main concern. Cloth prices were rocketing but the increases were due mainly to the removal of subsidies on cotton and wool fabrics and the rise in wool prices. Government policy was made quite clear, costs were to be kept as low as possible even if it meant reducing garment quality by lowering standards of production, not something which recommended itself to the buyers and sellers of young people's clothing. Statutory Orders to cover these and other contingencies flowed as fast as in wartime. By 1948 the List of Amendments to Schedule IG2 had reached No. 15 at which point they were mainly increasing the range of cloths, extending the uses to which they could be put and raising the prices. Manufacturers struggling to keep track of the seemingly endless legislation had an extra obligation thrust upon them. In 1949 Schedule IG2 had grown into IG3 and IG4 and the List of Amendments and additions had swelled to No. 16 and two additional appendices to Schedule IG4 followed soon after its publication. It was Schedule IG3 that compelled manufacturers to adopt the recently launched BSI size nomenclature and standards of manufacture to which it was linked. As noted in Appendix I the BSI sizing system had been critically received and was eventually to flounder due to lack of support but meanwhile it had the backing of law which firms ignored at their peril. The eager adoption by the BOT of the size standards was the more galling in the light of the discussions which had gone on for three years over including buster-rompers, a useful two-piece for infants, in the Utility Schedule. Knitwear and hosiery manufacturers were almost as tightly controlled as in wartime and Making-up Directions for certain woven materials were still being sent out to makers-up on an individual basis. Understandably the cost of this to the country was not going unnoticed.

The dimensions of the utility mark on babies' footwear had long been a cause of grievance and was occupying the time of BOT officials. The heavy utility stamp was out of place on tiny shoes but the Board insisted that it must be included; as a concession the Board agreed that it could be reduced to a radius of less than *one-quarter inch*, but not less than *one-eighth inch*, a mathematical calculation guaranteed to infuriate the producers concerned.

At the end of January 1949 came the big news, garments made wholly or mainly from woven wool cloths were off-the-ration, good news, indeed, except as usual for that hard done by section of the community, the infants, for the cloth of the utmost importance to them, utility No. 236, reserved exclusively for their garments, was to continue to be rationed because it was selling so well abroad there was insufficient for British babies. The older children were also affected by gaberdine, the only other woven wool cloth to be similarly restricted as it, too, was in high demand overseas and home requirements had to take second place. Knitted garments and cloths were not freed from coupons, a further sacrifice on the altar of exports and there was much ado about linings, with complicated arrangements between suppliers and shopkeepers with, for non-utility, hand-on-heart compulsory declarations, in writing, that the material would be used solely as linings and reminders that it was an offence in law if those conditions were not observed. The system of issuing coupon floats to manufacturers continued because of the some on, some off the ration policy for cloths. Many months were to go by before coupons finally disappeared, their end hastened by the decline in sales due to rising prices.

The stranglehold on knitwear producers continued with the revisions to the Utility Schedule reaching Schedule K which replaced Schedule J—and its supplement—but not entirely as some of the things in Schedule J had not been included in Schedule K (altogether it ran to 600 Specifications) so reference would have to be made to Schedule J—and so on, and on and on. Then came Schedule L which introduced the proviso that the garments must be made in accordance with the principles of 'good hosiery manufacture' and a Panel of

Assessors was appointed to ensure that this was observed—and in no time at all Supplement No. 1 to Schedule L was published, and then Schedule M.

These were the mechanics of clothing, or not clothing, the child population but beneath the surface a hot spring of fashion was about to erupt, one that no Government could contain however hard it tried. No one anticipated that between 1945 and 1949 fashion would burst out of its unnatural confines at a roaring rate and once again dictate the clothing habits of the nation.

# CHAPTER 18
# The New Look

The New Look in 1947 – one of its first adherents was teenager Princess Margaret – ridiculed and rejected at first, as is the way with extreme fashion, blazed a trail which all were to follow within a remarkably short period. Its influence was not confined to the longer length although this, of course, made the deepest impression. Its curved lines introduced a softer silhouette and ushered in a return to dressiness and femininity. The rounded shoulder, nipped-in waist and longer length were going to be adopted, albeit in fits and starts, by the teens but the children's wear designers, as always, were in a quandary. Still largely in a world of their own which concentrated on producing apparel, not fashion, they were but dimly aware that alterations in their field were wanted. Reluctant to accept that the basic cut of a tailored coat, for example, could, or need be, altered, they compromised and to placate the increasing pressure from store buyers tried to graft the New Look on to the old. To the classic tailored front they added a back of gores and umbrella pleats in recognition of the call for skirt fullness. Conversely the straight coat back was retained but the front had a nipped-in waist and stiffened canvas inset to curve out over the hips but the exaggerated, square shoulders, pointed collar and revers were retained. Turn-back cuffs with three-button fastening sticking out at the sides quarrelled with the customary narrow sleeve pattern. Compromises of this nature served neither to please those wedded to the past nor placate others who wished to move with the times. They revealed not so much an appreciation of current trends as the obstinacy of designer/pattern-cutters, that ultra conservative body of men. At least the gores, seamed to the waist and then swinging free, broke away from the all-too-familiar flared coats.

Peplums had been revived and with them emphasis on the hips either with the peplum itself or a narrow frill all round, or with an inset of contrast material or colour from the waist to the hip. Kept to a discreet minimum on dresses the effect was not unpleasing but on coats it was occasionally hideously overdone. Coats for two to four years had pie frills let into the

*Loath to believe that the tailored coat could be improved and reluctant to concede that the New Look was anything but a passing whim, makers clung to their old patterns and tried to graft the new on to the old with unfortunate results.*

waist, these of necessity were either double thickness or edged with several rows of stitching, or peplums finished with wide bands of strong contrast colour.

A happier trend for the teens was the softer line suits in the characteristic New Look idiom with softly curved shoulders, dolman sleeves, tight-waisted hipline jackets and full skirts. In

*Another attempt to satisfy the demands to catch up with fashion, ungainly peplums on an old pattern, cruel to the average young girl's hipline.*

other suits buttoning to the neck, a longer jacket and all-round belt were challenging the revers and d.b. fastening of the severely tailored costume.

The situation was better in dresses where modifications were easier to achieve. There were the peplums and hipline emphasis and the bell contour conveyed by close fitting waists and canvas linings at the tops of the hips to convey the bell outline. Adding the finishing touch and the prettiest for years in girls' dresses was the lingerie detail which peeped beneath the hem. This was something really new, and slightly daring in its delightful hint of petticoat finery. An inch or so of finely pleated net, white or pastel, insertion ribbon lace, guipure or double rows of narrow lace dotted with velvet bows was enough to convert a full skirt into the latest fashion. Another interpretation in the same spirit, on flared or full circular skirts, featured ruching in self or contrast colours round the hem, equally feminine and charming for girls of all ages although lacking the spice of the petticoat peepers. Both versions looked best in taffeta and velvet, the latter particularly for the bell line. The lingerie detail was often repeated on the sleeves where it was treated in a similar manner, the sleeves themselves running at that moment from short to bracelet-length to allow for the inclusion of the frilly finish. Rounded shoulders were achieved by following the kimono sleeve shape with the sleeves cut in one and joined across the shoulder possibly with a slight padding introduced but nothing as bulky as the former shoulder pads.

Tiers of gathered panels, reminiscent of the crinoline, gave a satisfactory fullness to other frocks, especially for the younger girls not yet ready for sophisticated bells, godets and gores. Coats for the same age group followed similar lines with horizontal tucking and channel seams defining the crinoline inspired shape. Fashion had decreed the curved lines and full skirts and, to set them off, slim waists, not much in evidence in teen figures and practically non-existent in the less mature. The nipped-in waistline could only be achieved with help in the tightening up process or by emphasising the hips. A canvas interlining accomplished this by holding the skirt away from the body but the older girl invested in a 'waspie', a lightly boned band which encircled the waist and, not quite achieving the Victorian wasp waist after which it was named, toned

*The teens and in-betweens got their New Look suits—rounded hips and full, long skirts—in utility, not what the Government intended when it was first introduced.*

down any youthful thickness. Stiffened petticoats in rustling taffeta, paper nylon, organdie or just plain fine net (very scratchy this if not lined) all helped the skirts to stand out. A further aid was the belt: the nondescript plain buckled, narrow kind contributed nothing to the dress and in its stead had arrived stiffened belts in self or strong contrast colours which were not just a means of hiding the waist seam but wide at the sides, curving to narrow fronts and backs, clinched the figure in a highly satisfactory manner. Collars were changing, too, mainly because manufacturers had adopted a stiffening process which enabled the collar to be cut to any shape and remain beautifully smooth throughout its life but later this method was to be largely superseded in children's dresses by a less expensive interlining which served the purpose just as well.

A major outcome of the Paris shows was the advent of the jigger coat, the merits of which were accepted immediately without controversy yet it was the complete opposite of the familiar, full-length tailored garment so long associated with Britain. The jigger broke all the rules for the younger generation: it hung loose at the front with no fastening or had a single button at the neck, wrist-length it had wide sleeves, deep cuffs, high rounded yoke and godets at the back for swinging fullness. The effect was to make the coat stand out from the dress or suit beneath. It provided a topcoat without the restriction of a close-fitting full-length coat and was an alternative to the suit jacket for teaming with a skirt and adaptable enough to go with jeans. It looked just as good in baby pastel wool velours, not hitherto worn above the toddler stage, as in big muted checks and it could be prettied up with pussy bows of velvet or moire taffeta at the neck in a manner never possible with the no-nonsense tailored variety.

The jigger gave the girls, too, something for spring which was not identical with the coat they had worn all winter except for the difference in the weight of the cloth and about which they were becoming increasingly restless. Infants were not so fortunate, no mini-jiggers were made for them and there was mounting criticism of the tailored coat for spring.

Logically following on the jigger was the full-length swagger and with it came the three-way fastening which by simply omitting the waist loops and leaving slits in the side seams enabled it to be worn loose, semi-fitted or belted all round without any unsightly loops to look as if the belt had been lost.

Despite rationing, despite shortages, despite the lack of money, fun wear for children had arrived. Brief-cut shorts and play tops, bare midriff sun-suits, no less, sun dresses with bolero jackets, co-ordinates through from the dress to the sun suit were in bold stripes and eye-dazzling colours. With them went coollie hats with wide, wide brims and tiny flat crowns which perched on top of the head, anchored by ties under the

*It was with great reluctance that manufacturers put swagger coats of this type into their ranges a few years after the war ended.*

chin. Girls' trousers, ankle-length and sensible were transformed by the advent of the pedal-pusher, above-calf length with turn-ups. The length of the leg, freed by this invader from restraint, travelled from above knee to the ankle but almost without exception with turn-ups which somehow seemed to impart a carefree spirit. Having injected styling into this stereotyped article attention was inevitably drawn to the top to go with it, not only that it should be smart but that it should complete the outfit rather than act as a mere accessory. Designs which achieved this introduced the waistcoat, fitting over the trouser top and jauntily pointed. More advanced were the one-piece affairs with belted, figure hugging waistcoat tops or variations on the bib-and-brace front. That they were every one in minute quantities so that few girls would ever be able to buy them merely increased their attraction.

The younger children were not unaffected by the upsurge of interest in fashion. Not, of course, for them the New Look, waistlines remained where they had been for a long while, not far from the armpits although there was a slight move towards lowering them. Tailored coats were getting competition from the full-length swagger with fullness falling from a high back yoke. Worn on its own it was a welcome development in outerwear but forming part of a set the style looked incongruous over wrinkled, baggy breechettes. Just as incongruous with any coat were the hats which completed the sets and it was no wonder that mothers were highly critical of their shape and lack of appeal. Having surmounted the hurdles of Government restrictions it seemed that the manufacturers were content to have something 'run up' which could be plonked on to the child's head—of whatever size since the measurements never varied presumably on the principle that a good big one would also fit the smallest head, which it did, the brim coming down over the eyes like blinkers. It was unfortunate that most of the cloth hats owed their origin to the poke bonnet, charming in days gone by but sadly whittled down to an ugly deep crown and heavy brim which suffered badly in the rain, anchored under the chin with a depressing loop of the coat material and finished with a meagre self or velvet bow trimming, the whole contributing nothing to the appearance nor comfort of the wearer. Faced with wholly justified criticism the coat makers blamed the hat firms who supplied them on a cut, make and trim basis, they in turn claimed it was not their fault, whenever they put forward suggestions the coat producers did not want to know. Unable to ignore the devastating truth that mothers were leaving the hats behind in the shops as they were not worth taking away, coat houses looked around for restyling ideas, hopefully not entailing too much alteration, and one company went so far as to commission a leading women's milliner to design their matching hats. It was no easy task to inject fashion into a child's hat without making it ridiculously sophisticated for the young face beneath and perhaps the results were somewhat too fanciful for mass-production but at least they showed that there were other ways of covering girls' heads and the *couture* approach did set makers thinking. Meanwhile most of the parents had no alternative but to pay for the hats they spurned as they were sold as part of the coat set.

As a result of the resistance to the dreary cloth hats, balaclavas in self cloth for boys and hoods attached to coats for girls were seen as welcome alternatives in breechette sets. So many women had knitted balaclavas for soldiers during the war that they had taken to buying helmets for their baby boys knowing how warm they kept ears in the cold weather. Having been converted to this cosy covering they were receptive to its replacing the discredited paddy hat, the usual shape for boys' matching headwear, for winter. The girls' hoods were not confined to the smaller ones but spread through to the teens. Brought in first in the late 1940s the hoods were either completely lined tartan or faced with the collar material, velvet or check cloth. Far removed from head covering like this was the 20th century version of the Juliet cap, with a stalk sticking up at centre back, worn by the bobby soxers of America and taken up with enthusiasm by British girls. American influence was again reflected in Breton sailor hats with wide, off-the-face brims and streamers dangling down the back, a flattering shape set for a long life. For the younger child there were Puritan bonnets cut out of felt with appliqués of flowers in bright colours. Felt was a material coming to the fore for skirts and waistcoats with original appliqué treatment but whilst it had considerable charm its success was short-lived as it could not be washed, only dry-cleaned.

No criticism could be directed in that period to separate

millinery, fur felt hats became perky with a long, long, feather stuck in the petersham band, shapes were varied, tricorn, off-the-face fur felt berets with big bows either side and Paris inspired bonnets in glowing jewel velvets for dressy occasions whilst Mexican hats trimmed in dazzling colours joined the coollies for beach wear.

*Pyjamas for the older girl varied only slightly from those of their tiny sisters'. Warm interlock fulfilled winter requirements for what was described for all ages as 'Kiddies' Nightwear'.*

Older girls' footwear was improving with suede or grained leathers and one-inch barrel heels but for the younger ones lace-ups and one-bar sandals predominated.

Girls wanted pretty underwear to go with the femininity of their top clothes. The befrilled half-slips were there but everything they wore had to be dainty with frilly necklines, bows and embroidery in place of the unrelieved art. silk slips, knickers and vests. The girls rebelled at the nightdresses with peter pan collars they wore the year round with simply heavier or lighter materials to mark the seasons. Nor were they content with shirt top pyjamas, hardly different from their brothers' in style or fabric, or wrapover dressing-gowns which were identical. Candlewick with embroidery and ribbons and quilted satin dressing-gowns were preferred and the small quantities reaching the shops were quickly snapped up. Such delights were not for everyone. There were girls up to 16 years whose wardrobes included not pretty bras and suspender belts but fleecy lined bodices with rubber buttons identical to those of their infant sisters and enough were bought for the BOT to include teen size bodices in the Utility Schedule.

Customs and Excise were not softened by the natural instincts of young girls and in the course of their duties issued a forceful reminder that opera top petticoats and slips were not exempt from purchase tax even if they were below the maximum measurements. They were, said Customs and Excise, not considered suitable for girls.

Boys were not favoured with fashion diversions, their knickers, for example, remained unswervingly just above the knee. Unfortunately for the schools they, too, were left behind in the fashion stakes. Those who were preparing to break away from the old uniforms were warned they should consider themselves lucky to get any official school wear at all let alone trying out sweeping alterations in colours and styles.

It was noticeable that where supplies were adequate and mothers could pick and choose they began to express their discontent with hackneyed styles. They looked beyond the fact that they could get garments in the right size and material: they looked to price and fit. The latter point became important not on grounds so much of appearance but from a practical aspect involving width of chest, neck opening and cuffs which were not keeping pace with children's development. Fault finding had spurred on designers to correct a few of the shortcomings, more pronounced in the infants' sizes than elsewhere where they reflected an ignorance of the mother's viewpoint. The number of buttons on boys' buster suits was a case in point giving the mother unnecessary work when the child was being dressed and daunting to a child learning to dress himself so a real effort was being made to introduce elasticated waists on boys' knickers, both woven and

*Mothers' grumbles about the number of buttons on buster-suits resulted in the introduction of pull-on trousers and tuck-in shirts which cut down dressing time.*

knitted, so they could be pulled on quickly. A loop inside the crossover backs of knicker straps which stopped them slipping off the shoulders was considered so momentous that it was covered by a patent. Girls' frocks acquired loops at the backs to hold the bows at the waistline instead of drooping depressingly below. Attention was paid to the type of button put on children's coats. It was the practice for cloth covered buttons to predominate but in wear these were often unsatisfactory, the material pulling away from the button and harder substances in shades to match the coat material were adopted.

Mothers were especially dissatisfied with the monotony of breechette sets in plain velours in a limited, unexciting choice of colours. Their complaints were answered in part by the fortunate emergence of corduroy velvet as a fashion material for women's wear. It was a rare cloth in that in varying weights and colours it could be worn by babies through to the teens. It stimulated designers, too, to produce a tough and tidy garment for small boys, the trouser-overall, virtually a copy of father's bib-and-brace dungarees, manly with workmanlike pockets and correct turn-ups.

The efficiency of the siren suit (it now had additional names, e.g., shelter suit, pixie suit) and the monotony of the breechette set led to experiments with a coverall based on the snow suits of America and Canada which were fully able to withstand the rigours of winter. The British versions bore only a slight resemblance to the wartime models produced to meet the emergency. Instead of dressing-gown type velours, the outer materials were showerproof, they were fully lined and had zipped legs and pockets.

Women shopping for second or third babies were becoming disenchanted with knitted pram sets identical to those they had bought for their first child. This was a reaction which hardly penetrated the complacency of the knitwear producers who apparently regarded the fact that babies came into the world without clothes as sufficient reason for going on making the same old designs. They might be new to the baby but they certainly were not to the mother, nor is it any exaggeration to say, the grandmother. Only after repeated pressure by store buyers was buttercup yellow added to the eternal pinks and blues. Mothers of small boys were critical of knitted jersey suits never altering in style nor colour. The indifferent cut of the knicker, buttoning so high over the jersey top that it was reduced to a yoke, contributed to the depressing appearance of an outfit which covered the body but hardly flattered the wearer. Manufacturers of knitted underwear, surely the most hidebound, had gone on making underpants oblivious to the fact that they were longer in the leg than boys' knickers. As a consequence mothers either had to turn up the hems of the underpants or their offsprings suffered the indignity of white frills round their knees and derisive cat-calls of '*droopy drawers*' from their schoolmates.

There were hosiery and knitwear manufacturers, of course, who were prepared to experiment even with universally accepted baby articles. The firmly entrenched shawl had continued down the years as an essential item in the baby's layette but at last someone thought there could be a better and easier way to keep the child covered and produced a cape with hood, a top-to-toe wrap much easier for the mother to handle yet allowing freedom of movement to the baby. The capes were knitted, invariably in white and the grander ones for christenings were in botany wool in a cockleshell pattern, the hoods edged with swansdown and tied with satin ribbon. The dolman sleeve brought in with the New Look spread to babies' knitted matinée jackets by the late 40s where it was a decided improvement on the set-in sleeve. Round the feet the prospects for infants were brighter. The virtues of the baby bootee compared with the ankle strap shoe were being recognised. The bootees being laced up the fronts, kept on the feet much better and they were dainty and serviceable in chamois lined, washable Morocco leather.

Fashion was moving, but slowly in some quarters, the classic twin set, for example, continued to command appreciation of its high quality but the low-set three-button fastening of the cardigan was being compared unfavourably with the American style which buttoned right up to the neck. This was considered to be too revolutionary for girls and they were only allowed, at first, a compromise between the two, more than the three conventional buttons but stopping short of the all-the-way USA fastening. They were to get their high-buttoned fastening, however, due mostly to the arrival on the scene of a smattering of small firms producing children's knitwear with strong Continental connotations. Unlike any made before for children in Britain the garments were in highly original stitches with raised designs giving more body to garments than was usual, the colour combinations were vivid and gay without being too bright for youngsters, edges were crocheted in bright contrast, embroidery and trimmings bore no relation to tired bobbles and flowers and, a complete departure this, they had white grounds hitherto dismissed as being too prone to catch the dirt. Several items were co-ordinated so that a complete set, jumper, scarf, hat, skirt, gloves, skilfully following a theme could be purchased. The biggest impact was made, however, by the buttoning-to-the-neck cardigan-jumper which became identified with this knitwear.

On the woven side a remarkable feature of the immediate post-war years was the emergence of several baby and infant clothing houses specialising in smocked and hand-embroidered dresses. They burst upon the scene with collections of brilliant smocked frocks, outstanding in their styling, colours and choice of materials; they largely scorned the puff sleeve and peter pan collar, preferring a delicate ruffle round the neck and sleeves with touches of embroidery which emphasised the dainty line. The whole of the bodices, back and front, were smocked in patterns and rich colours seldom seen before and glowing velvet and satin ribbons picked up the tones in a way the limp, narrow art. silk ribbons generally employed could never do.

Little girls were seeing for the first time in their lives coats with fur trimming, mainly of beaver lamb. There had been no sudden influx of fur collars and cuffs, the limitation on the supply of appropriate skins preventing that, but after the first tentative try-outs fur trimmed coats were given a push forward by being included in the Utility Schedule with, surprisingly, ocelot creeping in to join beaver lamb, not only for the collars and cuffs but for pill-box hats and Victorian muffs to complete infants' coat sets. The utility concession opened the door for a return, after many years absence, of babies' bonnets adorned with white swansdown, a trimming closely associated with christenings.

Already influencing fashion on their own account were the developments in man-made fibres. A number of these were of the utmost benefit to mothers. The quick-drying, non-iron nylon seersuckers quickly became established for dresses and blouses and the plain colours of the first arrivals were joined by stripes, checks and florals. Other fabric weaves, satins, taffetas, chiffons and voiles, were coming on the market but by far the swiftest acceptance was gained by the nylon tricots. The advantages of the open construction which overcame the criticism that nylon was cold to the touch and did not 'breathe', won for these materials a lasting place in children's under and nightwear, blouses and baby frocks and, in fact, for every garment where easy-care outweighed other considerations. Nylon for swim suits met resistance from those who held firmly to the belief that wool with its comfortable warm feel was the best material for British waters but the nylons were gay, plain or printed. Whatever prejudices people might have they were soon to be overcome by the impact of elasticated swim suits for children. They solved so many problems: they not only fitted awkward figures they stayed firmly in place however active the fun and games on the beach and they could be grown into, instead of out of, with no detriment to their appearance. Shirred in nylon, rayon and cotton in an assortment of finishes from satins to voiles, these elasticated suits brought a sparkle into girls' bathing costumes which they had never possessed before.

As well as the progress in synthetic materials there were advances in the treatment of fabrics from natural fibres and the older rayons. Conspicuous amongst these was the American process which glazed the surface and added a crispness and body to the cottons and spun rayons but the sheen was not the only reason for the speedy adoption of this finish for girls' dresses. Its shining surface was less likely to soil, it was guaranteed shrink-resistant, did not crease nor crumple as did untreated fabrics of similar texture and the lustre was not affected by washing. Not surprisingly the process met with immediate success and remained the dominant factor in summer cloths until many years later the vogue for softly draped materials returned.

In the meantime for both nylon and cotton materials 'waffle' surfaces enjoyed a long spell of popularity. In a way the developments in natural and synthetic fabrics, altering as they did the visual aspect of dresses in particular, disguised the old familiar lines and postponed the day of reckoning.

Fashion on a less frivolous note affected babies' comfort. The trap feeder entered a new stage, the 'trap' was raised to cover point instead of along the bottom to catch escaping particles on ill-judged journeys from spoon to mouth. Disposable napkins were as much a part of the baby's layette as terry and muslin squares as young mothers looked for ways to ease the chores of baby care and lighten the burden of travelling with an infant. Various waterproof holders of disposable napkins were making their debut in neater shapes than the old pilch but they were not always so effective. Changing the napkin, of whatever kind, meant trouble for mother and baby and alleviating this was the purpose behind the introduction of a bib-and-brace coverall with grip fasteners on the insides of the legs which popping undone meant the whole of the lower part could be lifted and the nappy changed quickly without disturbing the baby unduly. On similar lines was an adaptation of the tunic suit with plastic lined pants replacing the usual knicker, fastened at the sides with poppers for easy opening. With baby boys in mind the

*Once the wartime shortages were over mothers became more critical about the design of babies' clothes in particular and garments like this for easy nappy-changing began to appear.*

tops were straight cut shirts, buttoned high at the neck, with short sleeves. Easy to wash in cotton seersucker they had another feature which appealed to mothers, each set had an extra pair of plastic lined pants.

Opposition to synthetic pants for babies, and they had several disadvantages not least a tendency to harden in use and also make the baby hot and uncomfortable, was largely overcome by the introduction of nylon film which 'breathed' but whilst letting in the air was completely waterproof and retained its softness through repeated washing. The terry napkin shortage lasted into the 50s with Harold Wilson, as President of the BOT, getting bogged down with statistics purporting to show how much better things were, then having to explain a 'typographical error' when the evidence showed they were not.

School uniforms, as always, were in the news. The Minister of Education made a statement in the House of Commons on the '*undesirability in present circumstances of prescribing a school uniform*' and reopened the old argument on the pros and cons of official uniforms with the protagonists equally convinced that their premise was the right one.

The resurgence of interest in fashion had inevitably lead to a call for a reappraisal of the maximum measurements laid down for purchase tax-free garments, primarily to accommodate the longer length. The definitions had remained virtually unaltered since they were devised eight years before but Customs and Excise could no longer remain oblivious to the altered outlook on children's apparel. The admission that the measurements would have to be examined in the light of fashion fancies was the first step along a stormy road travelled by weary Customs and Excise officials, angry, frustrated traders, and bewildered parents who at the end of the day were footing the bill. The outcome of the Customs and Excise investigation was an increase in the tax-free length for coats from 39 to 42ins. (99 to 106cms.) and dresses from 38 to 40ins. (96 to 101cms.). Taking the opportunity of tidying up other measurements and specifications, Customs exempted, within certain definitions, white, blue and pink carrying shawls for babies, coloured blouses for school as well as white, and extended the exemption to several new garments, backless swim suits, for example, which had arrived since purchase tax was introduced. The older girl who wanted different styles from her younger sister received support, no doubt unwittingly, from Customs who dropped the stipulation that garments in the maximum measurements must be made from sizes 33ins. (84cms.) (dresses) and 34ins. (86cms.) (coats) upwards in order to qualify for tax exemption.

Almost unnoticed during that post-war period a garment slipped into the country with no hint that it was to become an integral part of every child's life nor that it would be of such consequence in establishing a company as the largest manufacturer of children's wear in Europe. The garment, aptly described as a T-shirt, was coldly received. Mr. Eric W. Pasold, head of a hosiery firm mainly concerned with producing 'Ladybird' children's vests and knickers and, when permitted, dressing-gowns, brought back the idea of a T-shirt from North America where it was an accepted everyday article. To British retailers it was appalling, its stark white simplicity, unadorned crewe neck and short sleeves were identical with a man's vest and in the prevailing conventional climate regarded as 'most unsuitable' for a child. Store after store in Oxford Street turned down the shirt and then Eric Pasold persuaded the buyer of Swan & Edgar Ltd. in Regent Street to take 20 dozen for her children's section on a sale or return basis. The buyer never had cause to regret her decision and the department achieved fame as a source for 'Ladybird' T-shirts, supplying eventually the sons and daughters of the original wearers. It is not hard to understand why retailers rejected the shirts, they had no sales appeal, but if ever a garment was created to please both mother and child it was the T-shirt, simple, washable, unisex and inexpensive.

Over the years the plain white was joined by pastels, then a variety of multi-coloured patterns and striping and the T-outline was softened somewhat by shaping the sleeves but basically the article remained unaltered, it served its purpose too well to require interference.

# CHAPTER 19
# The End of Controls and the Beginning of a Revolution

As the months, then *years* went by and the anomalies in the Utility Schedule were not corrected and there was no allowance for the rising cost of raw materials it finally dawned upon the trade that the negotiations in which they were engaged continually with the BOT were a complete charade. When it seemed that the children's wear manufacturers had woken up to what was going on, and it should be recorded that for years they had sat round the table confident that their views were being listened to in all sincerity, Labour Government spokesmen at first explained away the delays in price adjustments by stating that they wanted makers-up to use up their old stocks of materials. This was received with cynicism, there were no large stocks to be got rid of, and the better the manufacturer the less fabrics he was likely to have left on his hands. The true explanation was not long in coming out, the price of children's clothing was a sensitive area, any increases quickly became the target of adverse publicity in the national Press, directed at the Government. To prevent this, the policy was to stall any rise in prices however justified these might be in the hope that sufficient goods would come through albeit of indifferent quality.

At this point, six years after the war ended, the trade's patience was exhausted. In 1951 the Central Committee of the Hosiery Industry, the body advising the BOT, resigned and the National Children's Wear Association withdrew from the Light Clothing Federation, the organisation formed at the direct request of the Board, because it had been almost entirely impotent so far as children's wear was concerned. The NCWA in informing its members of the decision pointed to the fact that negotiations for prices of infants' and girls' light outerwear, underwear and nightwear had been going on for two years. In forthright terms it stated that the BOT had consistently maintained an attitude of apparent co-operation with the trade but actually doing very little to meet the urgent requirements put to them and the tremendous work done by the Federation and its technical committees had been almost entirely fruitless. The Association was scathing about the chaotic state of the utility scheme which had long outlived its usefulness. How far the NCWA was justified in its criticism can be gauged by the fact that for boys' knickers alone 539 specifications had to be observed, covering sizes, materials, styles, prices and so on at every stage of making and distribution. For *three years* discussions had been going on about getting buster-rompers included in the Utility Schedule.

The attitude of the producers was oddly at variance with that of Members of Parliament who in the middle of this held a debate on the utility clothing scheme during which their speeches served only to reveal their ignorance of the work entailed in the making and distribution of children's garments and the negotiations which had been going on with the BOT. One Member, a Conservative no less, advocated standard clothing for every boy or girl up to 14. Ten or twelve items would cover the whole field, he maintained, at practically the cost of production and went on, with some courage remembering how many women voters were in his constituency, *'Let us discourage the production of some useless and expensive fripperies which are given to children by indulgent mothers who hope to see the beauty that is no longer theirs reflected in their girls'*—fighting words indeed.

1952 opened with the publication of yet another long-delayed IG Schedule so full of glaring mistakes, accidental or deliberate, that the department responsible lost all credence. The remaining price controls on non-utility were removed except for nylon stockings—and children's clothing. The official explanation was that the BOT was waiting for the effect of the removal on other clothing to become clear. Bitter words flowed during the weeks that followed. So it went on until in March to the astonishment and delight of all concerned the Government, conceding that it could no longer cling to legislation devised in time of war, scrapped the lot, the utility scheme, price controls and all, seven years after the war with Germany had ended.

The ending of controls was the beginning of a revolution in children's clothing until after twenty years the wheel turned full circle and boys and girls were to be once more dressed in miniature copies of adult garments. The introduction of fashion reflected society's changed attitude towards the child but it reflected, too, the changes in society itself, the family motor car, the working mother, the decline in churchgoing, the disappearance of the nanny, all were to have their bearing on what boys and girls would wear and it hit an industry neither physically nor psychologically prepared for such an upheaval.

Years of Government controls had brainwashed manufacturers into thinking that production was all-important and any pandering to passing fads a hindrance to supplies. Women's wear firms who knew their prosperity was inexorably bound up with fast-moving fashion adapted speedily, children's wear manufacturers did not but then they had never thought of themselves as being part of the fashion industry. They, and others, had a fixed image of the schoolchild, retained from pre-war, dressed in staid, unobtrusive but well-made garments, slightly grander for Sunday-best, and enchantingly transformed if they were fortunate for the party season, a concession naturally not extended to the boys. Propping up this fixation was the iron hand of the school uniform. It set the tone of what a child should wear and in the majority of families left scant surplus for additional clothing.

In the past this had not bothered anyone unduly, the cost of uniforms had but not that there should be next to nothing for fancy clothing. The picture was quite definite, once attending school the boy or girl became a 'schoolchild' and that description extended from five years to fourteen or older, until he or she left and went out into the world and was swept into the orbit of fashion. Until that moment the child marked time in his or her allotted category. To break from that deeply entrenched belief was not only a question of accepting that the child at school wanted more than covering against the elements, it was also a matter of the construction of the industry. The trade was not geared for coping with a fluctuating market, nor were its cloth suppliers whose choice of patterns endorsed the *'children's clothes don't change'* maxim with unrelenting monotony.

The basis of the industry was skill in grading, labour and working to a price. Grading was on a scale never known in women's wear, extending from the babies, through to toddlers, from five-year-olds to the teens with a knowledge gained over the years of development at every stage. No wonder that makers jealously guarded their patterns and were slow to admit that they could be outdated when children's heights and girths began to expand. It took longer to train a machinist on children's clothes than it did women's and at the end only those with an aptitude for the work were of use. As for prices, these had to be keen to comply with the public's attitude towards the child at school. If fashion was to become an important element then a new factor, design, must rank with the other basic requirements. Keeping up with fashion was a costly business liable to throw any firm off an even keel and reflecting this risk element must result in higher charges.

This was already a labour intensive industry. No one outside could have any conception of the trade's diversity. Pre-war, a children's wear wholesaler, for example, could handle as many as 100 brands, entailing 500 labels and a host of different coloured boxes. The labour involved in sorting and despatch of branded goods was out of all proportion to the cost of the garments. In a warehouse there could be 15,000 different items of babies' and children's clothing. A company specialising in baby and infants' clothing, pram and cot sheets and so on, could have in their building no less than *one million* different articles. This figure would not include the stock required to fill orders but merely the samples to show retail buyers. In the layette department alone one thousand articles were carried. A baby in a dress, seemingly so simple a proposition, yet one firm alone offered more than 200 different styles in baby frocks and in baby pants they carried a choice of 64 in four sizes. The traveller for a juvenile wholesale house had to be a brawny individual, his sample cases could contain 1,400 items. It was no surprise that the road to fashion was trodden so reluctantly.

Coat firms were the most hidebound. Their interest was mainly in the quality of the cloth and they could not see why plain velours and checks could not continue indefinitely, tailored to patterns which served their purpose which, in their eyes, meant to cover the child adequately. The maxim was, *'Nothing looks nicer than a little girl in a tailored coat'*, and what was good enough for their daughters and grand-daughters was good enough for everyone. They closed their ears to adverse comments until the most stubborn were completely out of touch with events and went out of business. Yet during that period it was the coat manufacturers who set a fashion for the whole world to follow. The British tailored coat was to be found in wealthy households in many countries and just as the makers had attracted an international fame they achieved the same distinction with a garment which was a complete opposite, casual, loose fitting, shapeless and practically colourless it had been inspired not by the leaders of fashion but by the rigours of navy life, for in 1950 a manufacturer produced a miniature duffle coat for a child and made history, an honour for which there have been several claimants to be first in the field. The success of the duffle was immediate and soon it was being worn by all ages. It was to oust the breechette set and with tartan trousers became the standard attire of the up-to-fours.

On the Continent it was adopted gleefully and spurning the prosaic 'duffle' description christened 'Le Montgomerie' with a fine disregard of its naval origins but a tribute to one of its most distinguished wearers. Unfortunately the duffle coat proved to be too popular and rather like an ageing prima donna refused to retire. Too eminently suited to children's needs in every respect the manufacturers could not imagine that it could be supplanted. Continental firms were more imaginative and whilst retaining the basic design introduced vivid colours and replaced the traditional toggles with novel strappings and fastenings with an altogether livelier result than the British counterpart which continued on its beige coloured way, with navy as the sole alternative which, greatly daring, had been brought in for school.

On the dress side the smaller firms with greater flexibility were less opposed to new ideas, the larger companies supplying the wholesale were not so receptive. The output of the big firms was based on long runs, a limited range of samples and minimum variations in style, to bring in a fashion element would destroy this smooth operation. Knitwear and hosiery makers were in a similar position. They found it difficult to adjust to a buyer's from a seller's market and were confident that what they were doing was right and any fault-finding was trifle and transitory. Their minds were closed not only to fashion, but in outer and underwear to the claims of the post-war child with increased height and weight and earlier maturity.

Wholesalers were to lose most by the onset of fashion. Dependent on the mass-producers already referred to, used to dealing in numbers and cloth content, the majority were male buyers who saw no call to adopt flighty Parisian ways. Those who were far-sighted and enterprising received meagre help from their suppliers, some went into the business of wholesale distribution on their own, sponsoring manufacturing units to produce the garments they could not obtain elsewhere.

There were store buyers, too, who were reluctant to be swept into the fashion stream for personal and business reasons. Behind their resistance was annoyance at children and parents who were critical of their hackneyed stock and at heart they disliked the 'little madams' who came into their departments. Retailers could not hold back the tide, however, and it was they who had to reflect the wishes of their customers and press for more interesting garments. Shops and stores were at the receiving end of the growing independence of children. The buying pattern turned upside down. Pre-war, shops had to sell to mothers, post-war to the child. It went further than that, in the past retailers had acted in an advisory capacity to their customers who looked to them for help on what was 'suitable' and respected their views on what was being bought for youngsters. This relationship was to be reversed, parents and their offspring came into the shops knowing what they wanted and if it was not there they were not to be persuaded to accept substitutes, they went elsewhere. It was the child who dictated the purchases and the mother ended up not daring to buy anything without the child being present.

Buying for the baby underwent the greatest revolution. The baby linen section had always been tucked away in a quiet corner where the expectant mother could order the complete layette under the direction of her own mother, the dictates of the all-powerful nanny, and the shop assistant. They were all to be usurped by the clinics whose word became law. Such was the hush-hush atmosphere surrounding an expectant mother that when backless windows in small shops became the vogue after the war women complained that they could be seen purchasing baby things and the window backs had to be restored. It was not uncommon for baby wear specialists to open in the evening so that a woman could look through layette items in complete privacy, coming back next day to make her purchases. Who could have foreseen that in a few years buying for baby would slide out of its privacy into self-selection in full view of the public, and the word 'layette' begin to disappear from the language?

Specialist shops were to spring up all over the country to challenge the multiple stores and local general drapers and provide the boutique lines which the chain stores could only offer to a limited degree. Hitherto the corner shop, selling baby linen, knitting wools and underwear was the local alternative to the general stores and shops, the children's boutiques were another matter altogether. They were started by young mothers who, unable to get the styles they wanted for their toddlers, made up their own designs and spurred on by the admiration of their friends opened shops. Others recognised the potential in neighbourhoods where no exclusive outlets for children existed and moved in. Finally the country was covered by a vast chain of specialist shops along the lines of a highly successful French organisation which put the promotion of this section on a brisk businesslike footing. Rising transport costs helped to get the local specialists established. Shopping trips to cities became too expensive for mothers when money for lunches and ice creams as well as fares had to be found.

The road to fashion was a bitter journey for some but the will of the public to take their children along that path could not be denied and Continental firms stepped in to fill the breach. Imports had a quality of originality and elegance which had so far eluded British producers, save for an inspired few. The overseas firms dealt not in the cheap goods hitherto mainly associated with imports but top price articles and for these parents were prepared to pay. In knitwear the foreigners' stitches, designs and colours were outstanding, their jersey suits and dresses and rainwear, exemplary and they managed to breathe new life into every age group from babies upwards.

Yet the final push into high-fashion originated in the UK. Carnaby Street and swinging Britain swept girls' and boys' wear along with it to an exhilarating reputation as world leaders. The New Young Designers of the 60s were responsible. When they turned their unique talents to the junior scene they started with no restrictions nor respect for conventions and past practices. These young people succeeded as brilliantly in the children's field as their contemporaries did in the women's but it was the production ability of the established firms which made it possible. Only by the knowledge of sizing, grading and training of machinists held by experienced makers could the wildly way-out designs be interpreted for the mass market. In the end, high-fashion mattered and skilled designers assumed an honoured place in factories where before their presence was of no consequence but to get there it took twenty years to pull down brick by brick the wall that surrounded children's clothing from the adult world.

# CHAPTER 20
# 'Maids' Disappear

The teenager was the golden girl of the early post-war years. She burst out of the confines of childhood into the adult world and suddenly everything she did was news. Not for her the tail end of the children's section or the vapid 'maids' departments. She wanted to express in her clothes that adolescence had an identity of its own, and whatever anyone thought of her taste, it was *her* taste. That she should even think along these lines was sensation enough to the older generation and there was a tight-lipped reaction from retail buyers who disapproved of her choice. They had a point, inexperience coupled with a young girl's dreams resulted in some disastrous, often laughable, consequences as she spurned her one great asset, the bloom of youth, and rushed into women's garb. The critics were proved right in the end, the teenager's freedom won for her a tarty, vulgar image until it was channelled into the brilliance of a new design era.

Retailers knew the teens were deserting the juvenile departments and tried hard to woo them with special 'shops' and sections. Unfortunately they were starting from base, '*What did the teenager want*?', but the girls themselves did not know. Stores tried to find out through personal contacts, clubs, panels and discussion groups just what the girls had in mind but no real guidance was forthcoming. Meanwhile there might be great pressure in the national Press backed by that newcomer television, for fashions exclusively for the teens but they were still regarded as children in other quarters. Confirmation of this was given by a Judge in the High Court in 1951 when he ruled that a children's outfitter was entitled to cater for 'children up to the age of 17 years'.

In 1955 a Teenage Fashion Group was formed. It was significant in view of events that it was composed of children's wear manufacturers who went up to the bigger sizes, for the purpose of the Group initially was to specialise in 17-19 years. This is what everybody wanted, it was claimed. Before the year was out the Group had widened its scope to embrace 13-19 years, with the proviso that the emphasis would be on the 14-16-year-olds. There was no financial future in designing exclusively for 17-19 years, certainly not by manufacturers starting from the children's end. It might then have been possible for women's manufacturers who had the right experience but those who tried had similarly discovered that it was not a profitable venture. The truth was that it was not possible at that time, nor for many years to come, to specialise in such a section. There were girls in their teens who were at school and others who were going out to work: convention decreed that the majority of the former shopped in the girls' departments and the latter the small women's and the differences between a girl of 17 and one of 19 was far too big to be bridged by a single range.

So the 'maids' disappeared from the children's world.

# CHAPTER 21
# Public's Dissatisfaction with Design

In the beginning mothers were not unduly bothered, or even conscious of the stalemate in children's apparel. Their main concern remained the appropriateness and wearability of garments rather than their high-fashion aspect and the troubles that had arisen over babies' and children's development which had not been entirely rectified. To a degree the latter shortcomings were concealed by the next size up being purchased, as evidenced by the 'first size' for babies being left on retailers' shelves. To buy larger garments was not the answer, boys and girls were not necessarily growing in regular proportion to old conceptions of their height and girth and a higher standard of fit was being demanded. A common fault was the neck opening being too small to go over a child's head, tiresome enough in woven garments but disastrous in knitwear where even infants' jerseys with buttoning along the shoulder could not be pulled on. This was to be solved in vests at least a few years later when a hosiery firm came out with an inspired answer to the variations in head sizes, the mother's difficulties in dressing baby and the child's experience of being covered over for a few seconds until his head emerged through the opening. This was the 'envelope' neck with flanges either side which moved apart as the mother drew the vest over the child's head and went back into place round the neck to provide the requisite high neckline for warmth. This ingenious device was naturally approved and was extended to bigger sizes and other garments where adaptability and speedy dressing were welcome.

With the improvements in the design of footwear attention moved to socks and the damage which could be caused to the feet by hosiery which shrank or went on being worn long after the feet had grown too big for it. The man-made fibres were later to overcome the shrinkage problem but in the meantime it was realised that as much harm could be done by the daily restriction of socks which cramped the feet as ill-fitting footwear. In an effort to combat this one firm, after three years research, brought out a 'Footfit' shape which by simply rounding the top allowed sufficient room for each toe instead of the all-too-common pinching together caused by the familiar slightly pointed shape. The firm continued with its research, helped by medical and orthopaedic specialists and later launched left-right socks based on the principle that the inner border of each sock was straight to allow for the unimpeded development of the big toe but the advent of stretch almost wiped out the dangers of ill-fitting hose.

The pretty soft sole shoes for babies aroused no criticism but to one manufacturer at least they lacked the depth essential to accommodate chubby feet and after years of experimenting he produced the first soft sole shoe made on a last. By this means the toes could be blocked instead of the upper being stitched to the sole with no room for manoeuvre.

Waists on girls' skirts had always been a problem. Children requiring skirts of the same length could have wildly different waist measurements and only those whose business was dealing with young girls could appreciate the extent of the variation. Of the advantages the zip brought few were as beneficial as the adjustments it made possible in the width of skirt tops which went a long way to getting the chubbies fitted out with skirts from stock and thus saving them from embarrassment.

Slowly all the garments in the child's wardrobe were coming under review. History was made with the demise of the directoire knicker, the bloomers worn hitherto by every schoolgirl in Britain. The style and cut had finally been transformed and briefs had emerged with the balloon shape fined down to figure-hugging proportions and ribbing or bands at the legs cut high on the thigh instead of elastic just above the knee. The constant references to the older girls' dress aspirations fell upon deaf ears so far as the knitted underwear manufacturers were concerned and the mid-50s were reached before makers thought it necessary to offer 'sleeveless vests with lower necks for teenagers'. Girls continued to wear fleecy lined bodices but the front fastening went and they graduated to pull-ons, the smoother line so much better than the childish buttoning which often showed in a lumpy row through the material of the dress.

So much notice was paid to the teenagers that the sub-teens with no one taking up their cause had no alternative but to go on wearing styles which remained static and, most humiliating of all, classified them immediately as 'children'. Whilst it is true that the makers were only too glad to perpetuate the childhood image, thankful not to be trying to please the capricious teens, there was something to be said in their defence. It was on the in-betweens that advanced styling sat uneasily and parental opposition to too rapid strides towards maturity died hard. The grumbles about sub-teens' clothing persisted and unable to determine what the girls really wanted, manufacturers sought the advice of retailers and retailers sought the advice of mothers and their daughters through fashion shows, 'clubs', lectures and so forth sponsored by stores hoping to capture the trade and similar to those launched for the older girls. The novelty of being courted in this manner evoked a good response but did practically nothing to indicate their clothing ambitions, except for one thing. Contrary to the views expressed in the national Press, it transpired that the youngsters were just as conservative as their mothers were at that age and were not seeking attention-getters. They lacked the confidence to carry off advanced styles before these had become accepted. They did not know what they wanted, only what they did *not* want, and they did *not* want anything which allied them to their little sisters nor nondescript apparel which did not transform them into the pretty creatures they imagined themselves to be.

For much of the time clothing for girls of school age changed not because there was any trend, adult influenced or not, but because girls could not find what they wanted and rather than wear the same old styles they looked around for alternatives. In dresses, for instance, there were few smart designs and wool frocks were depressingly dull so the girls turned to skirts and jumpers which allowed for a degree of self-expression in colour at least and, happily, women were sporting them under the snappy title of 'separates'. The pendulum had swung away from formality to casuals, roll neck sweaters and jeans became the daily attire outside school. The timeless polo neck, long sleeve sweater had a great deal to recommend it but alongside this classic appeared a unisex sweater (promoted long before the term was regarded as trendy in the 70s but described in the 50s as 'suitable for boy or girl'). It delighted both sexes from four to 14 years. Simple in design and comfortable to wear the sweater was in a knitted fabric with ribbed cuffs and welt and a V-neck filled with a similar ribbed inset, this being elasticated to fit neatly round the neck. For years this garment retained its popularity and whilst this was due in some measure to clever publicity and its famous trade mark it would never have done so had it not been that the article itself was ideal from both the parents' and the child's point of view.

In the search for self-expression fads swept through the classrooms like wildfire, for no apparent reason, certainly seldom for their attractiveness. This was true of the elasticated belt craze although it did have one or two points in its favour. The belt could hardly have been less feminine for it was almost a facsimile of the businesslike belt holding up the trousers of the nation's small boys. Made of tough elasticated webbing, about two inches wide, it fastened with a prosaic metal clip but it was a godsend to girls whose skirts tended to slip below their waistlines, it prevented blouses from riding up and flapping untidily round the back, but best of all it achieved that coveted clinched-in look.

The tubular hat was another craze pulled on heads in every corner of the land. The birth of this bit of nonsense was attributed to a worker in a knitwear factory who finding a short length of circular knitted fabric ran a piece of wool round one end, tied it in a bow, turned back the other end into a cuff and threw it over to his workmate with a '*Here's a new hat for you*'. Apocryphal or not the hat was no more than this, except for the ends being neatened and two bobbles added to the wool ties, but it fitted heads of every size, looked jolly and took any amount of punishment. Fishermen's caps with bobbles on the tops were in a similar idiom and so were jellybag caps, but these were rather more finished and knitted in broad stripes in bright colours and extending into long points with pom-pon ends. Part of the charm of this carefree headwear was that it topped off the duffle coat in a way formal felts could never do.

Girls copied their baby brothers and bought clip-on bow ties in bright colours and patterns to give a perky finish to their too often plain blouses. The popularity of square dancing naturally led to a crop of dirndl skirts, tight-waisted and whirling appropriately at the slightest movement. Although too young to follow the callers' instructions tiny tots had their versions — on straps to withstand the boisterous efforts to 'set to your partners'. Skirts, generally, were even fuller, to the ultimate — the full circle — and nothing could have pleased the girls more. The length and line of dresses and coats were static having dropped, for the older girls, by 1953 from 39ins. to 46ins. (99 to 116cms.), the silhouette remaining a close fitted bodice and full skirt.

Through all the passing whims, the major and minor turns of public favour there remained one powerful factor, tartan. It was tartan, tartan all the way in the post-war years and into the 60s on the Continent as well as in the UK as much for its own sake as for the alternative it gave to plain wools. The Royal Stewart was seen everywhere then the Black Watch. Tartan was almost synonymous with infants' trousers, as coat linings and trews for girls of every age and when adults tired of it, it continued to be indelibly associated with children.

*Spanish produced baby knitwear in fascinating new stitches, pearly colours and revolutionary designs had a far-reaching influence on baby clothing in Britain.*

*A far cry from the art silk locknit petticoat of pre-war years: women had their glamorous half-slips, so did the girls, right down to the tinies.*

*In the middle 50s exquisite dresses in lace and net over taffeta, cut on traditional lines, were still being made for the sub-teens and teens but the girls were aching to get away from puff sleeves and bows.*

*Designers sought to effect a compromise for partygoers, cutting out the sleeves, simplifying the bodice and finishing the waist with a narrow buckled belt.*

*By the end of the 60s the old rules had been broken and for three- to six-year-olds there were wide necks, double layers of Cluny lace and such—to some outrageous—materials as burgundy moire velvet for high-fashion trouser suits.*

*By the middle 60s the children were sliding into the world of fashion in slick jacquard trouser suits.*

# CHAPTER 22
# The Impact of Synthetics

It was not style that was influencing events during the middle 50s but the man-made fibres and the benefits they brought to mothers more than any other section of the community. Easy-care took over and the burden of sock darning was lifted. Man-made fibres threw wide the door to fabrics hitherto rarely used and were to bring into existence garments never known before, accepted with alacrity by mothers no longer influenced by tradition. This decade was to see the beginning of the end of wool's dominant position in baby knitwear. The fibre houses were to inaugurate a new era, wide scale promotion of children's clothing on a scale no one manufacturer could afford and they were to back the New Young Designers who gave children's wear its final push into high-fashion.

Once established the synthetic fibres revolutionised clothes-care to the joy of the growing number of women who worked outside the home. Washability in layette items became of first importance once it was realised that it could be coupled with the requisite daintiness. Fine nylon and 'Terylene' woven materials and laces and nets replaced the silk crêpe-de-chine, laces and nets of the christening gowns. The synthetic materials were no substitutes but brought their own peculiar virtues. They could be as delicately embroidered as the natural cloths, laundered without shrinking nor changing shape, were easy to iron and could be stored to hand down without any deterioration in the fabric or the colour. Short dresses, buster-suits and similar articles lost nothing by the use of man-made fibres, performing their function with efficiency despite their delicate appearance. Pram coats in nylon fur fabrics were to be a cosy alternative to velours and just as pretty in baby pastels.

Of far more consequence than these, however, was the

replacement of wool by 'Orlon' as the leading fibre for baby knitwear almost wholly due to one characteristic, its built-in whiteness. Most fibres acquired through no fault of the washer a slight yellow or grey tinge disregarded in most clothing but noticeable in baby wear and becoming more marked when garments were kept for handing down. 'Orlon' retained its pristine whiteness however carelessly handled and coupled with its other assets of wash and wearability not surprisingly

rose to first place (an estimated 90 per cent) for baby knitwear and Britain was a wool only for babies nation no longer. A strong body of opinion continued to favour wool vests for the young ones for winter, and cotton for summer, however, preferring the natural fibres against the child's skin.

For schoolgirls one of the manifold blessings of man-made fibres was permanent pleating (the adjective was dropped at one stage as being too unequivocal and replaced by 'durable')

*Pleats were important in school life. Synthetic fibres, on their own or combined with natural yarns, with their durable pleating attributes opened the way to more varied effects.*

a boon for uniforms. To get tunics and skirts, pleated without restriction as to type, which could be washed repeatedly and left to drip-dry was miraculous to mothers accustomed to continual sponging and pressing over damp cloths or the expense of dry-cleaning with the added high charges for re-pleating. Pleats were important in girls' clothing since they gave the requisite fullness without bulk, could be varied to suit every age group and were neat and tidy on ungainly figures. When experiments proved that wool and worsted fabrics could be strengthened by the addition of man-made fibres without impairing the unique quality of the former the presence of synthetics in the classroom was assured.

Girls were not the only ones to benefit from the combination of natural and man-made fibres. The advantages of mixtures and blends were equally applicable to boys' outerwear and soon suits and topcoats were being sold made from these materials which were hard-wearing, fully washable and indistinguishable from pure wool suitings.

The blessings of durable pleating had a noticeable effect on baby coats. Clusters of narrow knife-pleating could be achieved in fine cream and pastel 'Terylene' and wool, the need for repeated washing having precluded fine pleating for pram and toddler coats in the past.

The adoption of man-made fibres in children's wear was swift and more was to come when the magic word 'stretch' began to be heard.

# CHAPTER 23
# Old Conventions Begin to be Broken

Help for the mother, comfort for the child and accoutrements for the post-war car travelling baby were to dominate the path to freedom and liberate the convention-shrouded babies' clothing from the long robe into shortening dress tradition and all that went with it. Items once considered vital were to disappear from the layette, like the veils of embroidered net which used to be laid over the baby's face to keep out the cold, and the bonnet, tucked and beribboned, was due for an early demise. The long robe lingered on but by the middle 50s had shrunk from 36ins. to 24ins. (91 to 61cms.) losing its place to the baby bag and the short dress. Initial reaction in some places to anything which saved mother's time was one of condemnation. It was supposed to be the mark of a dutiful parent if she worked and slaved over her baby whereas labour-saving devices were often much more hygenic than the old methods, as, for example, bibs. These progressed from the frilly bits of nonsense through terry towelling to plastics and the ultimate, disposables, an efficient means of dealing with sloppy eaters, although they never eliminated the fabric types.

Saving of labour was not always the main motive behind the ready acceptance of easy-care, it was the car which began to dictate baby's life style. Instead of being pushed sedately along the highways and byways baby was whizzing around the country in a car and wherever he went he must be accompanied by his equipment and this had to be adapted accordingly. Where the family went baby went, at home or overseas, unlike the old days when mother was tied to the house with a young child. The travelling baby spurred on the adoption of disposable napkins, and was behind mothers' insistence on simple outfits which could be washed out and dried overnight. Crease-resistance was another advantage when things had to be packed into the boot.

Here and there baby wear began to improve. By placing the leg holes of the baby pant to the front instead of the sides the voluminious shape was cut down without reducing the roominess where required or impairing its efficiency as a cover-up for bulky napkins. The pant had taken a first step towards fashion. Then the trimming was switched to the back—the part presented to the world when baby was crawling around—and what had been an unobtrusive and purely functional garment swept into the world of seasonal collections and new designs twice yearly. Frills and ruffles, Lurex stripes, non-chafe elastic, rose scented lanolin linings, the baby pant became a far cry from the rubber knickers of days gone by and

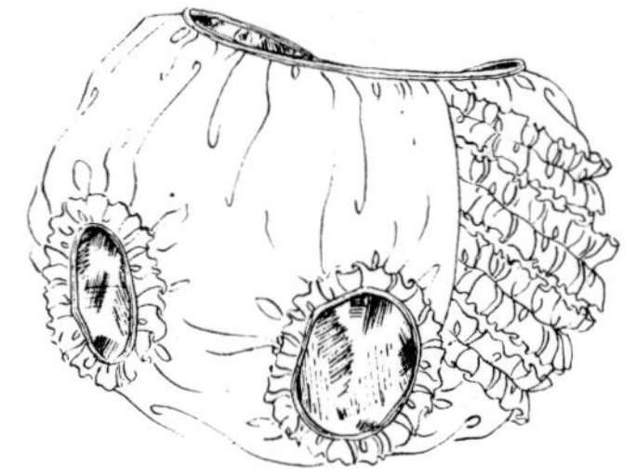

*Babies got their own new look in the middle of the 50s with frills on their pants across the back—where they showed.*

so pretty that dresses were made shorter to show off the pants. These decorative pants were so popular that eventually mothers complained that they could get none suitable for boys. Plastics which allowed air to pass through but retained moisture, thus affording maximum protection but obviating the hot and sticky nature of some plastic pants was another miracle fabric adapted to baby's comfort. The search went on for a means to cut down the nappy-washing chore. Pants with pockets to hold highly absorbent disposable napkins were one of the earliest successes.

Relief from nappy rash prompted another innovation launched in 1959, a nappy lining, not plastics, worn over the napkin and against the skin, which allowed moisture to pass through but remained dry and retained the properties through machine or hand-washing. The same material having proved its efficacy, considerably enhanced by developments which made it boilable, was later made into pants as well as a straightforward lining. Experts' views of potty training progress can be too optimistic and this was recognised by the introduction in the early 60s of training pants in terry towelling lined with fine waterproof vinyl for those not yet past the learner stage. Notwithstanding the convenience of the disposable napkins and the creation of diverse shapes, terry squares and nappy liners were to be by far the best sellers. Two

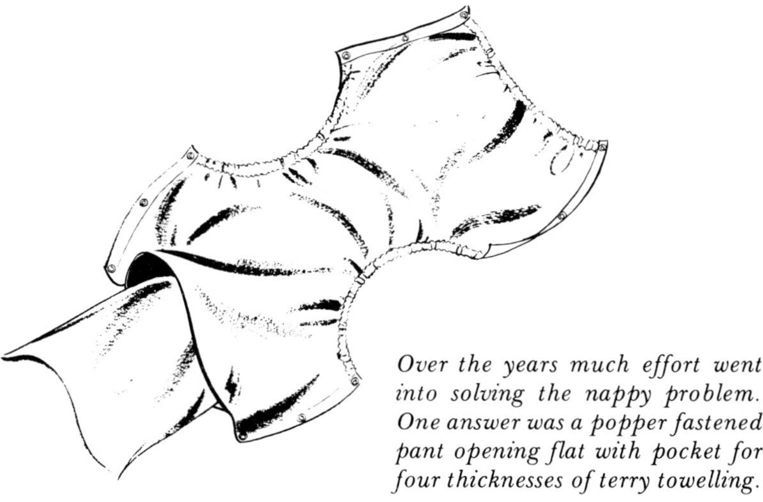

*Over the years much effort went into solving the nappy problem. One answer was a popper fastened pant opening flat with pocket for four thicknesses of terry towelling.*

dozen terry, two dozen gauze remained the mother's preference.

An advance in baby bags, as a direct result of suggestions from mothers, was the 'nightie bag'. This followed the same closed end principle but in wool and cotton mixtures and thus lighter in weight, kept the infant warmly covered however active tiny toes were at night. The promoters of baby bags always stressed that they were not intended for sleeping in at night and the 'nightie bag' was a cosy alternative to night-gowns.

The siren suit took a sideways glance at Scandinavian skiers and 'walking suits' came in for toddlers, knitted two-pieces with button-front tops, pointed collars and full trousers caught into cuffs at the ankles. Matching caps owing much to the snow scene completed the outfits which presented the orthodox breechette set with yet another rival.

British manufacturers were lagging behind their Continental contemporaries. Soon after the import restrictions were lifted, babies' and infants' clothes from Maderia arrived to relieve the monotony. This merchandise relied on exquisite hand-work which owed nothing to the traditional concept of handicrafts from that country. Embroidery and appliqués were created with the child in mind, the hackneyed chicks, ducks and elephants in almost entirely static poses of the home product had no place. Instead everyday incidents and domestic animals, kittens and puppies, raindrops and umbrellas, sunshine and puddles, were treated with imagination and humour emphasised by the incorporation of different materials to heighten the effect.

For slightly older girls Belgium had surprisingly become the source of hand-woven wool dresses with a 'tweedy' surface distinguished by their delicate appearance, favourite was a white ground and symmetrical pastel embroidery.

In 1956 a collection was shown in London which was to have a lasting impact on design. The show was brought to Britain

*A big impact was made in the 50s by dresses imported from Belgium made in hand-woven wool with delicate embroidery.*

from Spain, a country hitherto almost unknown abroad for children's clothing, by Mrs. Mildred Frey who had a background of the garment industry in the UK. Elegant, hand-made accessories were included in this first presentation but it was in the baby and infants' field that Mrs. Frey was to leave her mark. The knitwear for babies was a revolution, matinée coats with full bishop's sleeves, pearly in white wool lined pink in imaginative stitches far removed from the purl and plain of the British counterparts. Baby and infants' frocks in woven materials were as brilliantly conceived but here the skill was apparent, apart from the cut and the clever blending of colours, in the motifs expressing the spirit of childhood with appliqués of scenes and actions incorporating pockets, yokes and skirts so that the whole dress presented a balanced picture not an outdated pattern on which someone had sewn a chicken or rabbit motif. Flapper pleated dresses for the tinies originated in the Spanish collections. The frocks were sleeveless, cut straight down to box or knife-pleated bands at the hem. The long line allowed for more imaginative treatment of material or trimming not possible with high yokes and gathered skirts.

Naturally the Spanish imports were more expensive than the mass-produced British counterparts, and it would be invidious to make direct comparisons but they had the rare quality of conveying that baby was a treasured possession and their influence was to be far-reaching. Much of the outwork was done in the convents in Spain, the nuns showing a surprising talent for contemporary and uninhibited design.

Hosiery manufacturers were slow to realise that the Spanish imports had opened people's eyes to the potential charm of baby knitwear. Mass-producers tended to dismiss the imports as luxury items for the moneyed few but the contrast was not acceptable to mothers. Side by side with the Spanish matinée jackets and pram sets the British were seen to be twenty years out of date and the censure was not confined to the small sizes. Retailers and the public were complaining that in the bulk of the knitwear the shades and styles were the same as well before the war.

The natural fibres were to be eclipsed for a while by the powerful pull of the synthetics but the drip-dry, shrink and crease-resisting finishes on cottons and the shrink-resisting processess for wool, to be followed by machine-washability, were to restore them as keen competitors for the public's favour. Machine-washability was not to be confined to factory-made products, hand-knitters were to get knitting wools which could be put in the machine.

Another post-war innovation, silicones, had a major effect on children's clothing initiating the longed for injection of life into spring and summer coats. Silicones brought with them water repellent and stain resistant finishes for natural and synthetic materials and inspired designers to elevate summer wet weather wear to high-fashion, strongly influenced by Continental firms who had suddenly achieved eminence in this area. The silicone treatment arrived at the right moment, dissatisfaction over the classic full-length spring and summer coat which varied only from the winter edition in the weight of cloth was reflected in the decreasing sales. The almost unlimited choice of materials and colours to which the silicone finish could be applied provided the complete answer for showery or summer weather and sounded the death knell of the perennial tweeds.

The public was turning away from the symbolic tailored coat, high quality workmanship and cloths were no longer enough. Coat makers had always had a fierce pride in the fabrics they used, pure wool largely, weighted according to the season and there had to be a good reason for mixtures, but style and man-made fibres were combining to open the door to a host of cloths never previously considered as coming within the orbit of the children's coat manufacturers from synthetics to cottons. Surface interest and even washability was the talk of the day and where the siliconed showerproofs left off cotton duster coats took over. The short loose jackets were in and sweeping their way into fabric sources which had never been tapped for children's summer top-coats. In embossed cotton, when fully lined, they were demonstrably better than full-length coats in sober wools and working with cloths in sunny colours and stripes spurred designers, inspired by French *haute couture* to upset tradition and put short sleeves with turnback cuffs on jackets. They did the same with full-length duster coats, utilising similar materials and styles.

So old conventions were being broken in children's wear which was coming under increasing fire from parents, the trade and Press. Sizes for duster coats and duster coat and dress twosomes, still a novelty for girls, had later to be extended downwards to the one-year-olds, with sleeveless dresses and toning coats with three-quarter length sleeves, a departure for the tinies. It was not a simple operation to widen a size range, it frequently entailed extra work if the correct proportions were to be achieved and whilst parents might express interest in high-fashion for their infants they rarely wanted to pay for the skilled labour involved.

The silicone treated, showerproof cottons had revolutionised spring and summer coats and the natural outcome was that they would be carried over to winter. Quilted linings, fur fabric collars, cuffs and linings, allied to cotton outer cloths gave the requisite warmth and the ease with which the whole coats could be washed and dried restricted neither the design nor the colour and the rule of dark cloths for cold weather was broken by children in the palest of shades.

The short jacket of summer had become three-quarter (finger tip) length for girls for winter and it had to be chunky in heavy weight velours, meltons or camel in bright as well as dark colours. Fastening s.b. or d.b. deep turnback cuffs and collars were obligatory.

Double jersey started its triumphant progress. It was to prove immensely important for boys and girls. In synthetics and wool its lightness and warmth and recovery from careless handling were quickly recognised. For girls it had obvious advantages for coats and suits which were to become classic items for the younger ones. The square boxy jacket, s.b. fastening and peter pan collar usually with white overlay had the appealing asset of fitting all shapes and a happy knack of outlasting any fashion trends.

# CHAPTER 24
# The 1950s

Ever since the news of the fantastic Paris millinery had reached Britain after France was liberated hats had been in the news and this had a marked effect on young people's headwear, but it was the Paris collections in the spring of 1952 which had the most devastating result. It was then that half-hats were created. Head sizes were immaterial, the half-hat could be clipped on any head irrespective of hair style, no brims meant no tussles with gusty winds and the hat could be as fussily trimmed as the girls desired. This was one type of headwear that could be reproduced for girls without any strictures and it was, *ad nauseum*, for what seemed like an eternity. The interest in millinery rubbed off on to the youngsters and next year six-year-olds and upwards were acknowledged with a special hat range under its own brand name, smart bandbox label and copies, suitably scaled down, of Paris models. The main feature of this collection, aside from its refreshingly advanced styling, was that the proportions of the hats were adapted to young faces whilst being big enough for the head measurements which were almost identical to adult sizes.

Nevertheless millinery for most girls in the mid-50s meant a butcher boy cap cut with eight sections, with or without a tassel hanging from the centre, in bright colours and a variety of materials including suedette. The knitted hat had assumed a Quaker bonnet shape fitting snugly to the head and held in place by a metal band. Chunky stitches, vivid shades and swinging tassels turned this warm headwear into pretty toppers. Felt hats were subdued in comparison, small, and brims, if any, were turned up or back into a tight roll. They did not go so well with the growing casualness as did the knitted hats and butcher boy caps and were by no means as popular.

The New Look length had not been discarded by 1956 and in dresses there was no strong challenge to full skirts only for the older girls a compromise with a hint of the princess line in bands of self or contrast material coming from the side seams and tying in a bow over the bust, but the close fitting bodice continued. High bodices in contrast materials or colours set the line for frocks and, a big step this, matching jackets continued the theme, stopping short at the bustline and frequently upsetting convention by fastening down the back. The natural waist and full skirts continued but the length rose slightly. A direct result of the high bodice cut of the dresses and the short jackets was the emergence of the cummerbund. This not only hugged the waist and defined the line but filled the gap between the end of the brief jacket and the waist, providing, too, a splash of colour. It was especially effective for the younger sizes where the brief jackets could be copied but it was not easy to incorporate a high bodice with skirts which sprang from gathers at the waist.

The long torso line, or the dropped hipline, were the favourite terms in the mid-50s, bodices fitting snugly from shoulder to hip, breaking then into inverted or narrow box-pleated skirts. Vivid colours and black were sneaking into dresses and the pretty-pretty party frocks had a rival, separates in printed cord in rich, deep colours far removed from frothy pastels, but the latter continued to hold sway in a ballerina length (agleam with new fangled Lurex) which struck the right romantic note and, with dropped waistline, were in step with fashion.

The princess line was indicative of a move away from the natural waist which continued with the long torso line and predictably, at the end of '57 there was a switch to a straight look and the chemise or sack dress appeared on the scene for teens. Already being shown in Paris for the sub-teens the straight clean line for all its revelations of figure faults, more or less hitherto concealed, made the full skirts seem old-fashioned and lumpy and its adoption was inevitable in spite of the customary cries of horror and dismissal which arose. A natural outcome of the straight silhouette was a shorter length and those who had so vehemently opposed the New Look were the loudest in their condemnation of any raising of the hemline. The upshot was, of course, the shorter

*The torso line came in for girls no less than women and black was accepted in prints.*

length was in, the biggest switch for ten years. When it spread to tight skirts (and stiletto heels) shock waves swept over the country. Hostile store and shop buyers condemned the short skirts for the teens not on fashion but on moral grounds, others left the girls themselves to discover in time that puppy fat figures were not seen at their best in short tight skirts.

In keeping with the straight line came the sweater dress, a knitted tube bare of trimmings except for a narrow tie belt and not ideal for younger girls, but they did have one, in name only, so befitting their age group that it was worn for years and years, unaffected by adult fashion. The basic material was pure wool jersey, later double jersey. Neckline and cuffs were in knitted ribbing and a deep band of ribbing hugged the waist from which fell a full gathered skirt. The sleeves were full-length, the belt, if included, narrow and buckled. The secret of the success of this style was the ribbed waist, it fitted and flattered every girl and no amount of boisterous dashing about could disturb its neat appearance. The neckline might be varied slightly and tartans and checks join the plain cloths but the basic knitted waist just went on and on.

The advent of the chemise and sack was the beginning of the end of the voluminious stiffened waist slips but they died a lingering death. They gradually lost their layers of frilled net, replaced by stiff, crackly paper nylon reinforced with two or three hoops depending on the width of the dress, and along the road they had swept up the infants for in the end even the under-twos had their half slips. Meanwhile frilly underwear spoilt the smooth, straight dresses and soon children's chemise petticoats appeared, right down to the one-year-olds, dainty affairs falling straight through to a band of pastel ribbon, then finished with one or two frills at the hem, the effect somewhat marred by white interlock knickers showing through.

The pace of fashion was moving swiftly again and the current idiom was almost as important as the style itself. The sub-teens might not be able to wear the too severe chemise or the sack but they could the trapeze in which fullness started on the shoulders and, either through the stiffness of the material, or a lining, stood out from the body down to the knee-length hemline. Brief, square cut jackets topped these dresses, very plain but with the three-quarter sleeves unchanged. Coats responded well to the trapeze idea, deep turnback collars, big

*The trapeze line looked surprisingly attractive on the sub-teens.*

buttons, the wide clean line to the hem embodied the adult trends with surprisingly youthful results. Waistlines, banded and emphasised, dropped to the hips for those who wished to follow fashion and it was becoming increasingly apparent that both mothers and daughters wished to do so. Yet it was a strange paradox that until well into the 60s mothers were to resist slightly lower necklines for their daughters whilst the same girls were wearing beach outfits no whit less revealing than the women's.

The 50s had seen a great run on sun and fun wear. It started with sun dresses which followed the close fitting bodice and full skirted silhouette of the day but the tops were strapless kept up with light boning, or had narrow shoulder straps. Separate bolero jackets, small capes or deep collars, usually in strong colour contrast, converted the dresses into town wear. The tinies shared in this seaside gaiety minus, of course, the boned bodices. Sun dresses were considered very 'sophisticated' and by some mothers too much so but they were in fact quite serviceable with their double-duty purpose. Then came the bloomer swim, or play, suit with shirring in full swing and colours getting more and more exotic and swimming caps joined in, threw off the regulation image and adopted instead the flower decked helmets of the women. The play suits shrank to bikinis and mix-n'-match beach sets of minute proportions were accepted as 'cute' for holidays but the demure peter pan collar image lingered on for more sober occasions.

On the one hand girls were not only allowed, but encouraged, to imitate the startling brevity of the French Riveria but on the other hand were regarded as schoolchildren for whom fashion time had stood still. This was due almost entirely to the attitude of the makers concerned. In nightwear, for instance, girls had to wear to their increasing mortification striped coat jacket pyjamas, almost identical with their brothers', and their dissatisfaction was being reflected in a number of attempts to present alternatives in woven and interlock materials. Revolutionary among these were pyjamas with French porter tops, patch pockets and dolman sleeves in vivid blue, emerald and scarlet and they were adopted with alacrity. Interlock pyjamas were considerably enlivened by blouse tops instead of the humdrum V-neck and also 'pirate' pyjamas with fullness gathered on a high round neck, long sleeves and 'jeans' trousers, pedal-pusher length, with striped cuffs to match the top. Bright candy stripes on white replaced the conventional striping. Once established the design became a classic, sometimes called ski type, the length of the trousers varying with the times, and was copied, too, for nightdresses. For the older girl there were boat necks and short sleeves and a blouson fitting instead of loose tops to go with pedal-pusher trousers.

By the late 50s Italy and France were standing so high as style leaders in children's clothing that British manufacturers were entering into agreements either with established firms to make and sell under licence models for their collections or with individuals whose designs were making an impact on the Continent. Imports were popular because of the high standard of design and quality and for these the public was prepared to pay but imports at another level were to matter more in households, those from Hong Kong. Initially got out to a price and low-grade they were subsequently improved though not necessarily increased in price and knitwear, T-shirts, anoraks and nightwear from the colony were to have a strong position on the UK market.

Whatever the shortcomings of the British manufacturers of children's clothing they were enterprising enough to make history in 1957. The economic situation was grim and firms were being urged to export, Europe being the main target in view of the European Free Trade Plan. As sponsors of the highly successful parades of junior fashion at The Dorchester, *Junior Age* made the bold decision to stage a mini-version in Holland and for the first time children were taken to another country to model clothing. Strict legal formalities had to be observed on both sides of the Channel before permission was given for the trip, a hazardous journey as it turned out. The charter plane carrying the party overshot Schipol Airport twice in thick fog and had to return. A fortnight later a second attempt succeeded and the parade was held before an audience of store buyers from Belgium and Germany as well as Holland. The beautiful young models who travelled in their school uniforms, virtually unknown in Holland, captivated the Dutch Press which gave the show a wide coverage. The amount of business booked was impossible to gauge but of the interest aroused there could be no doubt.

The march of science and fashion might be transforming

their clothing but the little ones were as fond as ever of their fictional and real life heroes, excitingly extended to television personalities. Post-war youngsters were brought up in the television age. They were fascinated by the new media and their devotion to the lovable creatures presented for their entertainment was a pointer to the future. The Disney reign founded on films which these kiddies had never seen was being seriously challenged by competitors who shared the homes of their public.

Viewing at first was a special occasion and 'Telegowns' (housecoats-cum-dressing-gowns) forerunner of the one-piece cat suits, were created for the purpose. Once television was absorbed into the home and became part of the furnishings the novelty wore off and the idea of dressing-up to watch the box was forgotten except for one side effect. In those days friends and neighbours made a habit of dropping in to see the programmes and youngsters who were allowed to stay up as a treat but were already undressed and ready for bed had to have a respectable dressing-gown. The flurry of sales decreased as TV was installed in more homes or the nightly visitors wore out their welcome. Television characters such as 'Muffin the Mule' and 'Sooty' were to take their place as lasting sales attractions on a limited number of garments for the tinies, for another the fame was transitory but world-wide.

Through skill or chance entering the child's dream world could be a profitable business and as Walt Disney had found it in the past so he repeated his success in the mid-50s when he had boys and girls all over the world stalking around in fur caps with long bushy tails dangling down the sides. The expertise of Walt Disney's team guaranteed that the craze that had swept the USA after the film of frontiersman Davy Crockett's exploits was shown in a Walt Disney TV programme would spread to the UK. In America the adventures of the 'King of the Wild Frontier' had so captured the imagination of children up to the age of 12 that they wanted to imitate their hero. Boys and girls clamoured for copies of his coonskin cap and it sold in such numbers that rabbit fur was in great demand and there was a sinister drop in the cat population. Great Britain was not far behind America in sporting Davy Crockett's face on a multitude of articles from thonged trapper suits to tablets of soap. Nothing could have been further removed from Crockett's adventurous life than the school raincoat but one producer of this typically English unisex garment became a licensee, justification for the tie-up being found in a slogan, '*tough and dependable—like an Indian fighter*'.

No ordinary shop counter would suffice for this promotion, instead 'Trading Posts' were set up in stores throughout the country, to the delight of youngsters who had the thrill of seeing Davy Crockett in person when Fess Parker, who played the role in the film, visited Britain. It was a beautifully organised campaign, film, television and a theme song which went to the top of the Hit Parade and day after day reminded boys and girls of their wonder man and kept the interest going.

Not every attempt to woo the child with novelty was so successful. It appeared to be an inspired choice to put Ronald Searle's brilliant drawings of the 'Girls of St. Trinians' on cotton materials for children's dresses and separates, but it left the girls unmoved and never became the rage of the moment. The probable explanation was that the adults appreciated the satanic humour of the sketches—girls saw depicted their daily companions!

Children appearing in British films of the period gave a good indication of the adult conception of a typical British outfit. The child actresses' wardrobes were always understated to the point of dreariness and the aim was apparently to make their clothes as inconspicious as possible. Janette Scott was an established name in child roles and in demand as a photographic model but she was no style-setter and no one took an interest in her clothes.

The Coronation of Queen Elizabeth in 1953 whilst producing a predictable rash of tie-ups of a conventional patriotic nature, Union Jacks, crowns and much red, white and blue, had no real effect on the clothes children were wearing despite the publicity given to Prince Charles and Princess Anne ('Donald Duck's trip to see the Coronation' pattern on an apron was an extreme flight of fancy). There was scarcely a child in the land who did not have something already in red, white or blue and the Coronation outfits of the Prince and Princess reflected the current attire for special occasions. Charles had a suit in white silk with lace jabot and cuffs falling over his wrists and black Cromwell shoes similar to many seen on pages at Society weddings whilst Anne's lace dress with scallopped cap sleeves, ankle socks and plain shoes, were typical of any party-going outfit.

The Royal pair were closely watched but mothers were not easily persuaded to follow slavishly anything inappropriate for everyday life. It was left to the grannies to spend their money on dear little copies of a Royal ensemble as in the case of Princess Anne's coat, hat and muff set in green velvet trimmed with fur. The colour itself was against tradition and the dressy velvet a luxury normally reserved for 'best'. There was a certain interest in the muff, always appealing to small girls, but it caused no swing to its past glory. The Queen had shown before her preference for green but this did not break down the public's prejudice against it for children. The national Press quite naturally was quick to publicise anything the Princess was seen in (some of her hats were a strange choice and was it childish tantrums in the Royal household or an oversight that sent her out one day with the bows on the front of her hat and next, down the back?) but strangely enough she never equalled her brother's role as a style-setter.

The view that a confirmation frock was a special dress for one ceremony faded in the light of economic conditions and parents looked for styles reflecting current trends which could be worn on other occasions. Certain conventions were, however, observed. There were short sleeves for the venturesome few but variations were mainly in the fullness of the skirts and yoke detail and waists that could be covered later with colourful cummerbunds but the hand-faggoting, by tradition a symbol of the church service, remained. Roman Catholics maintained the practice of elaborate frocks and headdresses. Nylon had joined the silk and rayon nets for veils and the satin appliqués, flowers and crosses, embroidery and scalloped edges continued. As the years went by other church-goers took an increasingly practical view, aided by the onset of synthetics, and equipped their daughters in washable white pleated skirts, blouses and cardigans which would not be out of place for everyday wear.

*The confirmation dress with its distinctive hand-faggotting trimming went its classic way for years.*

# CHAPTER 25
# Colour Comes In and Stretch Yarns

Colour was increasingly a factor in children's clothing despite resistance to any departure from pastels and doubts as to whether strong tones were what the average mother wanted. Socks were a typical case in point. The striped hose for children being made in Italy had been seen and admired and after an interval during which it became clear that British mothers did not consider that broad stripes and bright colours were vulgar on little legs hosiery broke out of its understated white and pastel confines to become an attention-getter in its own right. After the stripes came the American inspired 'bobby dazzlers', ankle socks in screaming fluorescent colours which swept the country and offended school heads who regarded them as vulgar and garish and set the seal on their popularity by banning them.

Influence from abroad did not stop at the colour of the hose. A common sight on the Continent was kiddies in knee-high socks, kept in place by a narrow band of Lastex ribbing, the complete opposite of the heavy looking, three-quarter hose with deep turnover tops worn by girls and boys in Britain. It was certain that once tried out in the UK the Continental sock would becone established, as indeed it did, but with the emphasis at first for school on sober grey instead of the white favoured in France and elsewhere and quickly adopted as summer wear in Britain.

The advantages that synthetic yarns brought in the area of hosiery were manifold. On their own, or combined with natural fibres (nylon spliced heels and toes had given mothers their first insight into the shape of things to come) their strength was equal to all the demands of childhood and on one score alone they proved their worth they killed the cheap cotton sock which shrank in the wash and cramped growing toes, as big a menace as the too-small shoe. As stretch yarns were perfected they were greeted with acclamation, tough, non-shrink, felt free, easy to wash and dry, colourful and giving with, and not restricting, the feet they could hardly fail. Claims for stretchability were too wide at the outset with, for example, too many shoe sizes being spanned by one size sock but they settled down to realistic groupings later.

One-size gloves in stretch synthetics afforded equal opportunities of spanning an age group and adapting to growth. As with socks, gloves and mitts, enjoying a revival, in synthetic fabrics were easy to wash, hard-wearing and when fur fabric was developed, warm in winter. They were, too, considerably daintier for summer than the cotton variety, perhaps too fussy on occasion. Somehow English children, however impeccable in their tailored coats, never equalled the elegance of their French contemporaries who in dress or coat always wore beautifully fitted and expensive gloves as an integral part of their outfits.

The only people not enamoured of the post-war blessing of stretch were Customs and Excise who took a gloomy view of hose which kept within the maximum tax-free measurements when laid flat but expanded to take in bigger feet. Customs were, of course, to deal with this loophole.

It was in 1958 that the first tights for girls were imported into Britain and a new era had begun. Fully-fashioned in stretch nylon, covering the child from waist to toe, bridging the gap between socks or stockings and knickers, cutting out tight garters and bulky suspenders and, in heavier qualities, cosy and warm in winter, they had proved their worth on the Continent where they had been worn for years by children, mostly in white. The conservative British received them warily and they were slow to catch on, understandably since they were more expensive than stockings and one ladder ruined the whole garment but they were to become as indispensable to children as they were to women.

It was the stretch yarns which sounded the death knell for the swaddled baby in 1961 with the appearance in Britain of a Canadian import which was to sweep away the remnants of old theories about dressing baby. Stark in appearance with a minimum of seams, none at all armholes or shoulders, the article was made in a mixture of cotton and nylon with the texture of fine terry towelling. The garment covered the child from neck to toe, poppers throughout its length allowing for easy dressing and nappy changing. The fabric was light but warm and there were no washing problems and because of its elasticity it grew with the baby. This latter quality was not without its drawbacks. In the early days a few took the description too literally and went on using the suit until limbs were cramped inside a garment far too small. This was corrected by fuller information on the packaging emphasising the size limits of the child the garment was intended to fit.

There was resistance at first to the design, representing as it did a utilitarian covering with a collarless neckline and workmanlike fastening too reminiscent of grandfathers' combs to please fond mothers but once established the prettying-up process began. Inevitably the stretch terry coverall was adapted for other uses to spread into the realms of sleepwear and rival nightdresses, pyjamas and sleeping suits, and in the end was elevated to a major position. It was interesting that although such garments were to be available at various price levels people were prepared to pay for the better qualities. This was not entirely due to their better handle, the styles and colours were so good that they more than held their own against cheaper competition.

Stretch played a great role in bringing colour into infants' wear and colour did come creeping in. Babies and toddlers were already getting stronger colours for their dresses and these were seized by designers for contrast yokes, panels and hems to break up the plainness of whites and pastels and the clean lines were smarter for baby boys than the lighter colours and fancy smocking. There was a marked move towards indicating the masculinity of boys at the earliest possible moment. This led to the creation of the 'bocker' an advance on the conventional buster-romper and answer to criticism that this had too many buttons and buttonholes. The 'bocker' looked from the front to be a smart pair of bib-and-brace shorts but at the back the waist and legs were elasticated to provide the fullness to cover the nappy.

# CHAPTER 26
# To Follow Fashion or Not?

Whether to follow fashion or not, this was the question uppermost in the minds of everyone concerned with children's clothing in the late 50s and there could be only one answer but the hazards of keeping pace with the style-setters were becoming increasingly apparent. Just when the straight line was gaining ground the 'shirtwaister' dress came in, so called in *haute couture* circles but in reality the classic plain bodice, open neck and revers, natural waistline, gathered skirt and sleeves cut to three-quarter length, the prevailing vogue but it was just what the girls wanted, the seal of approval for the full skirts they loved and an excuse to hang on to those frilly half-slips. Happily the shirtwaister was at its best in the summer cottons of that period, floral patterned with roses rambling everywhere and mix-'n'-match prints beautifully colour-blended as right for girls as for women. The latter were mainly interested in gingham, elevated to world-wide fame by Brigitte Bardot but it had to be carefully handled for girls. There was scarcely a school uniform which did not include a gingham dress in pastel and white and contrary to past practice, women were wearing the sugar almond pinks, blues and greens and girls were choosing black and white ginghams. The glossy cottons, satinised, polished, sheen, supplied the perfect ground for rose prints and lifted the cotton frock out of the doldrums. Apart from the shirtwaister, skirts were flatter with stiffened interlinings or wide box pleats giving the width and enabling the beauty of the prints to be seen. Necklines were simple, boatline, almost straight across with only a slight curve but even this was sufficient for some mothers to dismiss them as too low (when the girls themselves were rebelling at the peter pan collar) especially when there were no sleeves either, and interest was concentrated on belts. These were wider,

*Horrifying to some, cut-away back and self flower instead of a chaste posy at the waist. An early 60s attempt to woo the sub-teens.*

stiffened and fastened in the centre with a flat bow or covered buckle, in self material they picked up the dominant colour of the print, the polished cotton gleaming like satin. The stiffened belt, narrowed in proportion, was copied for the smaller sizes but big and little sister had the alternative of cummerbunds which had not been ousted by the belts, rather they were improved by the rich colourings of the cotton. For winter brushed wool dresses repeated the theme with simple styling and self-covered belts. Coats were influenced by the broader belt and reiterated the line of the dresses, wide pleats held in by waist-hugging self-covered belts.

A more tolerant attitude towards necklines was taken over party dresses for older girls, lower ones being accepted as correct. Although they were designated 'party' dresses the term covered semi-formal frocks for the evening, the true party dress was slowly being confined to younger and younger girls. first to ten years then down to eight-year-olds.

The errand boy phase for hats continued, butcher boy caps, baker boy caps, with schools being urged by their senior pupils to adapt these in place of formal shapes. For out-of-school hours the current women's affection for Bretons, sailors and boaters affected girls' headwear. For them boaters worn straight on the head were covered in polka dotted material or white stiffened lace which softened the intentionally hard crisp straws favoured by the women. The stiffened lace was quite effective when left alone except for possibly a petersham band, but looked too fussy for the tinies when combined, as it often was, with posies of flowers, velvet ribbons, ruching and frilly nets underlining wavy brims. Whatever their qualities, price was the determining factor, hats came under the heading of extras so far as parents were concerned.

Bonnet shapes of pleated nylon were proving to be an admirable alternative to straw for summer for younger girls but sun hats for toddlers were criticised on the score of making the child's head hot because they did not absorbe perspiration as did the cotton paddy hat. Knitted headwear received fresh impetus from the talking point of the moment, skiing, and junior boys had benefited from the inclusion of stiffened peaks which, like the rest of the hat, were washable and meant they could have proper caps. Ponytail hair-dos had swept the land posing a problem for milliners but not for the makers of knitted Quaker, head-hugging bonnets, they left a hole at the back for the tail to go through.

The 60s were to witness the greatest upheaval in the attitude towards children's wear bringing about its most exciting phase, opposed by the diehards who clung to their belief that fashionable clothing for boys and girls was an evil leading the child away from innocent pursuits to precociousness and vanity. In reality it was the children who were changing and it was inevitable that this would be reflected in their dress.

In the early 60s conservatism had not been overcome, fashion inroads had not penetrated far as yet. The very word 'fashion' applied to children's clothes was abhorrent to some of their elders. One in particular voiced his objections over the air in 1963. A Minister of the Church he took strong exception to the inclusion of fashion in *Girl* comics published for ten-year-olds. Children of that age, he maintained, should be interested in playing games and not preoccupied with their appearance. In vain the other speaker, a journalist, pointed out that only one page was apportioned to advising girls how to make the best of themselves, the Reverend gentleman considered it morally damaging.

The girls had no style leaders as the boys had with the Beatles and the upsurge of fashion for men but there was no one powerful enough to exert a similar and widespread influence on girls' clothing. There were one or two big firms whose brand names could be found in every child's wardrobe but they did not set the fashion they wisely confined their production or distribution to 'safe' numbers on which they could get the long runs and steady sales which enabled them to stay in business in this most complex trade.

The continual disapproval in the national Press and lamentations on the shortcomings of children's clothing, often wholly justified from the consumer's viewpoint but making no allowance for the troubles which the trade faced, led a few of the big manufacturers of adult clothing to turn from time to time to the junior scene, confident that with their expertise they could succeed where evidently others had failed. Their efforts were well rewarded at first, the newspapers were enthusiastic, orders were good and everyone full of praise but after one or two seasons they quietly closed down the children's side. They had found, as others had done before, that the making of children's clothing involving complicated grading, highly skilled workers and collating of orders for manifold sizes and colours was an unprofitable business.

It was not the big adult firms who were to leave their mark. Stirring in the wings were the young people who were to overthrow all the old canons and give the final push into high-fashion turning London into an international centre for children's wear.

It cannot be said that the improvements in design and fabrics had brought noticeable changes in the appearance of British children for they touched but a fringe of the population. How a child was dressed out of school hours was a reflection of the mother's standards. By and large official uniforms were selected for their wearability and new materials, crease-resisting, permanent pleating, meant that pupils could remain neat throughout the rough-and-tumble of school life. Out of the classroom too many girls and boys looked as though their mothers had grabbed any garments which happened to be clean, or not-too-grubby, resulting in an odd mixture of school uniform and ordinary clothes with no regard for colour co-ordination or good grooming. It may be argued that there was no money left after the uniform was purchased but it does not explain the overall crumpled air of the girls, limp, unpressed hair ribbons, for example, in marked contrast to other countries. When youngsters were old enough to assert themselves about the clothes they wore and were able to take care of their garments there was a noticeable improvement. It used to be maintained that a mother who was immaculate spent all her time and money on herself and none on the child. Stand outside any shop where there are prams and a queue inside. The sparkling pram with a happy baby in clean clothes lying against a freshly laundered pillowcase, will belong to the woman shopper with tidy hair, careful make-up and immaculate clothes, not the woman whose hair has been hastily combed, frock hanging below her coat and run down heels. In both instances the women will have applied their own standards to their babies. It is rarely a question of money, in fact often the poorer the family the better the children are looked after.

As fashion filtered through to the babies and toddlers sleeveless shifts and the A-line of the 60s pushed high yokes and puff sleeves into the background. Dark checks introduced for winter dresses for the up-to-fives had elbow-length sleeves instead of the full-length hitherto considered vital and in brown and white or black and white were continued on lighter cloths for summer, a revolution in itself. This was as nothing compared with the big breakthrough in the early 60s, black

*A complete copy of the women's flapper pleated style, a delightful change for infants in the 60s.*

velvet down to one-year-olds. For the baby set was really with-it, their party wear was black velvet skimmer with a touch of lace at the neck and wrists of the long sleeves and white lacy tights. The shift for the tinies, a straight line culminating in a cluster of crisp pleats round chubby thighs had a charming air of frivolity. To be seen to advantage frocks had to be short and the pleated hems could not be let down. This was to cause a call for the 14ins. (36cms.) dress because it fitted the toddler better, as well as being short, and the mother's desire for the child to look her best overruled the folly of buying a frock which would soon be outgrown.

It was beginning to be understood that, handled carefully, mini copies of women's styles could be adapted happily for the up-to-sixes, dropped waistlines, low set pleats and tiny collars and ties could have an appeal of their own on wee girls. Babies twisted with the rest in the early 60s. The flapper pleats were replaced by ruffles for topicality and twist dresses could be bought for eighteen months to four years. The use of broderie-anglais with pale linings enhancing the pattern made some dresses every bit as dainty as their frilly predecessors. Typical of the fickleness of the public taste other cottons made a comeback for baby dresses the minimum-iron process being largely responsible. Mothers liked the whiteness of the natural fabric, its feel, soft but crisp, reminiscent of light starching. The short dresses to show off the baby pants shrank to 'angel tops', largely due to the Spanish influence, round neck, magyar cut, full bishop sleeves, these were to become the baby dress-ups of the future.

The scope in small boys' outfits was limited but ties were growing in importance. These were no obscure accessory, one manufacturer's range alone mustered 30 styles for toddler boys. Like their sisters they had their favourite make-believe characters and went to sleep in 'Noddy' patterned nightwear and perhaps it was the attraction of the characters that hid the need for their garments to be brightened up but eventually ribbed cuffs on pull-on tops and ribbed ankles on roomy trousers brought a tobaggon theme to the nursery.

When brushed synthetics were perfected they made a tremendous difference to nightwear. Fleecy lined materials had always been in demand for the younger generation, the teazling imparting a cosier handle to fabrics and to this was to be added, with the advent of man-made fibres, a dainty lightness on which frilly trimmings would not be out of place as they were on the brushed interlocks. Similar treatment was extended to underwear and petticoats for the tinies forsook their plain flannelette image for pastel pretties cosy enough to satisfy mothers who wanted heavier undergarments for winter. Nylon quilting had inspired designers to revolutionise dressing-gowns and create brunch coats (short housecoats) for infants to teens. Sweet floral patterned nylon, warmly quilted, was a formidable competitor to functional woollens and easy-washing (by hand or machine) and quick-drying properties allowed full freedom of design and trimmings took on a delicacy they had never had before.

As soon as the shortie length was established for dressing-gowns it spread to beach robes and the mid-calf style which had never been questioned before was rejected as frumpy and old-fashioned. When brushed nylon and nylon candlewick came along they set designers off on to a new tack unfettered by thoughts of weight or washability. As a result of this, lusty rival wool dressing-gowns broke away from the hackneyed crossover shapes to more feminine styles.

It was strange that infants' nightwear should be so stereotyped when novelty slippers were the rule rather than the exception, taking their inspiration from subjects as far apart as the furry animal kingdom to space travel with sufficient authentic detail to satisfy the sharp eyes of small boys.

Though apeing the adults might be frowned upon in some quarters the tinies were always allowed to have copies of their mothers' handbags, presumably on the grounds that these were toys. Whatever the reason, the makers kept abreast of *haute couture* and if the child's coat and dress did not reflect the passage of time her handbag certainly did with a rapidity on a par with the women's, reproducing faithfully shapes and colours, and, if on a cheaper scale, textures.

The thinking behind slippers and handbags was reflected in aprons and pinafores, a far cry from the white cottons with wing sleeves and tie backs which covered girls well after the 1914-18 war. Smocks with long sleeves aimed at protecting as much of the body as possible from paints, crayons and mud pies owed their origin to the overalls worn by French children. The styles progressed to tabards tying at the sides, workmanlike with good pockets to hold essential tools, enlivened with imaginative motifs. Tiny mites' preference was for pinnies, frilly affairs modelled on young brides' dainty bib-front concoctions. A sprinkling of glamorous aprons for the teens was around occasionally but price was a dominant factor and only inexpensive articles were acceptable, especially since girls had the greatest pleasure in wearing their mothers' aprons but as their dresses got smarter so did their pinafores and mini ties and flapper pleats were added even for babies from five months to two years.

By the beginning of 1960 the princess had been raised for girls' dresses to the Empire line, a grand name for an old friend, the contrast yoke. Coincidentally and similar in line the Baby Doll phenomenon percolated through to juniors. Prompted by the film it was one of the rare occasions when a sex symbol was adopted for youngsters and gained an air of innocent appeal especially on the toddlers. Party dresses were an obvious choice for the high fall from the yoke but it was in nightwear that the effect was greatest—and lasting. Pyjamas with short loose tops with tiny sleeves floating over trousers of

*Brushed nylon enabled winter nightwear to be as dainty as that for summer and continue the pretty baby doll style.*

minute proportions were bought for the tinies upwards. For winter nights, winceyette and brushed nylon replaced the frothy nylons and fine cottons, sleeves were three-quarter and trousers pedal-pusher length but common to the tops was the essential baby doll cut, gathers breaking from a high yoke and just covering the seat.

The dropped waist, hipline interest, held their own against the high line coats and dresses. Coats were wide and hiplines emphasised by seams or big patch pockets, the dresses with cuffed bands above pleats.

The leather look, genuine or most likely, simulated in vinyl, was everywhere and it was slowly being established despite Government disapproval that what the grown-ups wore the children could copy right down to the toddlers. At this stage the Continent was still important. The quality of design, colours and make of Continental firms allied to the build-up of trade fairs combined to create an individual European style for children's wear which had its origin in each country's distinctive abilities, Denmark raincoats, Italy knitwear and boys' wear, Spain baby wear, France *haute couture*, Britain tailoring. Europe had turned away from America with its apparent emphasis on mass-production and conformity. These influences did not manifestly affect the aspect of the child population. The tinies, true, had shed most of their cocoon of conventions and the teens were setting the pace but the bulk of the middle sizes were impervious to the ups and downs of fashion. In the matter of their clothes the teens had come to mean 17-19 years, the girl out at work, but as the years went by schoolgirls of 13-16 identified themselves with the older age group. The sub-teens were grouped as 8-12 or 11-15 years, depending on the manufacturer.

Out of school, sub-teens had almost another uniform for the winter, knitted hat close fitted to the face, swagger coat with fur fabric collar, Continental knee-high socks and black leather, one-bar shoes. The older girl was hatless, had a straight cut jacket with fur fabric shawl collar, chunky sweater, narrow box-pleated skirt, white Continental style ankle socks and pull-on shoes. For dresses they, or their mothers, clung to natural waists and gathered skirts.

Nylon stockings made their way down the age scale not without opposition from those who considered them too adult,

*A wrap-around nightdress with raglan sleeves, easier for mother to put on the baby.*

in or out of school. Ironically after girls had been complaining for years about being compelled to wear hateful black gym stockings as part of their uniform they were banned. In response to the girls' protests headmistresses had made concessions, light colours, fawn and beige replaced the loathed black until the Beatniks whooped in, part of the cult of the ugly exemplified by their black stockings. Any girl attending school in her old gym hose had no chance of getting past fierce school heads who regarded them now as 'too Beatnik'.

The patrons of the children's departments and shops had shrunk to a maximum of 12 years and these rebelled at the indignity. They could make their purchases elsewhere, mail order houses were winning increasing support from mothers. The firms had a highly developed sense of fashion and allowed no taboos to restrain their interpretations for children. Their in-depth knowledge of future trends in fabrics and styles rubbed off on to the junior side and the colourful reproductions in their catalogues and the extensive selection had a strong sales appeal. Coupled with the credit facilities it was no wonder that mothers found them hard to resist. In the main it was the above-infants' sizes which were bought from the general mail order firms, apart from the few specialist houses, mothers preferring personal shopping for baby wear.

By the 60s mother had been transformed from plain housewife to swinging chick. What the clinics advised counted with the expectant mother, not her own mother who was relegated to the background as not being with-it. The young wives who had grown up in a post-war period distinguished by its flood of discoveries to ease the work load of bringing-up children were not so concerned, as their mothers had been, with the longevity of garments, only with the convenience of the present. *'Can I put it in the washing machine?'* had superseded, *'Can I let it down and out?'*, and they wanted their toddlers to reflect their sometimes bizarre ideas on clothes. They were to get all they wanted with the advent of the New Young Designers in the mid-60s.

*This cotton duster coat and toning print dress was one of the first made for tiny girls from two years upwards.*

As casuals had ousted formality so co-ordination was to take over from piecemeal buying (even so matching wool coats and dresses for girls were not made until 1967). The co-ordination of apparel was largely brought about by the widening of cloth potential through the wash and wear capabilities of, and the inexhaustible openings for, synthetics and natural fibres. The heavy and light clothing production had moved closer together, coat makers taking on dresses and *vice versa*. As a consequence colour matching was inevitably facilitated aided by the advance in fast dyes and the stability of man-made fibres. It was a logical step to go on to add the finishing touch with hats, scarves and bags. It was the forerunner of the 'Total' look which some years later was to sweep women's wear. Co-ordination was ideal and had everything to recommend it but the price. Few mothers could, or would, pay for the whole outfit and most daughters were lucky to have two items which went together.

The square boxy jacket and pleated skirt had become the classic suit as had its predecessor the tailored costume but it was gradually becoming associated with the smaller sizes. Coats were losing their width and big buttoning to side fastenings and clusters of smaller buttons. Fur, natural and synthetic, was everywhere on collars, high round Victorian miss style, framing hoods, lining raincoats and quilted anoraks. The latter were brightening up considerably, the plain ones beginning to bore and multi-coloured patterns were substituted. The sub-teens were mad on skimmers and shifts as straight as they could force on their chubby bodies and they had won the must-have-a-sleeve battle. Paradoxically once the shift had begun to be seen around it almost seemed to be better for puppy-fat figures than the waisted frocks which cut them unkindly across the middle. They had slim underwear, too, slips sleek and trim down to a frilly hemline. Girls discarded their vests and the frilled half-slips were to disappear but in their long life they acclimatised girls to pretty underwear which had not been known before except for the moneyed few. Previously simplicity had been the rule for petticoats mainly to keep prices down but when full-length slips returned girls wanted them trimmed with the ribbons and laces to which they had now become accustomed. Yet fashion, ever perverse, resusitated an old woman's comfort, 'Long Johns', the knee-

*Departure from the hackneyed 'schoolgirl' costume, suit with straight line skirt and jacket, bracelet-length sleeves and cut-away collar.*

length knickers transformed in vivid nylon, lace edged and bow trimmed, which girls snapped up as avidly as their older sisters.

The gap between young girls' and women's bras and girdles was to narrow considerably. It became apparent that the limited demand for sub-teens' bras was insufficient to warrant the regular introduction of new styles as in the case of the teens' and women's foundations. One or two corsetry specialists retained the AA cup fitting and continued their excellent work

*As the outerwear changed, so did the underwear and baby girls from one year upwards had flapper slips to match their frocks.*

of keeping youngsters' needs in mind but the teens and women's models were so light and youthful that it was possible for girls to get something to fit their developing figures without difficulty. Because girls were larger A32 became the most popular first size bra. Whereas before the war girls had tried to disguise their developing figures, now they were proud of them and foam formed cups were included in AA fittings to help them on their way. Bras and belts (frilly bits of nonsense to hold up their nylons) had become essential for the 10-16-year-olds, the belts later to become obsolete as stockings were replaced by tights.

# CHAPTER 27
# The New Young Designers

It was early in the 60s that New Young Designers began to be noticed and by 1963 they were crashing through the taboos and conventions to create clothing for the tinies growing up in Swinging Britain. Fresh from art schools or the Royal College of Art they saw plenty of scope for brightening up kiddies' garments. Often having young children they did not regard parenthood as a reason to drop their individuality and unable to find what they wanted in the shops they were driven to create for their own or their friends' small children the same heady garb they themselves wore. Some opened boutiques to market their designs, others started modest manufacturing units to sell to the retail or through the post. The majority picked infants' sizes, the lovable stage, partly because they had their baby sons and daughters in mind; a few brave souls saw the gap and plunged for the in-betweens but none were keen to tackle the young teens.

So children's wear moved towards the completion of the full circle and boys and girls were once again to be dressed as their elders. From top to toe they copied the adults. Happily freedom was the lode star and there were no constricting corsets to hamper breathing nor layers of heavy materials which weighed down little bodies as in the past but fashion was to lead their feet into the wrong, sometimes dangerous, shoes.

Mothers, fathers, grannies and nannies—what they said was to matter no longer, from infancy girls and, surprisingly, boys, were to develop an awareness of fashion to an extraordinary degree and nothing short of their aspirations would suffice.

Although the media pounced on the New Young Designers with glee and gave unstinted editorial coverage to their work their actual impact at first was minimal. It was one thing to create way-out sensations for one child in one size but quite another to mass-produce profitably, however limited the production, and to grade sizes and train workers where inches mattered. The firms these newcomers set up were under-capitalised and the instigators learned the pitfalls of making a range which might extend from 14-40ins. (36-101cms.). They fell into the trap of trying to produce everything they were asked to, outer, under and nightwear, boys' and girls'. They were doing for children what their contemporaries were for women but they had greater problems to overcome. They were so advanced, too, that they could not hope to capture the bulk of the market. The cloths they chose, upholstery fabrics, curtain materials, black leather, colours, textures and weights never before used for any children let alone the tinies reflected their tastes alien to the thinking at the time. On the up-to-fours they put wide sleeves on dresses hitherto barred for fear they might catch on projections, they put on huge collars or left the necklines bare—trendy on a beautiful moppet but having a distressing tendency to make a plain child even plainer. So for a while the New Young Designers were dismissed as being too cranky to have a future but their talents were to revolutionise the junior scene and earn for the UK an international reputation as momentous in its way as the adults'.

The efforts of the New Young Designers received support from an unexpected quarter. In 1965 two collections were launched by the same manufacturer (Alexander Green Ltd.), an established dress firm, and the door to high-fashion which had been slowly opening was flung wide. Dramatically Cathy McGowan moved into children's clothing. Cathy McGowan was a TV idol of the moment sending viewers frantic as the hostess on a pop show for young people, 'Ready, Steady, Go.' Barbed wire fringe dangling over her eyes, she faced the cameras in a series of clothes which made her fans wild with envy. Many of the outfits she designed herself for the show and with fan mail running at 1,000 letters every week soon realised that copies of these and others could be marketed profitably under the Cathy McGowan label. She chose the right place to tell the world what 8-15-year-olds wanted to wear, the April 1965 *Junior Age* Parade at The Dorchester and trade buyers from overseas as well as the UK had their first shock—dresses four inches above the knee. Never had such short skirts been seen in London even on women (and they even embarrassed the young models). That was not all, some dresses had great holes cut in the sleeves. The length, the holes, these were attention-getters and food for critics but there was no doubt that her radical approach to designing was brilliant. She had gone outside the orthodox channels for materials, selecting from men's and women's houses cloths in dark, dull stripes and shirting checks. The hit was a shirt dress in Tattersall check West of England flannel, not the familiar tight-waisted, bunchy shirtwaister but a true shirt, straight up-and-down with pointed collar, centre buttoning, long sleeves, deep cuffs and breast-pocket, very simple, very clever. The straight up-and-down line formed the basis for other dresses in burnt orange corduroy or grey and white striped synthetics. She defied convention and reversed the fastening, buttoning the frocks the man's way. Waists were not defined but two-inch leather belts were slung way, way down the hips, anchored by tabs before they slipped to the hems. Her notions of how girls of 8-15 wanted to dress were derided—and copied.

Soon after, the manufacturer behind the Cathy McGowan enterprise, backed by a man-made fibre company, tied-up with Kikki Byrne already a name in women's wear for the Chelsea Look. This gifted designer conveyed in her work her fondness for children and she was talented enough to be able to introduce advanced styling without detracting from the youthfulness of the wearer. Her colour sense was extraordinary. She took black, bronze, olive green and white, caramel cavalry twill weave, mattress ticking stripes, velvet ribbon, shiny black shoe buttons and gilt ball buttons and turned out dresses for 7-14 years of exceptional charm and elegance. Her approach was quite the opposite of Cathy McGowan but both favoured straight lines, long sleeves and simplicity. A distinctive feature of Kikki Byrne's artistry was the high straight yoke and it was in her proportions, of collars and cuffs just that little bit deeper, that she showed her skill. Her collection was full of daring, culotte dresses, tweed trouser suits, city stripes, pie crust frilling, football dresses with wide contrast bands on the sleeves and deep crocheted collars on the most unlikely materials.

Mattress ticking stripes and shirts for schoolgirls?—it was a far cry from plain wool frocks in navy or red and children's clothing was never the same again.

Then things started to move. Junior fashion was going in every direction, there was Victoriana with feminine ruffles, but much saddle-stitched denim and black leather jerkins, popovers and French workman caps with high, full crowns or flat Danish caps for boys and girls alike. The caps matched the

*Mix-'n'-match had arrived for the eight-year-olds and upwards and if funds allowed hipster trousers, shorts and shift dress could be added to the items sketched.*

jerkins, the sweaters the tights, the Total look was spreading.

The following year the Junior Fashion Group of London was formed, a coterie of five firms, some new and small, others backed by experienced manufacturers, with a common object, to promote their unbridled originality. The Group was not content to concentrate on Britain it reversed the trend and tackled the Continent. There with a modest stand it showed for the first time at the *'Für das Kind'*, a trade fair in Cologne visited by buyers from overseas as well as Germany. The London Look of the Group, quite unlike anything seen at a trade show anywhere before, was pounced upon by the media but buyers were more cautious. After this initial sortie into overseas territory the Group went back next season with a devastating impact that shook Continental firms to the core. The Group's composite stand, sponsored by the Board of Trade, was in the advanced soot-and-whitewash technique thought way-out even for adults and their collections were equal to this sophisticated treatment. The creative talent of the Group's members was far ahead of any of the Continental companies and the colours exploded with a brilliance that blew the chaste blues and reds into the background. Buyers from the Common Market wanted to see this unique show and the Group's competitors were not slow to learn the lesson, for at the next Fair their stands were filled with the same 'shocking' colours but by this time the Group had moved on fashionwise, leaving the Continentals a season behind.

Across the Atlantic, American firms were turning their eyes to the children no less than the adults in Swinging Britain. News of the work of the New Young Designers had quickly spread and the 'London Look' was in for the USA. The situation was reversed, it was America which was importing from Britain, importing and making under licence for manufacturers had also realised the potential of these young people's ideas. Shops-within-shops sprang up in American stores and newspapers and TV enthusiastically welcomed the switched-on, zonky clothes. So good was Mary Louise, one of the earliest New Young Designers who had pioneered the breeching of fabric conventions and puff sleeve image, that she broke down the barriers in the USA against wool for children's dresses.

It was not only the feminine side that was in the news tiny boys were getting just as much attention and suddenly they had to be tough and manufacturers who had regarded their boys' sizes only as a rather troublesome sideline to the girls' were announcing the inauguration of special collections with suitably trendy trade names. Carnaby Street was beginning to mean something to the youngsters and the Street returned the compliment. In the middle of 1966 the first children's wear range was put on display in Carnaby Street when 'Kids in Gear' opened in the basement of the world-famous 'Gear' shop and tapestry brocades were the in-thing and the next year the Kids moved up the street to larger premises.

The widespread success of the 'Mary Poppins' film in the mid-60s and the expertise of the Walt Disney marketing team culminated in a flock of merchandise tying-up with the characters. Gimmicks like this fleetingly attracted attention but it was becoming increasingly apparent that fashion was the powerful pull for mother and child and not forced links with passing stunts.

Trade names reflected the changing children's scene. The make-believe world had lost its magical charm, the Pied Pipers took a different form, the lure replaced by aggressive, with-it titles, Mark One, His Nibs, Rave, Kinky Gear, 2ft and Trendy, Datesetters, Minitogs, Popchicks. The kiddiewinkies image for shops went and boutiques became Kids A Gogo, Guys and Dolls, Small Fry, Kids Togs. Wear became 'gear' and the formerly derisive kids took over from children in all walks of life. The word children itself became an anathema, the BBC dropped it for their long-standing radio programme and it in part forced the closure of the highly-regarded *Children's Newspaper* after 46 years, too few people wanted to buy it with that title.

The flower power people embraced the two-year-olds, complete with temple bells and one-year-olds had their caftans. There was nothing which could not be copied for youngsters, what the adults got their sons and daughters wanted. The one-year-olds had their mini-skirts—on braces, of course, tiny and sweet. Eight-inch (21cms.) authentic copies of tartan kilts wrapped round ten-month-old babies and older sisters wore the same length—like a pelmet. Baby's first dress, a minute 12ins. (31cms.) long, could be worn until she was two years old so accepted was the attenuated length. For the under one years angel tops and white lace tights were practically uniform but probably saved for outings, the stretch coveralls furnished babies' needs from the time they were born. The elaborate layette was gone but the desire to do more than just buy garments was by no means swamped, it was estimated that more than half of a baby's requirements was hand-knitted. Sleeves and collars were no longer compulsory for tinies, chalk stripes on gun metal challenged white crêpes and pastel smocked bodices. Play clothes became 'leisure' wear although boys and girls are never leisurely but it gave status to gear for out-of-school activities. Tailored trouser suits, slow to start and taking off in fits and starts, soon met the mood better than the full-length coat.

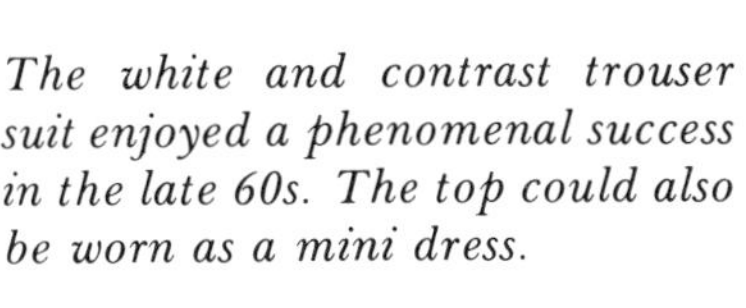

*The white and contrast trouser suit enjoyed a phenomenal success in the late 60s. The top could also be worn as a mini dress.*

Underwear was not left out. No sooner had the girls secured their feminine furbelows than they were off in another direction *à la* Mary Quant, stark simplicity in dark colours, navy and black for infants upwards with startling contrast appliqués of big bold flowers. Slips like this were cute to adult eyes how far they really pleased young girls is another matter. Nightwear designers took off on a fancy-free course, combined Bermuda shorts with baby doll tops, togas with slit sides in brilliant cotton prints over plain minute briefs, caftan shirts, baby doll tops over full-length trousers. For infants up to six there were chocolate coloured pyjamas, trimmed apricot. The caftan being around for dresses so it appeared for nightdresses and dressing-gowns, a warmly embracing alternative to the wrap-over or button-through.

*'Bunny Tops' in lacy 'Bri-Nylon' cuffed with genuine white fur for girls as young as three years were in marked contrast to the age-old party sock.*

The party dress as such for the in-betweens died, a shift with a deep hem of white feathers was more likely to be sported for festivities and feather boas were cuddled round little necks. Fashion terms were copied, somewhat ambitiously it is true, Dollybirds, Mods, Piccadilly prints, Op-Art, Mondian; sons and daughters followed the current crazes with the rest through the 60s. There were tut-tuts at applying the description 'Mods' in the mid-60s with its extreme connotations but smiles when the diminutive versions were paraded. This was one aspect, the picking up of current idiom but the New Young Designers had a character of their own. Although in tune with contemporary ideology they were an independent force thinking of, and for, boys and girls and it was the up-to-sixes who were the pacesetters.

The underlying sense of freedom and the emphasis on casuals had not come to mean a general sloppiness in dress. Compared with the severity of official uniforms it might appear that this was so but girls and boys in particular were studiously aware of the cut and fit of the moment and in their new-found vanity had no time for baggy garments for mucking about in. Loose in the right places, tight in the right places, anything else was out of the question.

Shoes could spoil the effect so these as well came under scrutiny. An expensive item in the family budget they could not be stretched as the socks to fit growing feet. Most schools stipulated some kind of sensible shoe and, together with the summer sandal, this normally sufficed but with fashion creeping in and daintier, colourful outerwear girls and boys, too, were rebelling against outdated footwear. It was not so easy to accommodate their wishes as it was with other clothing. It was essential that growing feet should have correct support and room to develop and opinions were firmly held about the damage that could be done by the wrong shoes, but eventually

*Casual footwear for schoolgirls met with bitter opposition at first but headmistresses were won over by compromises like this.*

the shoe manufacturers had to compromise (or, indeed, go out of business) and produce lighter, casual footwear and revise the sandal, not too drastically as to alarm parents or schools. This demand for fashionable shoes was to continue over the years and girls struggled to keep sling-backs on their feet until in the end the importance of correct footwear was brushed aside in favour of high-fashion for even the smallest toddler. Throughout each succeeding phase children's footwear kept pace, with boots, of course, promoted from a necessity to a fashion with special pairs for trouser suits, high laced in black or chukka style in mauve suede. When silver was the rage the ultra-conservative party Cromwell was right in there with it in silver, the high vamp and outsize silvery buckle even more in the clumpy idiom than much of the adult's footwear. Stretch, too, had penetrated party wear in silver and gold slippers. As it was the child who dictated purchases manufacturers could only endeavour to make shoes attractive to the boy or girl without sacrificing the sound principles of make on which they had spent so much time and money.

Babies' feet were to fare better. Lace-up shoes with high backs originating from America had been tried out and found to be an improvement staying on infants' feet better than the button-bar shoes which were apt to be sent flying by kicking limbs. Knitted bootees had a similar tendency. This hazard had been eased by a version which helped the transition from pram to floor. The soles were of soft leather, the uppers knitted like a sock with turnover tops which kept them anchored securely round the ankles. As the success of this principle grew other materials, such as nylon grosgrain, were introduced, the sole extended to form the whole of the shoe, but the knitted ribbing turnover top was retained.

Children's knitwear manufacturers had had to endure prolonged censure, not of quality but of design, in the post-war years. Their products were compared unfavourably with imports. The accusation that their colours were years behind trends had narrowed down to the equally damning, one season out of date. After having switched reluctantly from their characteristic fine knits to chunkies, when fine knit polo sweaters were demanded to go with tabards they only swung over after considerable pressure from shoppers. On the school front the classics continued, improved by the machine-washable qualities they had been given but slowly children's knitwear generally edged into fashion. The sweater dress, good for tinies and teens, not so happy on the in-betweens, provided a fillip to the conservative knitted dress but there was no determined and spectacular breakaway as there was on the woven side where the New Young Designers were busy. Then the Total look took over for youngsters in the autumn of 1966 and a galaxy of vivid colours and designs swept into being. Sweaters, long to the tops of the hips, and tights were vital to the co-ordinated outfits, skirts, jackets and coats were foils to their brilliance. Mix-and-match co-ordinates were at their height and so were skinny rib sweaters, high necks, long sleeves, tight ribbing, as far removed as possible from the chunky knits, and worn with hipster skirts. There was a great

*Knitted suits altered their sailor inspired image, jackets were restyled and lengthened, pleating fined down and colours blazed into brilliance.*

wave of V-neck, sleeveless pinafores and roll neck sweaters from toddlers upwards and there was no opposition to colour combinations such as grey/black/white harlequin patterns in a first size pinafore dress. Chaste white angel tops took on demonaic life when knitted in black with white shell edging and teamed with blazing red tights. The complete colour co-ordination achieved gave no hint of the extensive research

*Far removed from the days when beach wear meant a dress tucked into knickers; a bikini and brief jacket in floral printed terry towelling.*

which had been going on into dyeing and blending of natural and synthetic fibres of various weights and finishes required for the many garments involved in total co-relation.

Walking sets for infants forsook their plain colours and a single contrast or pale embroidery and blazoned forth in four-colour jacquard patterns for sweater tops over trousers tapered down from the toboggan widths. Small boys kept to the naval tradition but rose in rank to commodores and up to five-year-olds had knitted suits with d.b. jackets in the correct length in French navy, polo neck sweaters and long trousers with permanent front creases. Tights went berserk in multi-coloured bold patterns and so did knee-high socks and babies from six months got Nottingham lace tights in daisy patterns with an appropriate allowance in the seat for nappies.

*The simulated leather look arrived and four- to ten-year-olds could have gear like this.*

Against the background of high-fashion, easy-care and swinging chick mums it might be thought that the idea of a disposable layette which cut down the chores of caring for a new-born baby would have a rapturous welcome. In theory it looked good, a layette with a life of eight weeks, could be washed and drip-dried, costing approximately £7. The kit was a comprehensive one, bibs, angel tops, gowns, pram sheets and covers, plastic pants to hold disposable nappies, all sterilised and in a disposable bonded fibre fabric with a pastel spot pattern. This was to be the clothing of the future, cheap to buy, worn several times then thrown away, what more could be asked? Well, appearance for one thing. The garments in the disposable layette were made as attractive as their medium allowed which was not much but there was no disguising the fact that they looked like thin blotting paper. It would be a very cold-hearted woman who would contemplate wrapping-up her baby like a parcel. The disposable layette did not catch on. There were problems of manufacture with two or three companies involved which in the face of an obviously lukewarm reception there was no point in overcoming and the twentieth century layette never got off the ground.

The walls surrounding children's clothing from the adult world had not come tumbling down, they had been eroded bit by bit. How far the process contributed to the happiness and well-being of boys and girls is debatable. What is more important is that during the period 1939-70 the barefoot child was seen no more.

# CHAPTER 28
# Boys' Clothing

That fashion was restored to its former eminence as the dominant factor in women's clothing after the war was not surprising but it was altogether unexpected that boys would be drawn into its orbit. That hitherto ultra-conservative member of the community, the schoolboy, who in his early years wanted only to conform and later to copy Father at last became discontented with garments which were often ill-fitting (boys' measurements like the girls' altered but the sizes did not), uncomfortable to wear (short trousers which rubbed the backs of knees) and so drab that they depressed the wearers and the viewers. It was at this point that clothing for boys started to break away from its rigid confines and embark upon a fashion life of its own.

By the early 1950s change was in the air. Those manufacturers who leapt too far along the fashion road were to discover that it was just as unprofitable to be too soon as it was to be too late. The young male was not yet ready to accept too great a departure from custom and there was considerable opposition from those whose business lives had been bound up with preserving the tradition that individuality in dress was to be deplored. The tight-lipped criticism most often heard was '*too American*' and this was certainly true since the Wild West and its associations had a powerful appeal to young boys. The phrase '*too American*' went deeper than a dislike of another country's affect on the nation's clothing, 'American' in relation to apparel imported into the UK had come to mean, with notable exceptions, mass-production at its worst, flimsy cloths and poor workmanship with none of the durable qualities associated with British outfitting. Worst of all to the conservative retail buyers the clothes were in 'bad taste'.

A sudden crop of new ideas then, which threatened old values, was not wholly well received. Designs that were different were regarded as synonymous with cheap and vulgar and mothers who were very much inclined to seek guidance from outfitters over their sons' clothing also took this view. Nevertheless the revolution had begun. The full-length overcoat was losing ground to the duffle coat which supplied everything the boy required, warmth, freedom of movement, ability to take any amount of rough treatment, and because of its Naval history the right kind of masculine associations. There were reefer jackets, similarly nautically inspired, in navy with scarlet quilted linings. The lumber jacket's welted waist had given way to a longer length which covered the hips, offering another challenge to the full-length coat but not to the gaberdine raincoat which remained the most common wet weather wear.

Cut of jackets and trousers was studied instead of being mere repetitions of aged patterns, but these were not the breaks with tradition which were regarded unfavourably. The sources of inspiration responsible for a number of lines promoted for boys in the early 50s were the chief targets for censure. A typical trend owed its origin to the popularity of cowboys and Indians and amongst young boys bright check shirts, contrast yokes, white fringes and neckerchiefs offered a vivid and colourful contrast to unending grey flannel. Unfortunately it did not stop at bright shirts, the inhabitants of the Wild West were gun-toting, quick-on-the-draw fighters whether sheriffs or bad men and gun belts figured largely in promotion material depicting youngsters, stetsons proudly cocked, with guns at the ready. It was the time of the big days of the *Eagle* comic read by an estimated over two million children and the current hero Jeff Arnold in the 'Riders of the Range' series gave British backing to the American pioneer heroes. Shorts in tough drill had lasso throwing cowboys or rearing mustangs stencilled on the pockets, an inexpensive way to identify the tie-up and liven up an otherwise mundane garment, and other articles and accessories, belts and braces, bore motifs or badges similarly inspired. All, either obviously or by implication, were concerned with lives ruled by gun law and this was to prove the downfall of the cowboys' following in boys' clothing. Dramatically in 1953 the cowboy fell from hero to menace, knocked from his pinnacle by a blow from a totally unexpected quarter, the Craig and Bentley case in which a policeman was shot and killed. The controversy about the case remains but uppermost in the minds of mothers reading the account of the shooting was that the gun was held by a young boy and their immediate reaction was that their sons were not going to have anything to do with guns in any form, however innocent and playful.

The rest of the character merchandise linked with comics being worn at the time was not so affected, the less martial Dan Dare and his Spaceship offering fewer opportunities for imitation; jeans, windcheaters and so on were adorned with authentic motifs and Dan Dare suits included nothing more aggressive than improbable looking space guns not lethal, evidently, except in outer space, and bulbous helmets. Younger boys had their share of make-believe founded on comics, notably *Robin*, Walt Disney cartoons and, no less than their sisters, exciting television discoveries.

Character merchandise attracted the most attention because of its topical nature but except insofar as it reflected a bid for more adventurous boys' clothing it was not representative of the movement that was going on. The premise, accepted by the majority, that a modicum of style would not lead the wearer into evil ways, was resulting in small, but important improvements. Measurements were being modified to follow the proportions of the figure instead of the time-honoured room for growth (height and/or girth). Suits, trousers and shirts began to embody one or two features of the men's style leaders' in cloths never previously tailored for boys. By such means the transition from boy to man could be accomplished in a gradual manner. Hitherto the boy had been kept as a child for too long then plunged straight into the sober garb of the mature adult. The future held brighter prospects, however slowly they were to come to fruition.

Infant boys were helped to achieve a place in fashion by the attention given to everything worn by Prince Charles. Although his clothes were conservative in the extreme, with a strong bias towards hard-wearing, sensible boyproof articles owing nothing to regal finery, every item was hailed as out-of-the-ordinary by the national Press however long it had been in existence for little boys. The simple bow tie which finished the neck of his traditional buster suit was pounced upon as an innovation although buster suits had always had such bows. This did not stop them from being hailed as 'Prince Charles' bows and starting a new trade in separate ties. Occasionally the Prince did appear in an exclusive design which immediately provoked a demand for copies as, for instance, his miniature deerstalker. With no thought of another famous wearer, Sherlock Holmes, little boys began to stalk the country in this distinctive headgear with all the

*Pageboys' outfits hardly altered but they took a practical turn, the trousers could be shortened for 'best' and the lace-edged jabot removed when not required.*

advantages of the jockey cap and the added benefit of flaps to keep the ears warm. Most youngsters favoured the Stuart tartan for their deerstalkers but corduroy velvet in a rich dark brown ran it a close second.

Knitted garments worn by the Prince had many followers not only in Britain but all over the world both the patterns and styling being noteworthy in their own right. The Prince introduced broad lapels, double-breasted fastening and nautical brass buttons on a collarless middy jacket, a complete departure for knitted and even woven cardigans. The opportunities for following the Royal lead were wisely kept to a minimum but they brought this age group's clothing into the limelight with beneficial results.

The danger always in introducing any element of fashion for infant boys was that the result might be too girlish. That could not be said of an influx of fancy waistcoats which young boys sported in the 50s. Cut just like father's but in tartans—Stuart almost entirely—colourful checks and overchecks, Tattersall, pillar box red and camel they brought plain suits out of the doldrums. These were, of course, reserved for special occasions and on this score they were doubly welcome as mothers were becoming extremely vocal about the lack of party wear for their small sons. In sharp contrast to the abundance of pretty dresses for girls, fancy, frothy creations long established as a priority for all ages, boys (probably to their satisfaction) had no fancy dress-ups for festive occasions. A well-brushed suit and shoes and a clean face constituted the party-going preparations for most boys unless they had been pages at a wedding and had not grown out of their velvet trousers. In fact parents did not want their sons to go to parties in such fancy attire which would in any case have an extremely short life in the jellies and ice cream set, all they wanted was something unlike the everyday clothing and a good deal more colourful. Fancy waistcoats were ideal for this purpose and could be cleaned without detriment.

Boys' shorts for the above-infants' class were the object of growing dissatisfaction, European holidays convincing parents that their sons' baggy, knee-length knickers (and they were still called 'knickers' in 1956) contrasted unfavourably with the brief, well cut shorts of their Continental counterparts. Less tardy were the makers of boys' swimwear who copied the high-fashion trunks worn on the Continent. Miniature versions of men's swimwear, the boys' were in the same brilliant colours, boxer style or of a brevity never before seen on boys in Britain, and in gleaming satin finishes made possible by the progress in materials suitable for swimming.

Wearability rather than style continued to come first in the minds of the producers of British boys' wear. 'Terylene' and worsted materials were proving to be boy-resistant and this was regarded as of paramount importance. Nevertheless here and there fashion crept in. The inclusion of zips on self-supporting shorts in the middle 50s brought boys' wear another step along the road to adult attire. Boys' shirts were losing their tails, replaced by straight end coat styles which could be tucked inside, or left flapping outside their trousers, a shocking sight to the older generation. It did not stop with the older boys, for summer younger ones who would have been the buster suit brigade coping with a plethora of buttons were transformed in loose square cut pullover shirts with pointed collars and adjustable necklines instead of the babyish peter pan collar, and these were teamed with well-tailored shorts ironically much smarter than their older brothers'. Separate shirts for small boys had always been shaped, and rightly described, as blouses but at long last the elastic at the waist was being removed and the shirt lengthened in the proper masculine manner.

For generations the white cotton lining of boys' caps had tended to peep below the wool material of the top and no one had really cared until a young set of mothers who did not believe that 'boys' and 'scruffy' were synonymous, started to complain. As a result a patented method of incorporating the lining, or fused linings, which stayed concealed under the outer cloth came on the market.

It is true to say that during this period any progress in styling that was made was accomplished in the teeth of strong opposition from those who deprecated any attempt to introduce an element of fashion into boys' clothing on moral grounds and a reluctance to stir themselves out of the rut in which they had slumbered happily for so long. It was some years before the minority who had the courage and determination to produce garments which were modestly slanted towards an understanding of the post-war boy and his pursuits received the support they deserved and for some the interval was financially disastrous.

Fortunately for the boy, jeans and sweaters sufficed to meet the prevailing careless casuals mood. Sober jerseys were being transformed for instead of the dull pullovers whose main purpose was to provide warmth and not show the dirt there were Scandinavian-inspired sweaters in chunky knits with crewe necks and below, bands of vivid contrast round the body and over the sleeves forming a continuous line when worn. Interest was centred on these bands and from plain colours they progressed to intricate embroideries in wool, an idea which a few years before would have disgusted the average British schoolboy. For some reason the simple inclusion of this contrast had a husky masculine appearance which relegated the grey sweater to feeble schoolkids.

The shortie, car or scooter coat was presenting the first real competitor to duffles which were going strong in 1961 and again synthetics had had their effect. Fur fabric collars and linings, which would have been abhorrent to boys not so long

*Boys were quick to adopt the shortie coat, preferring it to long overcoats which flapped round their legs.*

before, were being worn by all ages. Son followed father and soon father was following the Italians. This was the big breakthrough for the boys. They had not been allowed to copy the immediate post-war style-setter, the Teddy Boy, a far from benign influence. The merest suggestion of narrowed trouser legs spelt drainpipes and was immediately stamped upon in the classroom, but the Italians in the 50s had achieved a reputation for good taste. True, their men's wear was sharper, sleeker, dandier in concept than the British male was accustomed to but it was elegant and had no sinister razor gang connotations. The Italian was the more fitted line for coats and suits, lapels were narrower, the buttoning higher, and buttons self covered. Materials were smoother and there was less of the rugged he-man appearance. Trousers were slimmer and one inch above the shoe to show the sock.

Here was a trend which was introduced with discretion and quickly captured the boys' admiration. They liked the elegant suits and coats which identified them with the men, their parents approved since slicked down hair and polished shoes were by-products of their son's graduation into fashion but were less enamoured of the fact that the boys considered a second wardrobe necessary, refusing to give up the casuals so indispensable to their activities. The standard dress for the up to eight or nine-year-olds was still gaberdine raincoat over grey suit, short trousers, three-quarter TOT hose and lace-up shoes, all obviously school wear, indicating that uniforms had to do double duty. Outfits bought with money remaining from compulsory purchases were carefully reserved for special occasions. Over nine there was a slight variation, hip-length jackets, check or plain, with zip fronts, grey flannel trousers, not noticeably influenced by current trends and obviously 'school' and regulation black shoes. The over-nines, too, reserved their extras for special purposes. Shirts, in whatever age group, were plain, white or grey.

The Italian influence gained ground and spread until five-year-olds had self-covered buttons on their suits. Schools were not prepared to give way and trouser widths caused controversy. Boys wanted their uniform longs to be narrow but headmasters disapproved of drainpipes. In the end the heads compromised and allowed some paring down but not much. There was no room on this elegant attire for badges and emblems identifying with a fictional or real life hero. Sophistication was there to stay, except for a sortie into '*Just William's*' adventurous existence. BBC television ran a series based on the Richmal Crompton books and a man-made fibre firm signed up the star, Dennis Gilmore, to promote casual wear. Wicked grin, freckles, cap askew, an obvious contempt for clothes, these attributes would not appear to be the obvious choice to promote garments but they certainly conveyed their boy-resistant toughness.

*Short wrap-over, dressing-gown and matching pyjamas in stunning colour combination, an idea which would have appalled boys only a few years before.*

Underwear was imitating Father's with athletic vests, trunks and briefs with cutaway sides for 6-15-year-olds to wear under their slimmer suits. Boys' pyjamas picked up the allover mini-paisley prints of their fathers for pullover and jacket styles.

True dandies rounded off their wardrobes with hats but these were in the minority, the means though were there, for headgear was apeing the elders' preference for snap brims,

*When fathers' hats livened up so did the boys' but interest in headgear was minimal.*

braid bands and side feathers youthful enough fortunately for youngsters and for fond mothers who were imitating the American practice of putting small sons in hats. When men took to wearing fut hats there were Nehru versions in fur fabric for the boys but this was one fashion in which they were not interested. Pageboys were not left out of this fashion surge, they kept their lace jabots, long sleeve blouses but their velvet trousers were tapered to the ankle like their brothers'. Pockets of resistance remained. Notwithstanding the full-length trousers and trews worn from infancy, schools were clinging to shorts for the junior lads as a demarcation line of seniority.

Nevertheless the principle had been firmly established, male garb was for all ages not just the adults. Dignified firms started to refer to their 'Mod' numbers and the farther down the age scale the better they were received. Mini versions of this controversial cult were regarded as amusing rather than menacing, Twist jackets with fancy linings which would have shocked a few years before were accepted as a matter of course. When the Beatles erupted on the scene it was not only the famous black leather which won adherents. The high buttoning, collarless round neck jacket without lapels was copied for suits down to three years—so was the tape finish, the open, one-button cuff and the cutaway front for older boys who also sported the black leather jackets and John Lennon peaked caps to match. Boys had their shoestring ties in grained pvc with help in tying the bow, this was held in place with a centre gilt ring and kept round the neck with elastic.

It took longer for Customs and Excise to give in. It was not until 1968 that they agreed a more generous tax-free measurement for classic polo neck shirts, unconvinced until then that these were suitable for boys but by this time the choice for shirts had widened to unfettered colourings and patterns for peacocks who had travelled far from the grey image days.

Wherever Customs were housed it was evidently not Swinging Britain for already Carnaby Street was achieving world-wide fame for its mini-versions of way-out gear. People were crowding in to buy kinky klobber for tiny boys, in the heavy brocades and flower power patterns. For a while the middle sizes were left out but inexorably they were drawn in, the only difference between their clothes and the men's being the size and the boys paraded home with pride their Carnaby Street paper carriers. The creaking advances over the years had conditioned parents into accepting that boys should not be kept down to their own notions of childhood. Far from taking no interest the boy was turning into a highly fashionable animal who was to spend as much time and money on clothes (and his hair style) as his sister, if not more. The Carnaby Street extremes were the chocolate cakes, but the solid fare of everyday clothing was affected forever. Other forces were to make their mark among them the New Young Designers who worked on boys' as well as girls' clothing and although in total their output was insignificant like Carnaby Street the effect was great. Where they differed from Carnaby Street was that they did not see the child as a copy of the man but as a boy with his own identity and life-style. They pictured him in his earliest years as a tough, larger than life character who had not yet fined down. Cowboys and Indians played no part, it was Blood and Sand, the desert and the jungle. The end had come, there were no shibboleths left to observe in boys' out-of-school clothing.

# CHAPTER 29
# School Uniforms

The old school tie tradition was faithfully upheld in the early days of the war, not that this word was used, the Government itself had set the tone by coyly referring to the 'emergency' in official proclamations and school outfitters took an equally calm and seemingly contemptuous view of World War II. A masterpiece of understatement was expressed in a circular letter sent out by one famous firm of school outfitters two days after war was declared and Britain was expecting to be devastated by Goering's bombers. '*In the present disturbing conditions*', the letter began, '*you may find it inconvenient to bring the children to London*'. The letter went on to remind the customer that the shop's record of sizes and '*all past transactions is so very complete and you need have no hesitation in ordering by post*'. (Alas, a bomb during the blitz blasted quite a few of the facts out of the files.) There was no flag waving nor fanfare of trumpets for the men marching off to war; '*Our staff*', customers were informed, '*is reduced by the necessities of National Service*'.

Despite this business-as-usual front it seemed that official uniforms would soon disappear. The immediate reaction was to tell children that they were no longer required to wear regulation outfits but to make-do with any suitable garments they had available. Predictably this brought a strong reaction from the outfitters who urged schools not to change their uniforms as this would mean that raw materials already used and labour employed in producing the garments would be wasted, and others would have to be made in their place. To scrap the uniform would be a mistaken policy of economy. It was argued that if all schools abandoned existing uniforms for something quite different 'the result upon the quantities, reserves and consumption of raw materials would be colossal'.

It could be claimed that the materials and garments could just as easily be used for some other purpose but in fact it was true that most would have been wasted. The specially dyed cloths which, combined with the styling, contrast piping and embroidery, might be wholly effective when worn by a body of schoolchildren would have looked completely out of place on a lone boy or girl. The logical outcome was for the stocks of school uniforms and the fabrics to run down until they were completely exhausted, replacement being impossible during wartime, but it did not work out like that. The uniform was fought for and treasured, there was a slight relaxation of the rules, a substitution here and a change there but overall most schools came through the war with their uniforms if not intact at least still recognisable.

Boys probably made the biggest sacrifice—a welcome one no doubt—as black jackets, waistcoats and striped trousers were replaced by lumberjackets and shorts. Some movement along these lines had already been felt before the war because of the influence of Stowe. Boys' public schools, surprisingly, were far in advance of the girls', swinging away from the hidebound conventions of the past to a new freedom 'based upon the theory that clothes possessing a proper regard for the principles of hygiene and freedom are as important to a boy's moral and physical welfare as modern sanitation and ventilation', as one school outfitter put it. A typical uniform of this type comprised wide leg shorts in blue-grey union flannel, shirt with open neck in blue grey flannel, lumber jacket in blue-grey in all-wool flannel with elastic webbing at waistband and zipp front, blue grey, all-wool 'golf' stockings. Other colours were available but blue-grey was most popular.

Despite the appeal of these practical and comfortable uniforms the schools adopting them were in a minority when war broke out. In 1940 Eton was clinging tenaciously to its distinguished uniform. Boys up to, but not including, 5ft 3ins. (1.6 metres), wore Etons—short jacket and long trousers, Eton collar (stiff white), black tie and black or dark socks. Boys 5ft.3ins. (1.6 metres) and over all wore tails and, in every case, a waistcoat. Their collars were double, turned-down and pointed of a special shape that fitted inside the waistcoat. Their narrow white cambric bows were inexpensive and thrown away when soiled. Only special categories, prefects,

6th form, rowing and boxing teams, were allowed to wear dress wing collars with double thistle and white dress bows. The boys had to wear shirts of white linen with double cuffs, all the year round. If any boy wanted a flannel shirt then it had to have a linen front sewn on to show at the neck and linen cuffs. Some houses allowed white cellular shirts to be worn during the day.

Sports coats were in browns or greys. Grey flannel trousers had to be in a dark shade as lighter greys were only allowed for the special categories already mentioned. Overcoats were double-breasted and had to be black or black-grey. As a wartime measure navy velour overcoats were *permitted* but it was made clear that black was *preferred.*

It was not only the public schools which were determined not to allow dress standards to decline. In state-aided schools in some parts of the country girls were not permitted to wear trousers and headmistresses were given the right to bar anyone wearing them from attending school if they persisted in doing so.

As the bombing drove the public and private schools away from the danger zones host schools offered them accommodation in 'safe' areas. Two schools might combine in shared premises for the duration but staff and pupils alike zealously guarded their separate identities and one way of making this apparent was by retaining individual uniforms. Thus a potent reason for striving to get the exclusive colours and styles existed in spite of wartime conditions. This had good backing from outfitters who, not wishing to lose the business when a school was evacuated to a safe area, kept contact with them in their new homes and continued to handle their clothing requirements.

Gradually the strongholds were eroded but every possible means of preserving peacetime rules was explored. In fact it was not until 1947, two years after the war ended, that one college conceded that owing to the difficulty of obtaining starch soft white collars would be worn instead of the hallowed stiff ones. More and more pupils, were, however, going back to school without all the items in their uniforms, a situation virtually unknown before the war when outfitters prided themselves on fully kitting out every one of their schools before term-time but the significant factor was that parents were prepared to wait for the correct garments to come through and not purchase substitutes which even in those times would have been regarded as unacceptable.

The schools themselves, particularly the private ones, were largely responsible for this attitude: they inclined to take the view that if mothers tried hard enough they would be able to get the items required. School lists were cut, but often the pruning was less than drastic. One boys' school reduced the number of shirts from six to four, three blazers to one and pairs of shorts from four to two. Many school lists, even two years after the war began, had an air of unreality about them, seemingly remote from the outside world of short supplies and coupons which had added a new complication. State-aided grammar school lists of compulsory clothing could entail an outlay of one-third or more coupons than a child's total allocation. The worry caused to parents trying to comply with these demands led the Board of Education to circularise schools and local authorities drawing their attention to the necessity to reduce the clothing needs to a more practical level, but the Board could only make suggestions not compel changes to be made.

There can be no doubt that in peacetime official school clothing lists were carried to extremes. One girls' private school insisted on four summer dresses in addition to the basic uniform, printed shantung, gingham, navy shantung with lace collar and speech day frock of cream shantung. Destined only to be worn in the summer months and rarely in the case of the cream shantung, no amount of letting out and down would enable them to be outworn before outgrown. Education achievements were not always the main consideration in selecting a school, regrettably there were parents who made their choice solely on the appearance of the uniform. Perhaps, however, it was not such a bad criterion for a pleasing uniform might reflect good sense in academic matters as well. Boys of this period showed little concern over their clothes whether in or out of the classroom but official outfitters noticed that when they were being kitted out for their first school although the garments themselves were regarded with indifference they evinced great pleasure in the colour of the uniform.

Being appointed the sole supplier, or even one of two suppliers, of a uniform which hundreds of pupils were forced to purchase was not the guarantee of easy profits which it appeared to be from the outside. Of course there was money to be made otherwise retailers would not have pursued the business with persistent approaches to school heads, offering new ideas, materials, greater service and keener prices but the securing of a contract carried with it much responsibility and involved an appreciable outlay in time, care and labour which whittled away some of the profit margin in a manner unknown in other clothing departments. Store managements regarded the school trade as a means of getting the customer into the store thus opening the door for sales of other goods for the family and by catching the child young, making it a customer for life. In fact it often worked the opposite way for children who disliked their uniform irrevocably associated it with the store and once their schooldays were over never wanted to enter the place again.

A tremendous strain was put on the staff of the departments, and the actual manning was in itself a problem since the demand was concentrated in the vacations and human nature being what it is, no one wanted to think about buying the uniform until the holidays were nearly over (providing the money was also a factor) and then parents flocked into the stores and shops complaining vociferously if the items were not available in the right sizes. Although these tardy people would seem to be unreasonable in expecting their requirements to be met at the last moment they were not entirely in the wrong. If an outfitter had entered into a contract to supply uniforms for an entire school then it was up to the firm to see that the garments were there when they were wanted and not expect parents to place orders in advance if they did not wish to do so.

The snags encountered by retailers were also experienced by manufacturers who had additional problems. Proof that making uniforms was not an easy road to amassing a fortune was given by the inadequate number of firms specialising in this trade. Many of the producers of juvenile coats, suits and dresses turned out standard blazers, grey flannel suits, navy nap coats and gym. tunics but there were only a handful of companies engaged in supplying distinctive uniforms exclusive to each school and several of the best-known were to disappear after the war. Where an industry remains small and attracts no newcomers it is a sure sign that the problems are greater than the returns.

Not least of the disadvantages for both suppliers and retailers was the constant effort of trying to please school heads who took a lofty view of their calling and could not, or would not, understand the limitations of 'trade'. Teachers could not be expected to know of the expense involved when only slight alterations were called for. Change for change sake was sometimes the reason for requests for variations but there came a time when the most conservative schools had to pay some regard to fashion. The exact size of the school hat, crown, brim and hatband, for example, carried its own menace. The deep, full-rounded crown had become completely out-of-date by 1939. There were headmistresses who were unaware of this regarding school wear as being quite outside the flippancies of fashion (and in this were encouraged by manufacturers who knew what modifications entailed) but others who recognised that girls detested the frumpish headwear asked for the crown to be made smaller. Lowering the top of the hat by as little as a quarter-of-an-inch necessitated the installation of new equipment for which, eventually, parents had to pay.

Amongst the hidden and costly work associated with school outfitting, almost unknown to the public, was the investigation and testing of possible cloths—wearability, colour fastness and so on—which might be considered suitable either by the head or the suppliers. Take, for instance, a gingham cloth: a sample would be sent to a typical laundry to be washed and ironed 100 times, the equivalent of a weekly wash over a period of eight school terms. Only if the cloth showed no signs of deterioration in colour or quality would it be included in the outfitter's school catalogue. Colour fastness was extremely important for a school where the purpose of the uniform was that it should be the same shade and not display a colour loss varying from the strong original to a faded version of its former glory and, incidentally, revealing the age of the garment to the embarrassment of the wearer.

Headmistresses—and masters—had often to be steered away from fabrics which although presenting a good appearance proved after testing to be inadequate for the rigours of school life however genteel the establishment. Styling, too, was a matter for discreet guidance, particularly where the resident art mistress rather fancied herself as a dress designer. The comments sent with the interpretations of someone's well-meaning arty-crafty ideas, so good on paper, revealed nothing of the storms which raged in the clothing factories. All this was hidden when finally a sample was submitted to the school but how much can be guessed from this extract from a letter sent to a girls' college. '*There was a little difficulty in attaching the top button of the neck opening in the position agreed as we could not get it high enough to close the collar neatly. There was a tendency for the latter to roll downwards. So we have devised a small tab which seems to solve the problem quite effectively.*'

Details which might be regarded as expensive extras were recommended by good suppliers because they would prove cheaper in the long run: the stripes down the sides of the black trousers compulsory in boys' boarding schools were of pure silk as this wore better and did not crease. Pure silk was also used for sewing seams because it lasted longer. On the other hand school heads would often insist upon expensive handwork where it was totally unnecessary and served solely to satisfy their ego and disdain of mass-production. In vain outfitters would point out that beautiful, intricate crests would increase the price considerably and by dropping one or two colours, embroidery charges could be reduced, or a different finish for the blazer edge would cut costs and production time. All too frequently schools were not prepared to sacrifice face value for economy and suppliers were blamed for high prices.

It was by giving good advice on how to choose a uniform wisely that stores and shops built their reputations and enlarged their clientele. One London outfitter alone was the official supplier for 565 public, private, preparatory and secondary schools in 1936. They were not necessarily, of course, the sole suppliers, frequently a second source, often in the locality of the school, was also appointed. There were schools who ran their own shops either in conjunction with, or in opposition to, the official outfitters and in the 30s the National Association of Outfitters estimated that uniforms worth seven million pounds were purchased from these outlets. It was to be expected that official outfitters whose livelihood largely depended on their sales of uniforms should be bitterly opposed to schools usurping their position but the most important question was whether the parents benefited. Being able to purchase the clothing through the school or its shop in the vicinity was a great convenience, more often than not obviating the necessity for a trip to a city retailer, or indeed, to London. Official outfitters did, however, send experienced personnel to the schools to check on present and future requirements. From the heads' point of view in running a shop they had the burden of obtaining, and maintaining, the right type of supply, never an easy task and an incredibly difficult one in wartime, then the resources behind the established retailers and their ability to obtain the right goods or satisfactory substitutes proved to be valuable assets.

By 1941 it was realised that it was not going to be possible to get replacement of uniform items for pupils, or to provide them for new scholars, unless the dwindling supplies were augmented and a fresh source found. Now at last those lengthy official clothing lists proved to be of service and the outgrown before outworn garments to be of particular value. Private and public schools appealed to old boys—and girls—to turn in their discarded uniforms and even their old school ties. This was the beginning of a scheme which not only helped parents over coupons but also ensured that the fullest possible wear was obtained from every garment. The Board of Trade gave its official blessing to the idea of passing on school uniforms which had been outgrown and put into operation a licensing system whereby retailers could buy secondhand uniforms and sell them to pupils of the same school without charging coupons even if they were sold above the permitted selling price. (Secondhand clothing could only be sold without coupons if it were below a certain price level which for obvious reason was set very low.) School heads had to nominate the outfitters they wished to operate the scheme for them and it worked extremely well. A number of schools preferred to run their own shops for secondhand clothes but with the co-operation of the local outfitter who operated a system of selling to the shop and crediting the parents' accounts. State-aided schools ran children's clothing and shoe exchanges, all with the active encouragement of the BOT.

Lack of supplies of headwear had naturally affected uniforms since every school which had any pretensions to an official outfit at all always included a hat or cap. In many state-aided schools the uniform was compulsory and even by 1943 had not been waived, on the contrary there was just as strong a feeling that standards should not be allowed to slip as there was in the public and private sectors. Despite this the Board of Education felt there should be some relaxation so far as headwear was concerned and asked Local Education Authorities to review the policy of directing that a special style of hat or cap should be worn. The memorandum from the Board was couched in mild terms with no hint that they had full powers to decree that uniform hats and caps be discontinued.

In common with the rest of the children's clothing it took years before supplies of uniforms were restored to normal and as wartime sufferings faded official outfits had a stormy passage with critics of style and price on the rampage. Claims of low quality and high prices, prompted more by emotion than hard facts, were proved to have no substance but not before a ding-dong battle had ensued. August, the silly season for the national Press, was the month for regular appearances of attacks on uniforms in general. It was significant that one chain store held up as the ideal provider of school wear tackled the subject extremely delicately selling only one or two standard articles in a limited size range and resisted any temptation to extend their selection. There was a strong element of political bias in the attacks on uniforms certainly the excesses in some private and public schools were to be regretted but parents did not have to patronise those establishments. Privately many mothers were thankful that the question of what to wear for school was settled and not the subject of daily argument or the continual paying out to keep up with the Joneses but parents did resent being forced to buy what and where at the schools' dictation.

Buying the whole outfit together made the outlay more painful than if the items were bought piecemeal as required. That the child would already possess underwear, nightwear, and so on as part of the ordinary wardrobe and it would not be necessary to purchase these articles was frequently overlooked when the lists were examined. That the bulk of the garments were better-made and in better materials than could be obtained generally was also disregarded. It was customary for holders of school contracts to give immediate credit even if the fault was obviously the wearer's. An outfitter took it as a matter of course that parents counted on a uniform being wearable five days a week for more than two years. A serge tunic was expected to last for a minimum of four years or more and it was not unknown for cotton frocks to be handed down through the school lives of first, second and third sisters. The higher up the social scale the more careful parents were in this respect. Holiday time trunks of school clothes would be sent to outfitters for repair in time for next term.

The blazer was an early target of post-war abuse. This jacket had taken on a different character since the days when it was a proud proclamation of one's upbringing. With the spread of uniforms to state-aided schools the blazer had acquired another role. Parents could not afford the luxury of a jacket reserved for light wear and it was called upon for daily duty, a purpose for which it was never intended. Complaints grew that blazers wore out too quickly. Fortunately the advent of man-made fibres led to experiments to impart their strength to flannel cloths without destroying the smooth cherished appearance of the garment. Not all the results were satisfactory in the early days, the hardness of the synthetics rubbed the soft wool and white streaks showed through. Meanwhile school outfitters endeavoured to remind the public that the life of the blazer must be limited if it was not treated with respect.

In the early post-war years there was a remarkable attempt by the British Colour Council to cut down the expense of official uniforms. Schools insistence on exclusive colours was a major cause of high prices entailing special dyes and money tied up in stock (not infrequently lost when a school changed its outfitter—or its mind—and turned to another shade). The aim of the BCC was to sponsor a series of guaranteed basic colours for woven cloths to which knitwear, hosiery, trimmings, accessories and so on could be matched or contrasted. After mammoth research by the BCC's Children's Wear Divisional Committee the shades were whittled down to 16. Given this foundation the mixing and matching would have provided an infinite choice of single or several combinations to meet the extreme wishes of schools all over the country. Despite the good reception these basic colours received they made no real impression. The idea that colour matching could be assured was welcomed by manufacturers to whom co-ordination of several materials and continuity of supplies was a constant worry. The producers found, however, that faced with a list of 16 colours from which to make their selection school heads spurned the thought of 'standard' shades. These, they considered, might be good enough for other schools, but their pupils must have uniforms in colours quite distinctive from any other establishments in however remote a part of the country. So one way of reducing prices petered out for lack of support.

It was the private schools in the main who insisted upon outlandish colours and mixtures for trimmings and accessories, the state-aided institutions had naturally to take a more practical view of classroom apparel. Modest grants assisted the less fortunate pupils to purchase minimum items of uniform but the money involved tended to fluctuate according to the economic situation. A clause in the Education Bill which came into force on April 1, 1945, raised the school-leaving age to fifteen and the same Act gave powers to Local Education Authorities to provide needy children with clothing and footwear. Devaluation of the pound hit, at the end of the 40s, help to needy parents. The Ministry of Education announced that expenditure by local authorities for the provision of uniform grants would not be recognised for aid. The decision brought such protests from local authorities and teachers who told the Ministry how important it was, especially for girls, that they should be able to conform with the rest of the pupils that the cuts were restored the following year and in subsequent years the grants had to keep pace with inflation. When more state-aided schools began to adopt uniforms the scope of the grants was enlarged.

The murmurings about the archaic attitude towards the correct attire for school began to get louder but teachers were adamant that there must be no deviations from their iron control, fashion had no place in the classroom. In the event they were proved right but it was not before the late 60s that a formula was finally found that suited both teachers and children. During the ensuing years, apart from the increasing fashion awareness of the girls—the boys were not so heavily involved—four factors were to force school wear out ot its hallowed position; the school head's right to dictate what should be worn was to be challenged by the parents through the Parent-Teacher Associations; the switch to comprehensive education; the development of man-made fibres which were to release school outfitting from its bondage of restricted colours and cloths; economic conditions.

Not surprisingly it was the senior girls who were the first to rebel and sixth-formers were allowed some freedom, striped instead of check cloths, for instance. Too much attention was paid to the grievances, adolescents always take a critical attitude and if it had not been uniforms it would have been something else. Many were the weird and wonderful methods put forward to send the senior girl to school clothed in her heart's desire but few had lasting value. Behind a great deal of the pressure to update school wear was the resentment at money being laid out on garments which could only be used for a specific purpose. Children on principle hated to wear their uniforms out of school hours and parents, too, disliked them doing so for fear they would get spoiled. As a result side by side with the desire to throw off the frumpish image of the average schoolchild came a call for dual-purpose articles which would not be immediately identifiable with the classroom. The speed of the progress towards liberation was slowed down by the rigid rules imposed by the purchase tax regulations which kept the exemptions to outdated cut and colour and helped to perpetuate the institutional picture of the schoolchild.

It was soon evident that the box-pleated navy blue serge tunic so completely associated with the British schoolgirl was going to be a war casualty. Instead skirts and tops, more flattering to developing figures, were to take its place. The tunic was not entirely ousted, a pinafore style was taken up, chiefly for the younger ones, the seniors favoured skirts and blouses. Skirts, too, were worn by the juniors, frequently with button-on tops for extra warmth in winter. This was the type of uniform which was wanted, it could quite easily be worn during out-of-school hours. Garments of this kind signalled the demise of the school crest which had previously had a prominent place on the tunic and this expensive embellishment faded away. Increased automation which meant that a number of badges could be machined at the same time increased production rate and cut costs but badges on tunics came to be regarded as luxuries.

Rationing and shortages of gym stockings had caused a switch to ankle socks in the early 40s but this was thought by headmistresses to be a temporary measure and one to be dropped as soon as conditions permitted and stockings could be made compulsory once more. The hose commonly used for school was full-fashioned lisle (not wool) in the extra long gym length but a considerable number of sub-teens wore three-quarter socks. When peace came girls would not give up their ankle socks and they became an accepted part of the uniform, fawn predominating for winter, white for summer. Not every article prescribed was extravagant. Machine-knitted wool gloves, inexpensive and able to take whatever punishment was meted out, figured in nearly every uniform list as a more practical alternative to elegant leathers.

Boys' outfits had gradually changed. Freedom, not fashion, was the dominant motif but their childish Eton-collar (euphemism for simple points) jerseys were giving way to V-neck pullovers and slipovers. The grey flannel suit was so widely worn as to have become a uniform in its own right. The aspect of both boys and girls was to be considerably enhanced by the wearing of crease-resisting washable ties. Interest in headwear fluctuated but never died right out. Velour hats for girls lost their exalted position although this headwear had a brief spell of popularity when brims got out of hand assuming dramatic tricorne lines, contrast petersham edged, heavy and dominating the uniform, and the face. Girls disliked big brims always hard to cope with on windy days and perhaps this is why there was a switch to skull caps but by far the most consistent millinery was the 'New Yorker'. As the name implies the origin of this headwear was American. Made in felt the crown of the hat was small and rounded and the narrow brim turned down all round. The official hatband sat very well on this headgear and there were few heads it did not suit, so much so that it had a lasting place in school life. The hat was copied in panama for the summer in the place of the old wide brimmed hat. The Breton and sailor with ribbon streamers and the boater were to be revived principally for the juniors, on seniors hats of any sort were to be discarded. For those who wished to lose no opportunity of identifying the school there was something entirely new, a swimming cap which combined two official colours.

By the late 50s the effects of the transition from single schools to huge comprehensives were being felt. Despite the belief held in certain quarters that the principle of official outfits would be discarded immediately the establishments were grouped into one unit heads carried on the uniform tradition looking upon it as a means of developing rapidly an *esprit de corps* essential with such vast intakes of pupils. In most cases the comprehensives did not adopt the uniform of any one unit in the group but devised their own. Starting from scratch they were not bound to perpetuate traditional oddities which time had outgrown and simplicity governed their thinking. It was noticeable that where official uniforms were not compulsory the majority of pupils chose to wear them. The pattern was clearly emerging, new pupils were keen to have their special outfit and wore it happily until they were about 13 then they started to rebel. Boys were not so concerned, for the most part they had a neat blazer, grey flannels, a nondescript shirt, black shoes, tie and cap and thought no more about it.

It was becoming increasingly apparent that girls were not going to be content with shapeless garments which observed the rules of freedom of movement and room for growth. The four-inch (10cm.) tolerance so well observed and monitored by heads was not, in the children's eyes, so necessary as good appearance. Dresses with bunchy waists and roomy bustlines were no longer acceptable, closer fitted lines were wanted and in tune with fashion they were to be achieved. More and more senior girls got open necks to their blouses and dresses. The tailored sleeve replaced the puff and the back ties gave way to stiffened belts. Knitted scarves with horizontal stripes were superseded by University style woven types with vertical striping, double the price but it did not stop girls from having them. (Mini scarves, less pretentious but incorporating official stripes, were being sported by wee pupils at nursery schools.)

The synthetics were making considerable inroads into the classroom both on their merit and combined with natural fibres. Whether because of their arrival or by coincidence there was a swing away from that traditional school material serge, to smoother finer textures such as barathea, able to stand up to term-time belabouring of desks and satchels and the wearability required was given by the strength of the man-made fibres allied to the wool yarns. Once it was discovered that nylon meant white socks that could be washed and dried overnight then the fawns and greys were relegated to a back place. Heavyweight nylons became the rule rather than the exception for stockings. Nylon macs with warm linings were to be adopted by the most conservative establishments instead of the gaberdine raincoat but the latter held up against this formidable rival.

Objections to the compulsory uniform snowballed and it began to be blamed for all manner of repressions and frustrations and complexes until a foreigner might easily have imagined that British youngsters were encased in strait jackets for the whole of their education. At the root of a lot of the hostility was concern over the cost which might, for example, be as much as £120 for a girl of eleven at a boarding school. The truth was that the bulk of the garments were hard-wearing and practical but their design had stagnated as clothing for school was regarded as a separate entity divorced from normal clothing requirements, a view wholly supported by head teachers. The critics were often women who had been boarders at exclusive academies where fetishes abounded and were honoured as evidence of the institution's aloofness from the common herd. Since design was at the heart of the matter the *haute couture*, amidst much ballyhoo, was called in to create fashionable ensembles for the classroom. The results were disastrous and one noted couturier must have wished he had never accepted the commission. The Press received his suggestions coldly but not so mothers, they were scathing in their comments to the newspapers. The designs, one for juniors and another for seniors, revealed an ignorance of the true nature of clothing for school and mothers immediately spotted that the outfits would be difficult to look after, were too elaborate, would not suit the average figure (not the pretty, well-shaped models on whom they were paraded) and, worst of all, they were styled on current trends which would quickly become outdated. One or two similar attempts to demonstrate what ought to be done served only to highlight the pitfalls of relating school wear to high-fashion, the repressions and complexes were forgotten and the industry and the schools were left to adapt to changed conditions in a less traumatic manner.

Those without a background of the realities of classroom life were apt to disregard the teacher's viewpoint. The prospect of being confronted with hundreds of girls attired in shocking pink, for instance, was enough to cause any teacher to take a jaundiced view of an artistic creation designed to improve the schoolgirl's lot. Life at boarding school had problems which had to be taken into account. Natty little ribbon or velvet trimmings might look smart and practical if they could be removed for washing but whoever could keep track of bits and bobs like that in the school laundry? Drip-dry finishes, popular though they were, had caused some headaches, all those blouses and frocks hanging up until they were dry posed a dilemma in the washroom. In making their selection headmistresses had to keep in mind not the good lookers with well-proportioned figures but the lumpy ones on whose fat arms, for example, cap sleeves would be disastrous. Three-quarter sleeves which copied the prevailing fashion and lasted for years had to be neatly finished so that they did not crumple up under the ubiquitous cardigan.

With school uniform so much in the news it was not surprising that it rated questions in the House. Members of Parliament tended to pay more regard to exaggerated Press reports than the facts and emotive terms like 'monopoly racket' made further headlines. In 1956 no less than seven MPs leapt to their feet in the House of Commons to question the Minister of Education and demand immediate Government action. The rumpus had been caused by an article on school uniforms in the BSI's *Consumer Report* inviting mothers to submit information on satisfactory and unsatisfactory purchases. Samples received were later exhibited. Unusual for the BSI the garments were not submitted for testing and complaints were taken at their face value, always dangerous where children are involved and in this case they were apparently all boys. Reference had also been made by the BSI to a large and welcome response but it transpired that out of a circulation of 20,000 only 135 letters (less than one per cent) were received some of which did not mention school uniforms and many were complimentary, supported the practice and had no complaints against type, price or quality. Nevertheless the BSI moves gained considerable publicity and, in fairness, so did the NCWA's reply which amongst other comments pointed out that no professional research organisation would attach the slightest importance to the Report.

Later that year another MP raised the matter in the House in a much more constructive fashion. The Labour MP who put the question, Mrs. Joyce Butler, did not oppose uniforms. On the contrary she brought some sound commonsense to bear upon the subject. She referred to the growing number of children attending secondary grammar and secondary modern schools who were being required to wear uniforms. This she described as an excellent thing because it prevented a snobbish approach to clothing by parents, provided neat and tidy garb and prevented any outlandish costumes as was sometimes the case where there were no regulations. Her complaint was that parents were forced at the dictate of the head, to buy from one particular shop. This monopoly meant that there was no incentive to be competitive. She had especially in mind members of co-operative societies who would prefer to patronise their own stores. She pointed out that a head teacher often chose an outfit of an unusual colour or type in order to make it distinct from other schools and this was understandable but added greatly to the cost of the uniform. Manufacturers, she said, would prefer to supply standard colours and materials. She felt that head teachers should be encouraged to keep uniforms simple and down to as few items as they possibly could but primarily she wanted the Minister to send a circular to Local Education Authorities requiring them to give greater freedom of choice as to where uniforms could be purchased.

In reply, Dennis Vosper, Parliamentary Secretary to the Minister of Education, confirmed that the wearing of school uniforms was on the increase and emphasised that the spread to secondary moderns did not stem from statutory requirements but was a natural growth. He then went on to say that with regard to the contention that uniforms of good quality should be available at a reasonable price, there was an absence of evidence to the contrary. There was a conspicuous lack of complaints on the subject. Parents, he said, were not slow to complain to their MPs or to the Minister but during his two years in office he had not received a single letter on the subject. He had himself been to a number of schools and asked specific questions on the subject and could find little evidence of a really serious problem. First, he said, do the schools themselves set too high or too expensive a standard? Secondly, do the manufacturers and retailers respond with satisfactory garments? He had found satisfactory and attractive uniforms particularly in girls' schools at very little additional cost because they would have had to be purchased in any case. He had been informed by the BSI that whilst manufacturers did not admit that there was any large volume of unsatisfactory garments they recognised that a minority of poor quality goods might prejudice the reputation of the trade. They thought that, in part, it might be because parents buy for appearance rather than durability. He ended by referring to work that was going on to try to produce a cloth that would meet the need.

It was blazer cloths which Dennis Vosper had in mind but it was to take many years of discussion and research before a British Standard was to be published for these materials. The object was to provide a general purpose standard in order to assist Education Authorities to specify and parents to buy blazers of adequate performance for school use. Despite the difficult dyeing processes required in the manufacture of coloured fabrics these were covered by the Standard (BS 3838) as well as black and navy blue woollen and blended woollen cloths. The qualifying tests for the Standard were severe, tensile strength, seam slippage, colour fastness to light and wet and dry rubbing, abrasion resistance, shade change after abrasion. The use of abrasion testing as an index of wearability marked the first time it had gained official recognition in a British Standard.

Up to the middle 60s the gulf between the school and the outside world had apparently hardly narrowed yet comparison with the past revealed that minor improvements had resulted in an overall effect of smartening up the British schoolgirl image. The check cottons for dresses were no longer sacrosanct but reflected something of fashion influence in the shape and size of the pattern and sported overchecks as well as plain pastel with white. Stylised prints, neatly symmetrical, had been welcomed as alternatives to customary ginghams and zephyrs but guaranteeing continuity was difficult. Stripes, always a part of the school dress world, were much bolder and broader and some daring teachers were allowing black on white. The battle of the hemline had been won and tunics,

*Designed to please senior school-girls, dropped hipline and plain neck, but such styles entailed many 'specials' to fit buxom growing girls.*

skirts and dresses had been shortened. Built-in permanent stiffness stopped turnback and peter pan collars from getting limp and crumpled.

The girls had their own ways of adapting to current trends: when the sloppy look was the rage they bought their official sweaters two sizes larger but in sharp contrast to the burning desire to do away with tradition girls clung to their school ties which they considered smart. Yet though the cry went up for change and Parent-Teacher Associations held lengthy examinations of the many samples submitted it was nearly always the clean, classic garments which were finally selected in preference to the artistic designs which were so clever on the drawing board but failed lamentably on the human form. Submitting samples which committee members could examine added to the costs but suppliers had found that it was better to let them see for themselves how a sketch would look made-up.

It was obvious that if uniforms were to be modernised suppliers were the only people with the experience to carry it through successfully. It was up to them to find a formula which would satisfy the schools, parents and the fashion-conscious children and yet provide apparel which would stand up to the tough school life. To do anything else would mean short-lived attire and a host of complaints. It was now understood that school wear could not keep pace with fashion unless parents were prepared to pay the expense of repeated revisions to satisfy passing whims. The trade had an unexpected ally. The swift acknowledment of the blessings that man-made fibres brought to the classroom had alerted the producers to the vast potential of the market and in exploiting it they introduced for the first time promotion of school wear on a national scale that no one manufacturer could afford. The fibre houses backed suppliers with lively, clever and informative publicity through every advertising channel and because of the expert handling of the subject invested prosaic garments with a crispness and polish never before achieved. They encouraged research into suitable colours and styles and brought them to the attention of the media. Of course they made mistakes, the art student gimmick, for instance, it sounded inspired to invite creations from swinging youngsters but the result was a collection of impractical gewgaws. They were on firmer ground with the experienced manufacturers

*Revised school tunic, in tartan 'Terylene' and wool worsted, a fabric which cut out washing problems and increased the choice of colours.*

and their support stimulated designers and gave them confidence to go outside their usual classic ranges. A new spirit entered this much maligned business and the results have stood the test of time.

The changes were not, of course, solely due to the influence of the man-made fibre houses. Already by the middle 60s the orthodox summer frock was being affected by the H-line and the shift which had penetrated the full-skirted stronghold. Plain neck, smooth line to the hips and pleated skirt, the H-line was the direct opposite of the orthodox dress, its drawback was the number of specials it entailed—every one cut by hand—necessary to fit the sleek line of the less than sleek schoolgirl figures. Confined at first to the seniors it heralded the skimmer which spread to the juniors and became in itself a classic for the up-to-elevens.

By reason of the colours and the crests, uniforms had always been co-ordinated but mix-and-match of high-fashion brought a new dimension and this, and double-duty, was made easier by the entry of synthetics. Matching of yarn for knitwear and woven and knitted cloths could be guaranteed and because of easy-care endless exciting colours could be adopted which could be worn outside the classroom without being immediately recognisable as uniform. The brighter shades were better suited to young people than the dark 'serviceable' tones, tunics, blazers and skirts in petrol blue instead of navy, jade green instead of bottle and for blouses and dresses a host of brilliant combinations hitherto out of the question, gold, flame, orange and lime, employed with discretion. Wool was not entirely driven out by the synthetics, its use was essential combined with man-made fibres for warmth and body. Some prep and public schools kept to pure wool maintaining that their special colours could only be obtained in this yarn. Later machine-washability gave wool knitwear a new life.

Schools were slowly allowing sixth-formers freedom to wear what they liked or laying down guidelines, skirt and blouse, for example, with some direction as to colour. Others added a tunic for the colder weather but incredibly a few nervous heads clung to the puff sleeve on dresses. The rigid rules about lace-up shoes for seniors went and any kind of casual footwear if practical was allowed, in black. No sooner had this concession been established than lace-up footwear came back for adults and the girls wanted lace-ups, somewhat to the heads' disapproval. The girls showed the same contrariness over their hose. Having insisted they be allowed to wear nylons instead of socks they elected to switch later to the former despised three-quarter white Continentals.

Boys, far into the 60s, were uninterested in the clothes they wore to school and even the senior boys did not complain except to insist that their trousers must be tapered. Knickers were still being sold for school but limited to the youngest boys. Three sizes only sufficed until by the end of the 60s the six-year-olds went to school in longs. Boys prep schols began to abandon the grey flannel suit in favour of sweaters with official colours or just polo neck jerseys and trousers which need not be confined to the classroom and that trademark of the British boy, the cap, lost its grip but was by no means entirely eliminated. The prep boys followed the seniors' lead and many turned away from belted d.b. raincoats. Straight, s.b. proofed raglans, anoraks and duffles filled wet weather requirements. Senior boys kept to black footwear but already the styles were identical with the men's. Conservative schools went on clinging to turn-ups but most went by the end of the 60s and jeans were recognised as qualifying for official uniform, but black trousers, jacket with badge and plain shirts were as far as some schools were prepared to go.

At the end of the 60s girls' uniforms if not swinging could no longer be described as frumpish. Waisted summer dresses had virtually disappeared. The skimmer went from strength to strength—mandarin collar, tailored sleeve, high yoke and straight fall to the hem and front fastening buttoned or zipped. Care was necessary here, the hoop ends craze for zips hit a snag, they were too great a temptation for boys to pull. Synthetics were superseding the time-honoured poplins, zephyrs and ginghams. Jackets, with or without school badge, teamed perfectly with skirts or tunics, the latter, indistinguishable from ordinary pinafore dresses, like the frocks were on skimmer lines with zipped neck fastening. Culotte dresses in whipcord and stretch jump suits and leotards were an enormous improvement over the old-time games wear but wrap-over skirts and shorts, in fact the whole gamut of school wear, had taken on a crispness and variety made possible by the easy-care good nature of man-made fibres. The

*The late 60s version of the school costume, blue whipcord worn over a yellow and green striped roll-neck blouse.*

'navy gab' was now trench coat styled in natural or synthetic fibres or a mixture, and quilted or interlined with detachable fleecy lining. Cloaks did not die out, they were not only back in fashion but coat or ankle-length were too useful for boarding schools where classes were in different buildings. Domestic science and cookery overalls became cover-ups with turtle necks, long sleeves and patch pockets, roomy and straight without waist definition. Almost all the Sunday-best extras were being dropped.

Uniforms altered and so did the structure of the industry. Economy was forcing manufacturers to take a long hard look at the school trade so overweighted by labour costs. Mergers were absorbing small firms into the realm of big business and the complex trade was coming under the eagle eyes of financial controllers. The expense of troublesome exclusive dyeing grew and continuity could no longer be guaranteed. As a result more and more companies concentrated on stock lines and standard colours. School heads had to temper their ideas to availability. Not that the choice was so small, one manufacturer carried over 500 fabrics for summer dresses alone.

As the garments improved the spotlight turned away from compulsory uniforms. Fees not fashion were occupying parents' minds and economic conditions proved more efficacious than publicity at pruning school regulation lists for as fees rose, clothing requirements fell.

# APPENDICES
# I Size Nomenclature

The mass-production of clothing for children brought with it one formidable problem which was to remain unsolved, that of size nomenclature. Generally manufacturers had evolved patterns which overcame the many difficulties of grading to suit the development stages from birth to 17 years and were providing garments which fitted the majority of the child population. What at first sight appeared to be the minor question of how to identify the sizes of those garments became a major stumbling block. Because of the tight knit nature of the trade the matter was looked upon as a whole rather than as in other sections such as women's wear a subject for individual treatment according to garment type. Retail buyers were largely responsible for all babies' and children's clothing and producers often made some articles of both outerwear and underwear. In women's clothing there was greater division and specialisation and stores would have one buyer for coats, another for dresses and so on. They were, therefore, inclined to be concerned only with the best sizing method for their own lines but the juvenile buyer saw her business as a complete entity and naturally wanted co-ordination throughout her stock. In this she was reflecting the wishes of her customers to whom the figures in their children's clothing were meaningless often having no relevance either to the dimensions of the garments nor the boys and girls or representing stages of growth.

Ideally the answer to the criticism expressed on every side would be to have a common symbol for all garments worn by a child at one time. Had the sights not been set so high in the beginning agreement in each section at a time might gradually have been possible from which a common symbol might eventually been derived. Why was there such a state of utter chaos over the size marking of children's wear? It had arisen simply because the provision of clothing for children had passed so swiftly from the hands of the mother and the dressmaker. The firms who had started to mass-produce boys' and girls' clothing had labelled their articles by whatever means suited their work. Often it was one actual measurement taken somewhere on the garment itself, sometimes it was just an arbitary set of numbers signifying the smallest the firm made up to the largest. This did not mean that they necessarily started from babies and went to the teens; they may have commenced at, say, the first school age of five and finished at 13 or 14 years—or 15 or 16. Largely the size range depended on the type of garment and the age group for which it was intended. Few producers immediately made through from infants to the teens, they started and ended where they liked, frequently introducing another size and sex according to the additions to, and growth of, the family of the head of the company.

It will be seen that the numbers on the garments from one firm going from one to eight might mean they covered approximately five to 12 years, but another supplier using the same digits would be catering for infants from three months to five years. Yet another would intend them for one to eight-year-olds and in some cases the explanation seemed to be that they were the only labels in the factory at the time!

There was no co-ordination within a company itself. A well-known hosiery manufacturer had five different size markings on his seven garment types:

*Child aged two years*

14ins. (36cms.) Vests (length)
12ins. (31cms.) Knickers (waist-crutch-waist)
12ins. (31cms.) Briefs (waist-crutch-waist)
30ins. (76cms.) Pyjamas (length)
22ins. (56cms.) Jumpers (chest)
22ins. (56cms.) Cardigans (chest)
20ins. (51cms.) T-shirts (chest)

If the mother of such a child had an older girl of seven years she would find that this daughter's knickers and briefs bore the number 14, the same as that on the vests for her two-year-old. The most common marking for knickers was 12-26, the old outside leg, but the same companies which used these figures sized their briefs with the petticoat or slip lengths so to the uninitiated children's briefs could be bought ten inches longer than the knickers, for some would carry the number 36.

There was no harmony between nightdresses and pyjamas, the former went in three-inch (8cms.) rises, the latter in two-inch (5cms.). Pyjamas could bear a number which denoted the overall length or the waist to ankle. Blouses were labelled from 20ins. (51cms.), in two-inch rises to correspond with the dress lengths, or 13, 14, 15, etc., or from 00-0, 1, 2, 3 and upwards. Frequently sleeve lengths on blouses varied considerably although the body size was the same. Much of the knitwear and some jackets and blazers would be labelled according to the body measurement of the child it was intended to fit but slacks, skirts and other items would combine a body measurement with a garment measurement, e.g. waist (body) and length (garment measurement). Many infants' items were keyed to the dress or coat lengths as chests and waists had no meaning and this was generally understood by the mothers, so much so that it was hoped at one point that it might be possible to bring all the older children's articles in line with this policy.

To some extent boys' wear had its own co-related nomenclature. For some years boys' outerwear had been marked with 'Leeds sizes', a term everyone in the trade understood. The nomenclature ran from 00000-15 and covered 1-20 years: by adding five the number could be converted to the approximate age but boys' underwear was not marked in this way and could be just as confusing as the girls'. The break between infants' and boys' marking was subject to the individual whim of the manufacturer or the wholesale distributor.

Surely an actual measurement should be the basis for the size marking? To start off with this was the most efficient for length, waist, outside leg and so on seemed straightforward but resulted in just as wide confusion. As detailed earlier, first some manufacturers gave the actual measurement of the garment itself; others gave the measurement of the body it was meant to fit. The result was that the retailer would have two garments both marked 36ins (91cms.) chest, one would represent the exact measurement of the garment and the other the size of the chest it was intended to fit and since tolerance was about 4ins. at that time, would measure 40ins. (101cms.) Then there was the way the measurement was taken. A coat length, for example, surely that was quite simple? On the contrary, length could mean front shoulder seam to hem; shoulder to hem at back; base of throat to hem, front; collar seam to hem at back; or just '*from that bone that sticks out at the back of the neck*' to hem.

It might be thought that once the different manufacturers' methods were memorised the difficulties were largely overcome but this was not so. Big changes were to come in this new industry, fashion arrived and with fashion came change and change meant new lengths for outer and underwear. Mostly manufacturers continued to put on the same numbers as they had always done although these soon had no relation to the garment measures. In some instances they were dramatically different, girls' knickers altered so much in cut that the old measurement, the outside leg, was so wildly different from any part of the garment that it became an arbitary figure, but nevertheless one of the most widely used and understood size symbols.

Two other factors prevented the achieving of a uniform mark throughout a child's wardrobe, type of material and type of garment. For certain articles good fit was essential, leaving on one side the British parents deplorable habit of buying to grow into, coats and dresses were expected to fit but not such items as underwear or nightwear. Since it was not so important to have a 2ins. (5cms.) rise, less sizes were made and both manufacturing and retailing costs were kept down. As for various materials, at the time the knitwear held pride of place. Here the elasticity of the fibre meant less sizes needed to be carried than for frocks or coats or clothes from woven cloths and when stretch arrived actual measurements of garments became irrelevant. Of one thing there was no doubt, the greater the success of the firm the greater its sales and the impact its method made on shopkeepers and the public.

It had always been the nomenclature which aroused the wrath of parents and distributors. If a child took, say a size 4 vest then every article he or she required should be similarly marked. As the child grew a larger size would be required, either 5 or possibly 6 and this would apply to all clothing requirements. That manufacturers should be incapable of devising such a logical means of indicating the sizes of their garments seemed incomprehensible to outsiders. Those who have on occasions entered into the controversy convinced that it was obstinacy, apathy or the narrow-mindedness of the trade which prevented a simple and easy solution soon found a subject so complex that there were very good reasons why it had not been resolved. Manufacturers do not mind what method is adopted to indicate the sizes of their products, they will put on whatever suits retailers, provided, of course, that these are the buyers whose orders make it worthwhile. The outstanding exception to this will be examined later. However, no manufacturer wishes to have several different methods of marking similar size garments going through the factory causing unncecessary work and the possibility of mistakes in despatch. Producers are as anxious as anyone to have a uniform method to which every one of their buyers would work, so are the wholesale distributors who would prefer not to have a variety of systems passing through their hands, but to neither of them is the matter so important as to the shopkeeper. The unfortunate retailer buying from many sources had to be familiar with every single size designation, train staff to understand the meaning and interpret it for the customer who might be shopping without the child or ordering through the post.

The first attempt to introduce a standard method of size marking was made by the trade journal, *The Children's Outfitter* (later *Junior Age*) in 1937 when it called retailers together to discuss the subject. As a result of this meeting a committee of distinguished retailers was formed under the Chairmanship of M. S. Pocock, Managing Director of The Treasure Cot Co. Ltd., to see whether size standardisation could be achieved. Twelve months later the Committee presented its suggested Size Chart as a Recommendation and asked for comment. In the majority of cases the chart gave one measurement, agreed as the most important, per garment and the articles which the Committee thought were of a size that the child would wear at any one stage of his or her development were keyed to that number. The Committee believed that it had gone at least some way to achieving the aim of a mother being able to quote one size symbol for all her child's clothing requirements. Since this was the first time that children's wear sizes had been co-ordinated in this way and the chart was the work of retailers of high-standing and long experience of school and fashion clothing it might have had some chance of success in standardising size nomenclature or at least forming a basis from which to work but it was April 1938 and the prospect of war hung heavy over the land. This was not the moment for bothering about labels, industry was more concerned with how long it would be possible to go on making anything at all.

The results of the beginning of the many attempts by the British Standards Institution to solve, with the aid of interested parties, the problem of the size nomenclature of children's clothing were published in 1949. They marked the start of a long, and occasionally bitter, controversy during which sometimes the BSI changed course, sometimes the manufacturers but always remaining at the receiving end of altered nomenclature or method were the distributors and the general public in whose name the work was done but who benefited not one iota from the conclusions reached. Retailers in particular had much cause for complaint; after being presented with the news that at last a solution to the sizing problem had been found, they realised in time that it was no remedy at all, a conclusion that a number of them arrived at once the system reached counter level. The big retail groups gave every backing to the BSI in an endeavour to simplify methods of marking which they knew annoyed the, and added to the work of, children's departments, until by the 70s some decided to go their own way.

Although in 1949 it was agreed that the sizing situation was chaotic and should be resolved as soon as possible, the British Standards Institution did not get wholehearted support for its efforts. There was good reason for this on the part of the manufacturers. The Government regulations controlling clothing were still in force and it was anticipated that standard size marking methods linked to body or garment measurements launched under the auspices of the BSI would be adopted for Schedule IG thus making them compulsory for utility. Hitherto the makers-up, through their representatives on committees dealing with various clothing categories, had negotiated with the Government on the basis of their own experience and knowledge of clothing needs. The producers had no wish to introduce a third party to those round-the-table discussions in the form of a Standard, the ramifications of which, once put into operation, might adversely affect their production.

Coat manufacturers were, and remained, vehemently opposed to anything which savoured of standardisation. Having the longest tradition of quality tailoring and jealously guarding their patterns and grading secrets they feared, as did others in totally unrelated industries, that 'standards' would result in their high quality articles being identified with lower-priced goods. To the argument that the British Standards would only lay down minimum measurements their reply was in such circumstances the minimum became the maximum. A further reason for the reluctance of manufacturers to co-operate with any body whose object was the introductions of a set of rules, however useful or praiseworthy they seemed to be, was the widespread suspicion that this was a step towards nationalisation of the clothing industry. The Socialist Government had announced its intention of setting-up Development Councils for a number of trades and it was feared that a Council of this nature would provide a central organisation which would be cognisant of the entire clothing industry, assessing its weaknesses and its strength so that nationalisation could be accomplished with ease. Added to this was the fact that the manufacturers themselves would be providing the money to run the Development Council through compulsory levies imposed by the Government. The Development Council for the Clothing Trade was in fact set up in October 1949 although '*it was not unanimously supported by both sides of the industry*', said Harold Wilson, then President of the Board of Trade, in a masterpiece of understatement when moving the Order in the House of Commons.

The children's wear trade felt more vulnerable to State control than any other section of the clothing trade. The utility scheme was seen by some as a means of providing the minimum clothing needs at minimum prices. Critics could point out that whatever may have been the intention originally this was no longer the case. Nevertheless there was a belief this was the right policy for children's clothing. Standardisation as a means of supplying the community with its requirements was much talked about and there were many determined advocates of standard clothes for children. Lewis John Edwards, Parliamentary Secretary to the Board of Trade, in April 1949 called for as much standardisation '*as is consistent with differing tastes*'. Standard apparel for boys and girls would be practical, severe and plain in cut, be devoid of ornamentation, would decently cover the wearer and give protection against the elements. The general public had had enough of wartime severity and treated with indifference any suggestion that their youngsters should be dressed in such a depressing manner but there were some powerful supporters of the strictly utilitarian approach which added fuel to the trade's belief that the future might bring even more State control.

There was one human factor which was also responsible for opposition to any idea of a national, easily understood method of indicating the size of a child's garment. Wholesale and retail buyers who had spent their lives in the industry and who regarded the complexity of the system as being one of the tricks of the trade were not unanimous in wishing to see any simplification. By reason of their long experience they alone were able to interpret the many marking methods with speed and accuracy and this earned them the respect of others and gave them greater authority. If a nomenclature were to be adopted which even junior sales personnel could immediately recognise and understand the knowledgeable buyers would lose their special qualifications.

It was against this background of fear and suspicion that the BSI launched its British Standard for Toddlers' and Girls' Underwear and Nightwear. This attempt by a BSI Committee to introduce a national Standard was described by its Chairman as '*representing the first step towards the unified classification of children's wear*'. It was not, worse, it held back any progress towards the achieving of a national system for many years. This was no reflection on the Committee or its Chairman, R. C. Lang, who was sincere in his conviction that the best possible solution had been devised for size marking toddlers' and girls' underwear and nightwear.

Introducing the system Mr. Lang said, 'It is hoped that in time all children's garments (with the exception of boots and shoes, socks and stockings, gloves and hats) will be incorporated under these British Standards so that the whole of a child's underwear and outerwear can be covered by one single size designation at each stage of its growth. Thus if a child could wear a BS3 vest it could also wear a BS3 raincoat. There is a great deal yet to be done before this goal can be reached and perhaps at this stage two vital facts should be clearly understood by all who are interested in helping to clarify the present mass of nomenclature which faces parents today in the buying of clothing for their children. Firstly, the sizing of children's garments is a science and its basis is the body of the child. This basis cannot be satisfactorily found in any one firm's size charts, and the only logical approach is an anthropometrical one. . . .

'Secondly, it must be emphasised that this is not an attempt to regiment sizes but to regiment nomenclature. Thus, although fewer sizes are needed for underwear and nightwear, we must face up to the exactitude of fit which outerwear has always offered to the public. This should not be bridled. If the present British Standard sizes for Toddlers' and Girls' Underwear and Nightwear (which are primarily based on height) are amplified to cover three fittings—let us call them, for example, slender, normal and plump—they will offer a framework within which every outerwear manufacturer could work. It would be an exceptional fitting or size which would fail to find its own pigeonhole in such a comprehensive framework. It is to the public that we, as a great industry owe a debt. Children's garments offer to bewildered parents a nomenclature that embraces age, heights, girths, numbers and letters. Between the varying garments of underwear and outerwear for the same child there is rarely a connecting link to aid the prospective customer. If by establishing standards we are aiding 20 million potential customers, and if by such standards we can aid retail selling staffs (overtaxed by inexpert junior assistants), surely the results are worthy of our united efforts?'

The closing sentence in Mr. Lang's statement is significant for two reasons: firstly, it was a plea to the trade to adopt the scheme for without the support of the major manufacturers and distributors he knew it could not succeed; and, secondly, it expressed the belief of the Committee that it only needed a 'united effort' to establish the Standard which had been adopted. Unhappily the method put forward failed in the one thing vital to its success—the nomenclature. The Committee was handicapped, apparently, as committees often are, in that the members had been working for many months on the problem. The members were so familiar with the new designation that it appeared to them to be clear and straightforward. To outsiders it was completely illogical, impossible to memorise and did just what it set out to avoid, add yet another collection of meaningless symbols to the children's sizes scene.

The Committee had agreed early in its deliberations to base the new system on the results which had been published of extensive research undertaken by the US Government which had entailed the measuring of 147,000 youngsters. The results appeared in '*Body Measurements of American Boys and Girls for Garment and Pattern Construction*'. Although it was understood that this report revealed a relationship between height and girth, twenty more years were to elapse before a system of sizing by height was to be introduced into the United Kingdom for children's clothing. It was found that in the case of girls for each height there were five different groups of measurements. These ranged from two termed 'slender' to two 'plumps' with the middle group as 'normal': it was the latter group that the BSI Committee took as the basis of its system. The decision to use the American findings as the foundation for the new method was due to the fact that eight years before the makers of 'Berlei' foundations had measured pupils at a school in the Home Counties and the results closely resembled those published by the Americans.

There was no complaint about the Committee's decision to use the American work as a basis for sizing clothing intended for British children and, in fact, at first there was hardly any criticism at all of the Standard measurements. It was understood that it was quite beyond the resources of the trade and the British Standards Institution to undertake a nation-wide survey of boys and girls from infancy to school-leavers. Without the aid of Government funds such a task was out of the question.

'*The general use of the sizes given in this Buyers' Guide will give mothers an easy road to shopping*,' said the BSI when launching the first 'official' sizing system. The Standard started at a child of 2ft. 7½ins. (80cms.), weighing 1st. 1lb. (5.8 kilos.) and finished at 5ft. 6ins. (1.68 metres), weighing 9st. 2lb. (58 kilos.). The approximate ages were given as 18 months to 12-16 years. The nomenclature ran:

BS03 02 01 1 2 3 4 5 6 7 8 9 10 11 12

and therein lay the cause of the failure of this scheme for such a nomenclature could not hope to succeed. The Standard started not at birth, not in fact at any truly nationally recognised stage of development but at 18 months with a BS03 mark which meant nothing at all except that it was three steps down from BS1, the latter, again, represented no clear-cut division, no universally accepted break in manufacture or selling. The sizes then continued rising until the limit of BS12 was reached.

When the draft proposals were first circulated in 1948 there had been misgivings on the part of the retailers that arbitary figures which conveyed no idea of the age, height or weight of the wearer would be of little use to the general public. From long experience shopkeepers knew that unless they gave in their press advertising or catalogues some indication of what the size marking meant in terms which parents could relate to their youngsters it would be no assistance whatever. Despite the evidence that age was no indication of size many retailers maintained, and continued to do so, that age was the most helpful information for the mother. The BSI Committee were too optimistic in believing their solution was the perfect answer and, if it were, in the length of time it would take for the system to be understood and practised by the public. Not so the retailers who from past experience knew the kind of questions that would be asked and misunderstandings likely to arise unless there was an obvious connection between their publicised size ranges and the children who would have to wear the garments.

Why was the nomenclature adopted and presented then as the solution? Two reasons were advanced, (1) the symbol put on the garment did not matter so long as all the clothes required by a child of that height or girth carried the same mark and (2) manufacturers of underwear and nightwear started their children's (as distinct from infants') ranges at approximately 3½ years. Having devised the method from that age upwards, making it No. 1, it was then decided that smaller sizes should be included and the device of inserting an 0 in front and working downwards was regarded as an obvious course. The fact that by so doing the trade and public were being given two different principles to memorise was never appreciated by the members of the Committee who, for the first reason stated above, felt the actual numbers were immaterial so long as everybody used them. This was a fair assumption, provided that the figures ran in a logical sequence. As it was instead of a straight run through of numbers which paralleled the child's growth shopkeepers and parents were expected to learn a system of sizing identification in which the smaller the baby the bigger the number until at 3½ years it went into reverse and became the bigger the number the bigger the child. That the Committee had misgivings was shown by the announcement that it recommended that until the BS nomenclature was widely known an identifying measurement of the garment as a temporary expedient should be included on the label thereby continuing the practice which its efforts had been geared to stop.

The members of the Committee, which included at that time representatives of interested trade associations covering manufacturing, wholesaling and retailing, believed that they had accomplished a *framework* within which the industry could work. Minimum measurement were laid down for each size but within this framework manufacturers could make to their own specifications, provided these exceeded the minimum measurements in every case. From the table of size steps the makers could select which were convenient to them, i.e. where their collections were composed of less sizes than the 15 listed they need only make those which conformed to their usual production and mark them accordingly. Although ample opportunity had been given by the early circulation of the draft for amendments to be made it was not until after the publication that some of the minimum measurements were found to be incorrect. The Board of Trade, who were behind the move for size standardisation, did not hesitate, as predicted, to incorporate the British Standard in Schedule IG3 thus making it compulsory for utility clothing. The Board's alacrity was ill-timed for the Standard had only been in force for a short period when the BSI announced that they were to issue amendments for children's knickers. (In an endeavour to avoid a similar situation when later the Committee dealing with infants' and girls' light outerwear started work the members fitted samples on children before deciding on the measurements. It was while this research was being undertaken that, for the first time, the BSI Committee stated publicly that due regard would be taken of the selling value of appropriate designations.)

Meanwhile Customs and Excise were being subject to considerable pressure to amend Notice No. 78A which covered 'Young Children's' garments because of the influence of the New Look which by now had affected girls' coat and dress lengths. Although working closely with the BSI the Customs never adopted the BS designation for the purposes of purchase tax, preferring to lay down exact measurements and the method of arriving at them.

Every effort was made by the BSI to publicise the chosen nomenclature and educate traders and the public in its use. Some of the ways they suggested shopkeepers could operate the scheme were a trifle impractical, for instance, the retaining of one garment of each type in stock to provide a yardstick for new deliveries. No retailer was prepared to tie up money in a complete collection of non-saleable stock merely to serve as a marker. Nor were they disposed to agree with the proposal that they should go to the expense of installing weighing machines. It was difficult enough to persuade unwilling youngsters to try-on garments let alone mount a weighing machine as well. Despite the promotion the method received it never attained widespread acceptance. Underwear and nightwear manufacturers loyally backed it, printing special charts to help sales staff and the public to understand the meaning of the tables but they found even after several years that the marking could not be easily related to the size of the garment without reference to the charts. The most damning evidence of the failure of the BS size nomenclature was given by a member of the Committee responsible for its creation. After the system had been operating in his own works for years he could not himself say which size, height or girth the symbols represented without consulting the tables. Producers of some other garments also took up the scheme but with no success. The vast majority of manufacturers waited to see if it would be followed, found it was not and simply ignored it.

Early in 1953 the BSI staged a conference on garment sizing at which all sections of the clothing trade were represented. It was agreed then that any system should be based on body measurements but that each division of the trade must decide what the garments themselves should measure. To this end Sub-Committees were formed and one, a children's wear sub-committee, put forward at a second BSI conference, two proposals for altering the then current nomenclature which by this time had been extended to BS05-12 to cover six and 12 months and to include light outerwear. One of the proposals was adopted, that BS05-12 should be scrapped and replaced by a straight run from 00 and 0, followed by 1-15. (The Conference decided it did not want there to be any association with the age of the wearer and this sentiment the BSI ever after held sacrosanct.)

The usual practice was followed of circulating the proposals in draft form to interested bodies. It was at this stage that the trade associations, who were fully in accord with the necessity for a standard sizing method, decided that having watched the efforts to impose a system from outside, if yet another scheme was to be advanced their manufacturer members would want some assurance that it would have the support of the distributors and that it must be based on the most successful current trade practice, namely, two-inch rises for coats and dresses involving 16 sizes. The BSI plan introduced 17 steps for the same group of children which meant more stock to be held by the retailer and costlier garments for the public since the makers had to cope with extra sizes entailing shorter runs for each and added labour charges. To maintain that a producer need not make all 17 sizes was good in theory but not in practice; so far as dresses and coats were concerned a manufacturer could not elect to drop one or two 'steps' out of 17 and leave a gap in his range. The only way the number of sizes could be reduced would be for adjustments to be made in the measurements throughout to give even fittings for the whole age group.

Strongest advocate of basing any sizing system on trade practice was the National Children's Wear Association, the body with members in supply and distribution. At meetings called by the BSI in 1955 in response to proposals put forward then it was agreed that the body measurements should be reviewed to see if they could be adjusted from 17 to 16 sizes. In this event the garment measurements laid down in the original Standard would also have to be examined to ascertain what alterations were necessary. Nothing, however, appeared to have happened and there the matter rested for two years. In 1957 fresh interest was aroused by the appointment by the BSI of a Technical Officer whose duties included being secretary to the garment sizing committee. This officer was to concentrate on labelling of textiles, including sizing, and, therefore, to investigate the children's clothing aspect. In the interim the Drapers' Chamber of Trade had decided to find out from its own members stocking children's clothing in every part of the country what was considered to be the best method of identifying garment sizes, understood by retail buyers, sales staff and the public, what interval between sizes was preferred and retail experience of the Standard. The replies to the questionnaire the DCT sent out showed an overwhelming majority in favour of a symbol that was an actual measurement in inches either of body or garment. Far down the list came a symbol which was simply an identifying letter or number and way below this, age only. Almost all the replies wanted regular intervals, two-inch rises, between garment sizes throughout the range. Asked to comment on the BSI Standard a large majority said they had had no experience, or too little, to express an opinion, others found it confusing, muddled and difficult to understand and by some it was actively disliked. It was easy to see why shops wanted a measurement in inches either of body or garment. Apart from what appeared to be on the surface a simple method of identification it was the best one for sales staff to check.

Once the BSI called its Sub-Committee to meetings again it was apparent that the work had to be started afresh from the beginning. The scale of body measurements had to be realigned to provide for 16 instead of 17 steps to meet the wishes of the trade, agreement would have to be sought as to the garment measurements to which these body sizes would be linked, and what, if any, actual garment measurements would be shown on the size labels. Now that the system might be based on the dress and coat practice of two-inch rises by garment length this posed problems for knitwear producers whose main interest lay in the girth, i.e. chest. The difficulty here was in reconciling the smaller number of sizes made in knitwear to cater for the same age group as those wearing the dresses and coats. This raised another point, namely, the most essential measurement would differ according to the garment. In dresses and coats it would be length but this meant nothing in knitted outerwear where getting the fit right over the chest was vital. Even this was not straightforward since it was proposed that jumpers, blouses, jackets and blazers were to be put together in one category and marked 'body chest measurement' whereas for the smallest sizes there was a strong body of opinion that they should be indicated by the dress length measurement as being more helpful. It was usual for two or three lengths to be provided for the same fitting as the chest measurement was not of importance for the tinies and this freedom retailers wished to retain. Whether chest or length was the crucial measurement for vests was the subject of much discussion and then there were skirts, should these be marked with the waist and the length, or as was common, bear the equivalent dress size which was more convenient for the little ones who had no waists? What to do about waist petticoats, should these show the waist, length or length of dress? Length seemed to be right for nightdresses and dressing-gowns but there were shorties now on the market, should they have the length of the garment itself or the length it would have been if it had been full-length?—not so silly a suggestion as it may seem as putting on the actual size of the shortie conveyed nothing to the mother. Take pyjamas, would parents rather be told the chest or length?—which would help them most to get the right pair to fit their daughters?—and so it went on.

Manufacturers and distributors worked hard behind the scenes on knotty problems such as these and tried to reach agreement amongst themselves. By this time the 00's had faded away and an orderly sequence of 1-16 was forming the basis of the nomenclature. The BSI further complicated the situation by expressing the view that some provision should be made for figure types falling outside the 'average' body measurements and proposed they should be covered by 'broad' or 'chubby' scales but few manufacturers were interested in this. It meant doubling the number of sizes, always an uneconomic move. The only alternative would be to specialise in these categories but makers were not convinced that the sales would justify such a course, and they, together with the distributors, were of the opinion that with the variation in pattern cutting and 'specials' most children could be fitted satisfactorily.

What was becoming increasingly apparent in the discussions was that it was easy to reach perfect agreement and understanding on a sizing system for coats and dresses, i.e. length, which was equally familiar to mothers, but the problems presented by identifying the sizes of other garments by a single motif were insoluble. They were, therefore, being put aside. The result was that all that was being achieved after years of work was the addition of a symbol to the already established practice of indicating the size of a dress or coat by its actual length measurement. The bogy of 'standard' garments continued to be raised for the public would regard the body measurements as the standard size range for children whereas it was only a collection of average body measurements. It was believed, too, that the public would suffer since it would no longer get the variation in cut which enabled the different figure developments to be catered for over a wide range of patterns, something no maker could do economically on his own. Despite the fact that distributors were in agreement with putting a garment measurement on the label opposition came from the makers, who, whilst appreciating the assistance this would give shopkeepers, felt it could make no allowance for fashion changes and might involve them, vis-à-vis the retailers and their customers, in some disputes. Measurements, manufacturers believed, should be confined to the specifications for Standards and not be incorporated as part of the nomenclature, or they should be body sizes only.

Gradually some progress was made. The stature steps had been reduced to conform with the trade practice of 16 instead of 17 sizes and agreement had been reached that the nomenclature should commence at (1) for a stature of 29ins. (74cms.) to (16) for 66ins. (168cms.) (coat sizes 14-44ins. (36-111cms.)) but there remained the vital issues which must be decided if the various sizing systems were to be co-ordinated into a national nomenclature. These were:

1. whether to include one or more actual measurements of the garment on the label
2. if so, which measurements were to be given
3. whether to include the 'traditional' measurement which had no relation to any part of the garment but was nationally understood, as in the case of knickers
4. how to key all the different articles of clothing worn by a child to a common symbol.

It will be seen that the first three points involved moving away from the idea of one symbol for all garments and by using these means of identification instead of the body, the markings would become out of date with every turn of fashion. Worse, to follow the third suggestion would mean perpetuating a custom which the BSI, the public and most of the trade wanted to abolish. The fourth point, the *raison d'être* of the whole scheme, was proving difficult because of the differing number of sizes required in each group of clothing, for example, 10 knitwear and only 7 knicker sizes to be related to 16 coat lengths.

It was at this stage, 10 years after the publication of the first British Standard for Toddlers' and Girls' Underwear and Nightwear, that the blow fell. A co-ordinating size schedule had been prepared by a retail organisation and circulated by the BSI to interested bodies. It listed infants' and girls' light clothing, suggested their identifying measurement(s) and grouped them under their appropriate size symbol. The result was impressive and it seemed at first sight that at last the goal had been reached of one mark for every article of clothing a child would wear. To the National Children's Wear Association, however, whose members were experienced in making and selling fashion and school wear, the schedule proved conclusively not that it could be done but that it could not. Further it convinced the members that only a complete reversal of the approach to nomenclature would be successful. The basis should not be an endeavour to create a uniform size symbol for a child of a given weight and stature but for a uniform size symbol for garments in any one category.

The view of the NCWA was that the public wanted not so much the co-ordination of every article of clothing under one symbol but that the method of marking the size should be the same for all garments in any one group and be easy to understand and remember. The Association's case against the common mark throughout was compelling. The advocates of such a symbol had forgotten one important point, children do not develop in an orderly fashion increasing their stature and expanding their girth in the right statistical proportions so a size 8 type for coats might need a No. 9 skirt and a No. 7 sweater. Moreover, if the nomenclature were to be related to all children's clothing requirements, because fewer steps were sufficient for some clothing than for others, three different numbers could go on articles of the same size. The co-ordinating size schedule which had been circulated showed on close examination that a mother might purchase for her daughter knickers marked 12-13-14/28½ but when she wanted a jumper should she ask for a 12/32, or the 13-14/34?—and the skirt to go with it, should this be 12-13/24 or 14/26?

The many examples of the overlapping which would occur as a result of attempting to co-ordinate ranges of varying dimensions convinced the NCWA that to proceed further along these lines would not resolve the situation but only result in a size marking system that would be unworkable and confuse the consumer. The NCWA proposed that the current methods of size marking, range of sizes and identifying measurement(s) where they existed, be investigated and on this information it would be possible to get rid of out-of-date methods, decide on the most important measurement for each category of garment and adopt this as the nomenclature. Other trade associations supported the NCWA and it was agreed that the size numbers 1-16 would serve no purpose and should be dropped. Experience with the British Standard for children's clothing had shown anyway that such symbols were not universally adopted. Of first importance was the reduction of the multiplicity of methods of marking various garments which appeared to be an attainable goal. Because of the broad acceptance of the identifying measurements for each type of garment and the urgent need to simplify the sizing situation it was decided by the BSI that the NCWA's proposals, after they had been submitted in draft form to the other organisations concerned for approval, should be issued as *'Recommendations on the Size Marking of Infants' and Girls' Wear'*.

This was done in January 1960 in the form of two Tables with an explanatory foreword giving the background to the conclusions reached. Table 1 was divided into the type of garment, the identifying measurement to indicate size, and the range of sizes; Table 2 gave the stature steps numbered from 1-16 on which the Committee had based its findings.

So another official BS system was presented to the trade—and the vision of a mother purchasing a complete wardrobe for her child by quoting one number remained just a dream. Nevertheless the Recommendations (not, of course, a British Standard) were regarded as a step in the right direction but in reality hardly anything had been accomplished. Instead of a unification of size nomenclature the Recommendations continued the practices of different sections of the trade and gave them official approval, viz:

1. Girth measurement, in inches, of the *body* the garment was meant to fit (but not the actual measurement of the garment)
2. Length in inches—the nominal length of the garment, possibly close to its actual length, as in dresses and coats
3. Length in inches—the length the garment would be if it were worn full-length, e.g. shortie pyjamas, nightdresses and dressing-gowns and jeans
4. An arbitary number linked with a measurement long since discarded.

Complicated as (2) and (3) appeared since the measurements in inches would not necessarily correspond to any part of the garment being purchased they could nevertheless be related at some point to the child, e.g. a shoulder to hem measurement on a shortie nightgown would be some guide to the height of the wearer. No. 4 represented the greatest defeat for it perpetuated the custom which had prompted the moves to abolish irrelevant size symbols which had no reference to girth, height or any part of the garment. The Committee had been forced to recommend such a method in the case of knickers. The size was to be indicated in the time-honoured way as it was generally known and understood, by the old outside leg measurement abandoned long ago when bloomer legs were shortened. This measurement remained to indicate size although it bore no relation to the current outside leg of the garment. Try as they would to find a formula, waist-crutch-waist, waist, actual outside leg, measurement to the crutch when the garment was folded in half, and so on, the Committee could not arrive at a more satisfactory, foolproof way of identifying the knicker size than keeping to an outside leg length which no longer existed.

It was hoped that the very latest date for goods supplied to the shops marked according to the Recommendations would be autumn 1960 when a campaign would be undertaken to explain the 'simplified system' to the public. No such campaign ever took place simply because the Recommendations were so ineffectual. Some of the big stores supported the scheme faithfully but it made no real difference to the bulk of the producers and distributors and it is doubtful if the public ever heard of its existence. When the Recommendations were introduced the statement was made that height was the best indication of a child's size but this was not pursued until years later when one manufacturer, certain that only a major upheaval could bring about a satisfactory solution of this complex problem and with enough strength to carry it through, decided that height was, indeed, the only answer.

In the intervening period the size marking of children's clothes remained a controversial topic with the people most concerned willing to listen to any suggestions for reducing the multiplicity of the symbols or for devising a better way to acquaint the customer with the dimensions of the garments but no concrete progress was made. The BSI Recommendations continued to be applied by their loyal supporters but to such little effect that they had joined the other labels as being yet another system which had to be learnt.

It was not until 1965 that it looked as though the breakthrough had come. It seemed to begin with a retrograde step for the basis was age, dismissed on more than one occasion as unreliable but used extensively by chain stores as the best guide for their customers as well as by a number of makers. However, since the company concerned, Sharp Perrin & Co. Ltd., was a leading specialist distributor greatly respected in the trade and with a long experience of children's clothing, their views commanded attention. For three months the firm had been co-ordinating the size marking methods of garments handled by all their departments, a total no less than 130 labels for 55 garment types and this did not take into account items they manufactured themselves nor the baby linen which they felt was well-established and should not be interfered with. The starting point had been for the company's buyers to decide, on the score of their experience, which garments in their departments were meant to fit every age up to 14 years, then the results were co-related to the garments handled by other sections. This entailed marrying the various methods employed by their suppliers covering the whole gamut of actual and abstract measurements, girths and heights, in just the same way as the BSI Committees had tried to do so long ago. There were, however, two essential differences in that this firm was working with garments which flowed through their hands daily so that continual checking was possible and the symbol adopted, that of age, chosen because it was the one thing every mother knew about her child, was firmly fixed in their minds as the cornerstone of the method. They were, in effect, only attempting to put down on paper what they were doing the year round, selling articles to fit children up to 14 years. The fact that it took three months to accomplish the task showed how difficult it was despite the advantages the company had.

The results of the investigations were published in chart form as an easy guide for sales girls. The chart was divided into three separate groups, outerwear measured by length, outerwear measured by girth and underwear and nightwear. Complete as it was it left out several garments for older girls where changes of fashion made an age-size relation impracticable. To start with the labels were to carry one identifying measurement until such time as the system became so familiar to everyone that it could be dropped. It seemed as though this firm had set a pattern for the country which might one day solve the sizing problem or at least go a long way towards it, but a few months later another company exploded the old ideas by announcing that height alone was the answer and they proposed to convert to this immediately.

This statement would have had scant interest had it not been made by Pasolds Ltd., the biggest children's wear producer in the country, in fact in Europe, and one which had established a universally recognised brand name, 'Ladybird', and a reputation for advanced ideas and promotion. The decision to sweep aside past custom was prompted by retailers' complaints and because they themselves were irritated by the unsatisfactory nature of marking the garments produced in their own factories. Above all they wanted to make it easier for consumers. Hitherto they had put age on their labels to indicate size but they had come to the conclusion that this could no longer be regarded as a permanent solution. The alternative of garment measurements had no validity due to the spreading influence of fashion and, of more immediate importance, the entirely new factor of stretch fabrics. In their search for a more efficient system the company had been looking at the way it was done abroad with the possibility that Britain would eventually join the Common Market well in mind. It seemed that the countries which had adopted height were on the right lines. Sweden had devised a height system (with different fittings to provide for girth variation) and Switzerland had introduced a simpler version which was running smoothly. Examining the methods of other countries was helpful as a guide but although it would have been useful for their export trade to follow the same figures the size steps had to be adjusted to allow for British stature and, too, the Continent worked on the metric system and in 1965 metrication was still a long way ahead. The intervals between the height steps had to be carefully planned, based on a child's growth. To cover this the Pasold steps for infants were in two-inch rises for 1, 1½, 2, 3 and 4 years going from a stature of 32ins. to 40ins. (81cms. to 101cms.). After that the steps rose by 5ins. (12.7cms.) (corresponding approximately to the Swiss intervals) from 45-65ins. (114-165cms.) for ages 6, 8, 10, 12 and 14.

Baby wear could not be gauged in this way so the obvious solution was weight (already found to be working well for baby garments in stretch fabrics) and to provide for from one to 12 months the steps went from 8, 13, 18, 21 and 24lbs. (3.6, 5.8, 8.2, 9.5 and 10.8 kilos.): at the overlap of 12 months both weight and height were to be shown on the label. An extensive list of garments was included under the five-inch rises but this was too large a jump for others and extra sizes at 2½ins. (6cms.) gaps were fitted into the scale. Straightforward reference to height made no allowance for variations in girth. This was expected to be met by the child taking the size above or below depending on whether he or she was slim or chubby. In any case no manufacturer could hope to produce in a factory a big enough range to fit precisely every child's figure.

The nomenclature entailed a radical alteration to the labels going on the garments leaving the 'Ladybird' factories but not to the actual patterns and grading but the upheaval was an expensive process. It was admitted that whilst a mother might be fully cognisant of her baby's weight during the first twelve months it was unlikely that she would know an older child's height with any accuracy. The system was dependent on the child getting the right size by its height so to avoid the shopkeeper getting involved with *'She's-nearly-as-big-as-me-and-a-lot-taller-than-our-Jane'* hardly helpful estimates they had ready for retailers 'top to toe' wall measures against which the youngster's height could be checked in feet and inches and the nearest height step seen at a glance. It was envisaged that if the mother was shopping without the child but had made a note at home of his or her height it would be much easier to get a garment of the correct size than if she only had age as the guide. To this end the firm offered to provide a paper version of the height measure—and received 60,000 applications.

If the scheme were to succeed it was imperative that it must be clearly understood at the outset so the company circulated a colourful explanatory brochure to its retail outlets. Pasolds had the means at hand to let consumers know what was happening, booklets illustrating their products were circulated regularly to one-and-a-half million customers, an unrivalled medium for keeping the public informed. The mass media, home and overseas, gave the new system a good coverage finding at last a newsworthy story on this controversial subject. With so much to recommend it competitors and chain stores might have been expected to take up the height principle with alacrity but they were wary of yet another solution to the age-old problem and one, moreover, which involved the outlay of a considerable amount of money and disorganisation until it was established, if indeed it ever was. It was, therefore, left to Pasolds to go it alone whilst everyone else waited to see what would happen but there was admiration for the firm's courage in taking so drastic a step when they were not bound to do anything but perpetuate the antiquated haphazard ways.

Not everyone was enthusiastic particularly those who

disliked change on principle and the BSI were obviously chagrined at the company going ahead without reference to its own organisation. It had been obvious from the start that the BSI did not command the support required to instigate a new sizing system. This was partly due to the trade's reluctance to work with an outside organisation possessing only a theoretical understanding of the matter and partly to the presence at meetings of lay representatives whose ignorance of production and distribution problems was a disadvantage. For example, when stretch brought increased confusion over marking of hosiery, The Textile Distributors Association approached the National Hosiery Manufacturers' Federation and together they compiled a table of sizes and measurements, got the approval of every trade organisation likely to be affected and main chain stores and publicised them with sufficient notice for the system to be put into operation in an orderly manner. Women's as well as children's hosiery was covered and the linking of sock to shoe sizes was the agreed basis for both. It was appreciated that shoe size marking varied but not so significantly as to render the scheme unworkable. Both infants' and children's hose were included, from 0 to 13½ and 1-7½. The way to measure the socks correctly was laid down and traders were advised not to include ages and verbal definitions such as small, medium and large, as such additional information served no useful purpose and only *'confused and detracted from the critical criteria'*. The list of sizes showed clearly how the number had been reduced by the introduction of man-made fibres, for non-stretch hosiery there were 14 for babies' to teens', for stretch there were six, less than half to fit the same age group.

Pasolds were so large a concern not only in terms of output but in retail outlets due to their 'Ladybird' sections within shops, main stockist scheme and their own shops, although the latter were few in number, that they were able to launch their height method without delay at all levels. Other producers, especially those with a thriving export trade, or like Mothercare the specialist retail chain who intended to open branches on the Continent, saw it worked and switched over to height. Simultaneously in Europe more countries were following the lead of Sweden and Switzerland and adopting height marking.

Pasolds' bombshell could not be ignored by the BSI nor

could the growing evidence that its effect was spreading. The BSI's work had presumably reached an impasse since no public pronouncements had been made for some while but soon came a statement that a reappraisal of the situation was to be undertaken. Four years after Pasolds launched sizing by height in the UK, the BSI circulated to interested parties draft proposals for a revised nomenclature for children's wear, infant boys and girls and girls over five years. To begin with it seemed that the proposals would be generally acceptable since they linked age, height and weight. It soon transpired, however, that there was a deep cleavage of opinion between one organisation, the NCWA, and the BSI itself. The Association was insistent that if a fundamental change of this nature were to have any chance of success it must be related to some symbol which the public readily understood, in their opinion this was age, the most quoted item of information according to retailers. The NCWA was adamant that age must head any table of measurements and be mandatory on labelling until the height system was well-established but the BSI was strongly opposed to its use. It was generally accepted that age was unsatisfactory as a basis for size marking children's clothes and the Association was not proposing it should be continued indefinitely. What the NCWA was concerned with was the co-ordination of nomenclature and a method which would help the public and the trade alike without introducing another hard to follow series of figures and symbols. The BSI Recommendations put height at the top of the table of body measurements, then weight, then approximate age. Unfortunately the height figures, 36, 38, 40 and so on, were already in wide use on coats and dresses and had been for fifty years, but not for two- or three-year-olds, etc., as on the BSI table but for the sub-teens and teens. One referred to the total height of the child and the other number to the length of the child's garment following the universally established two-inch rise practise. It was this similarity which, in the opinion of the NCWA, would create havoc and confusion. If, however, the approximate age was moved to the top of the list, and made mandatory on labels, for a bridging period, the possibility of misinterpretation would be considerably reduced. This age figure could also serve as a size number which would at least have some significance. There was no quarrel with the Recommendations in general which had been agreed after lengthy discussions. The body measurements, numbering 21, starting from a three-month-old infant and ending at 14-15 years with obvious omissions at the baby stages, were accepted as were the height steps. Even more important was the agreement over the way groups of garments should be labelled, i.e. size/weight, size/height, or size/weight/body, waist measurement, etc., which had been such a stumbling block in the past but the argument about the importance of age as an interim size symbol dragged on and publication of the British Standard was postponed.

Impatient at the delay, several powerful retail groups and chain stores notified their suppliers that they were switching to height related systems and the manufacturers had no alternative but to follow suit without waiting for the BSI. It lent weight to the NCWA's argument that the stores intended to retain age as a symbol until the public was familiar with the meaning of the height procedure. Although height was the method now being adopted by more and more firms the result was by no means a uniform system for the country as a whole as each concern had adapted the size steps or overlapping groupings in the light of their experience. Since all had started off from Pasolds' conclusions the discrepancies were minor compared with the overall acceptance of the height principle. principle.

The whole issue was getting away from the BSI and the NCWA were so incensed at the unsatisfactory state of affairs that they seriously considered promoting their own sizing system. At length, at the end of 1970, BS3728 1970 was published officially with age as the size number at the top of the table, linked to height and weight. Height may be the right premise on which to found a size marking system for children's apparel. What is certain is that no method has a chance of success unless it has the full support of the industry itself and is based on a nomenclature easily understood in the factory, in the shop and, primarily, by the public. No method can ever be perfect which seeks to fit inanimate objects to the human body through every stage of child development and appease a mother's pride which will admit to her offspring being *'big for his age'* but never smaller than average.

# II Purchase Tax

Fashion came creeping in and the purchase tax picture of a child and his clothing splintered. The weary exercise of interpreting Parliament's wishes in regard to tax-free clothing troubled continuously both Customs and Excise and the traders. The problem was two-fold, (1) to keep pace with sizes, styles and types of garments and (2) prevent evasion: it was not always the authorities who were the most vigilant in the latter respect. Makers and wholesalers who observed the law, and were subject to regular visits by tax inspectors, were ever ready to call attention to malefactors who, by devious methods, exceeded the measurements or, by calling taxed garments different names, were able to sell at lower prices. Consultations, involving as they did detailed examination of each garment or measurement, took an inordinate amount of time and the adjustments when they were published were always irritatingly tardy.

From the advent of purchase tax the general public never grasped the fact that it was the iron hand of Government which controlled part of the price they paid for their school-children's clothing and maintained a strong suspicion that shops were to blame. It was not hard to understand this point of view, it was not until the middle 50s, for instance, that a slight relaxation in the rigid definitions of tax-free school blouses was published so that the tuck-in type was allowed as well as elastic or tape-threaded waists which the girls regarded as childish and disliked because they tended to pop up over the tops of the skirts. If the blouses were darted, however, to fit neatly round the waist then they were taxed. Two years were to pass before the school blouse exemption was extended to include darts at the waist. It was only at the stage when tuck-in blouses were exempted that the clause specifying that school blouses to qualify for exemption must be made from cotton, wool or spun rayon, was lifted, thus opening the door for nylon and other synthetic fibres—far behind the public's recognition of their aptitude for school wear.

The restrictions included other details as well, no bust shaping, for example, yet the Government's own statistics revealed that the height and weight of the average child had increased and girls were maturing earlier, and in 1959 the first bra for 10-year-olds was marketed in Britain. No stunt this, it had been introduced because of the number of enquiries for a lightweight support for 10-15-year-olds. (The imposition of tax had thrown up the difference in weight and stature of schoolchildren, at the other end of the age scale a similar trend had been noted, the first size in babies' pram coats had been 14ins. (36cms.). This was too small and 16 and 18ins. (41 and 46cms.) had become the starting sizes.)

How could the shopkeeper convey to a mother that the Government had laid down that her baby's gloves were only exempt from tax if they were made within the meaning of the Act, i.e. that they were mitts *'measuring not more than two inches from the finger end of the palm side to an imaginary line crossing the article where the thumb joins the palm'*, that if the children's gloves she bought in a shop were not knitted nor crocheted by hand the Government would collect five per cent of their value?

The Government had imposed on Customs and Excise the role of fashion arbiter, but what had appeared right and proper in the war days of the 40s had become archaic and meaningless. The ruling that loose jackets were not suitable for young girls remained in force until 1956 when Customs at last acknowledged that they had become part of the attire of the average girl and entitled to tax exemption and at the same time provision was made for swagger coats and opera top petticoats (that modest variation on the rounded neckline). They agreed, too, that children's hats sold with matching coats should be free of tax, the cessation of the utility scheme having drawn these back into the tax net.

Customs and Excise were in the position of the Dutch boy with his finger firmly in the dyke wall watching fresh holes appearing right, left and centre. The monotony of blue for a boy, pink for a girl, was being broken by the inclusion of lemon, to such a marked degree that Customs and Excise were asked to add it to carrying shawls exempted from tax, and so they did—ten years later in 1965, dropping at the same time the stipulation regarding material and make but not size. Babies' headwear and gloves had the rare distinction of being included in the Chancellor of the Exchequer's Budget Speech in 1955 when R. A. Butler told MPs, no doubt agog with excitement, that these commodities would be exempt from the purchase tax which they had borne for 15 years. What he did not tell the House was that the headwear was only for babies with head circumference not exceeding 20ins. Nor was this the sole criterion, colour and material would come in for scrutiny and caps with stiff peaks, or sou'westers were definitely out. The limits imposed on the gloves, which were not gloves at all but infantees, mittens or mitts ('*Children up to two years*', said Customs, '*do not wear gloves with split fingers*') were just as stringent even to the extent of a caution that the thickness of the material, fur fabric, for instance, could make a difference to the measurement. It was a pity these salient facts were omitted from the Chancellor's speech, it would have given the economic situation a new twist.

The older the girl the shorter the skirt and this had settled down about the knee in 1961. Inevitably Customs stepped in and lopped two inches off the tax-free maximum for coats, dresses, skirts and petticoats but not from regulation raincoats nor gym tunics and they did make additional allowances for lumber jackets and shortie coats and surprisingly increased the tax-free chest measurement for boys' jackets to provide for the draped look the lads were wearing.

The farcical rulings on babies' headwear continued with manufacturers and distributors having to cope with tax-free maximums which did not exceed '*13½ins. (34cms.) face measurement from tie to tie*'. The exemption for babies' gloves and mitts was replaced by a clause allowing gloves suitable only for young children's wear to be tax-free provided they conformed to intricate maximum measurements. It was officially recognised that it was not unreasonable that 'opaque' tights might be worn by girls, and these were dealt with. Previously they were exempt from tax only if they were suitable for children up to ten. It did not end there, of course, for fashion had moved on from plain tights and stretchable stockings and for the latter the exemption was widened to include other than simple 1/1 rib but any fancy work must still be in straight ribs. A few weeks later Customs gave in and extended the definition to include patterned tights, by now universally worn by girls of all ages.

The Government through its agents, Customs and Excise, clamped down firmly on the girls' yearning for pretty underwear. Knickers, panties and briefs to be tax-free must, they said, be in plain styles, simple colours and non-decorative, they could not have lace inserts nor panels. The severity of this must have shocked even the C & E for they added primly, *'The presence of lace edging up to ¾ins. (2cms.) width even if in contrasting colour is not regarded as taking the garment out of the plain category'*. The puritanical ruling was the outcome of stretch fabrics. Women's panties were mere bikinis, far smaller than the girls were wearing and as such were coming well within the maximum tax-free measurements. In this Gilbertian situation schoolgirls' briefs were bigger and tax-free and the women's smaller and taxed, so a few months later the measurements were reviewed, altered and Customs admitted that it was no longer possible to rely on size or style as a means of defining children's clothing. This acquiescence led to the unprecedented step of conditions being imposed on packaging and presentation. The use of stretch for shorts and trews forced reductions in the tax-free measurements, worse hipsters had arrived and by 1962 kiddies wanted them but Customs ruled that they were outside the scope of the young children's exemptions. Hipsters were taxed in all sizes just because they fitted slightly below the natural waist. The children's versions were only a mild acknowledgment of fashion, you cannot have low hipsters when there are no waists nor hips but the authorities disapproved until 1966 when they capitulated and acknowledged that these trews could have a place in a girl's wardrobe. The fashion roundabout had turned and certain low-heeled shoes for girls above size 3 had let in some women's so Customs insisted on four eyelets for laced shoes—and no tax-free gussets.

Paris raised hems to above the knee at the beginning of 1965 and put Customs and Excise into a fresh dilemma, to raise the 38ins. (96cms.) for dresses would penalise children who not only needed this length but wore their clothes longer than women, on the other hand to do nothing would result in tax-evasion and already women were being told that this was one of the side-effects of the short skirts. A compromise in the autumn left the length as it was but imposed a maximum tax-free measurement of 36ins. (91cms.) chest, dresses must not be sold as this, if marked above 32ins. (81cms.) chest they must carry the tax—girls' dresses were sold by length. The object of this was to provide for the tolerance required for school frocks. As abuses grew the inevitable outcome was the imposing of an additional restriction. In 1966 a chest measurement was laid down for full-length coats, raincoats and macs, except for some duffle coats (in one colour, for instance) and 'Regulation' school raincoats. This was another example of the Government penalising any move towards bringing children's clothing up-to-date for 'Regulation' was defined as *'double-breasted, belted and with turndown collar'* which effectively clamped down on any deviations from the long-standing 'navy gab'. It was particularly disheartening as for several years the older girls had been switching to a raglan in place of the belted style. The single-breasted, straight raincoat was not a gimmicky flash-in-the-pan but a classic example of restrained good taste and a flatterer for it was much kinder to puppy fat figures than the belted type which was becoming identified with younger children, who, incidentally, followed the seniors in fashion showerproofs which were almost entirely single-breasted. It was ironic that when the d.b. navy gab was being given preferential treatment as a non-fashion garment, French girls were crossing the Channel to buy this authentic British raincoat solely because it was more fashionable than anything they could buy in their own country and even after paying the fare was cheaper.

It was only a matter of time, of course, before the outerwear lengths had to be reduced as women's mini skirts reached the ultimate and the Government struggled vainly to honour the children's wear exemption and prevent evasion and there *was* widespread abuse by the end of the 60s. Abbreviated skirts and the domination of stretch materials were making a nonsense of the regulations. When the economy was bad there was always a call to tighten up on purchase tax evasion and a noticeable hardening towards any approaches to help parents of school children. Unfortunately in the late 60s the Treasury was so ill-advised as to announce that all leather or suede garments would be taxed unless suitable for boys and girls up to 10, and they went further and ruled that it would apply to simulated leather. Plastics with the leather look were being worn extensively by boys and girls of every age. The materials were virtually indestructible and inexpensive. There was a storm of protest that materials should be singled out in this way when they did not come in the luxury class. A Purchase Tax Action Committee was formed by the trade and there were signs that not only was this ruling to be questioned but the legality of Customs and Excise role in interpreting Parliament's meaning of 'young children's garments'. Within a few weeks the ruling was rescinded and the *status quo* restored, i.e. exemption would depend on the style and character of individual garments according to the size limits and other requirements as already laid down.

Thirty years of purchase tax regulations record the gradual breakdown of the schoolchild image so fixed in everyone's mind when the tax was first imposed.

# III Nightdresses

How Parliament came to pass legislation interfering with the parents' right to buy the clothing of their choice for their children was the outcome of a campaign prompted by the altruistic motives of public-spirited individuals and a national daily newspaper.

In the autumn of 1955 an MP, Mrs. Jean Mann, wrote a Report on 'Dangers in the Home' for the Royal Society for the Prevention of Accidents. The Report dealt with the causes of many accidents to children in the home but it was the number of cases of girls being burned through their clothing catching fire that received the widest publicity and led to a campaign which eventually forced Parliament to introduce a series of laws affecting nightwear. Mrs. Mann's Report aroused widespread public interest but it was a Dr. and Mrs. Leonard Colebrook who in 1949 first revealed the dangers of inflammable nightdresses. The couple published a Report based on a three-year study of 1,000 patients with burns and scalds at the Medical Research Council Burns Unit of Birmingham Accident Hospital which disclosed that inflammable clothing could be the cause of death or injury to children. This was almost entirely a British hazard caused by dependence on open fire heating.

In her Report, Mrs. Mann in expressing her horror at the statistics she had obtained, advocated in the absence of a material which would have the necessary non-inflammable qualities, the substitution of pyjamas for nightdresses. With an MP involved it was no wonder that legislation would be the end result. There were already in being by-laws which laid down that it was an offence not to have a fireguard where there were young children but this was a perfect example of a law impossible to administer since it could not be policed. With the advent of other forms of heating, guards had gone out of fashion and who could be so heartless as to haul up before the Courts the parents of a child burned, perhaps fatally, because of a fall into an unguarded fire? Nor, of course, did the presence of a guard give foolproof protection. Even if it were locked in place a child could still clamber up and fall over the top of the guard, then if non-woollen clothing, or a mixture of cotton and wool, was being worn it could burst into flames.

Mrs. Mann was evidently fully aware of the problems of developing a cloth which would be non-inflammable yet have all the properties essential for young children's clothing, not least that its price would not be prohibitive. Research had been conducted along these lines for some time but it was not confined to nightwear fabrics. Tragic cases of girls getting burned when they were wearing their beloved frilly net party dresses had made the public aware of the dangers of full skirts and unguarded flames and before the Report was published 'Flare Free' nylon net was on the market. An extensive advertising campaign was launched in the autumn, just when mothers would be looking for special occasion dresses, and commanded attention with a dramatic photograph of a child in a full-skirted party frock leaning over a Christmas tree aglow with candles to reach a present. The makers could claim for this breakthrough that this nylon net could not flare, there was no difference in the colours nor the variety, durable pleating was not affected and at no extra cost. Predictably the net met with instant success to the exclusion of the untreated kind, for women no less than children, but it was in the latter field that it was greeted with the greatest relief and gratitude. By 1957 a spokesman for the British Man-Made Fibres Federation could claim '*There is no inflammable net being produced in Britain*'.

Soon the outcome of investigations into anti-flame finishes for other textiles was to be available to the general public. Already in use for industrial garments, 'Proban', a non-inflammable process, was to be marketed for many types of materials with the greatest emphasis on nightwear. Nightdresses in non-inflammable materials did not repeat the success story of the party nets. It was impossible to distinguish the latter from untreated nets but this was not so with processed cloths such as flannelette. The tragic accidents which could be traced to children being burned when nightdresses flared up were not sufficient to overcome the resistance to the proofed materials. This was almost wholly due to the handle of the cloth. In going through the non-inflammable process the fabric lost the soft feel long associated with nightwear and acquired a stiffness which mothers believed would rub the skin. The safety element, substantial price reductions and powerful propaganda failed to move parents who thought, of course, that they took such great care of their boys and girls that they would never come to any harm—it would always be someone else's child.

In 1957 a Committee of the BSI set up to consider the inflammability rating of clothing textiles recommended the adoption of pyjamas instead of nightdresses for children but the public had already indicated that it intended to go on putting girls into nightdresses. The Committee had dismissed the proposal that fabrics should be labelled at point of sale with their degree of inflammability as this might cause extra danger by giving false confidence. The Committee urged that public attention should be drawn to the special fire risk involved in the wearing of long, loose-fitting clothing but it was clear that in the face of public reaction so far and the extent of the problem there was nothing that could be done at that stage except to bring home to parents their responsibilities. At the end of 1958 the Home Office stepped in and launched a 'Guard That Fire' campaign urging the public to have proper guards on their fires. The Home Secretary himself, R. A. Butler, launched the campaign with a broadcast on the BBC and all bodies, local authorities, Gas and Electricity Boards, co-operated in stressing that heating equipment must have adequate guards.

In the spring of 1959 came a British Standard for textiles for which some degree of flame-resistance was claimed (a low flammability fabric) measured against a special BS test. Government backing was given by regulations which made it an offence to offer for sale fabrics or garments claimed to be flameproof, or to possess any degree of flame-resistance, unless they complied with the Standard. Stocks of non-inflammable nightwear, meanwhile, piled up in shops and notwithstanding further slashing price reductions stayed there. Price was a factor and talk of *'a shilling or two extra'* was misleading, even a leading chain store with a reputation for keen pricing had to charge 50 per cent more for their small size nightwear than for untreated garments. In 1961 British Nylon Spinners Ltd. launched their 'Safer from Fire' labelling campaign which was to have a tremendous effect. Firstly, nightwear in the scheme did not have a special finish and the soft handle was unaffected, flame-resistance was inherent in the fibre which melted when directly in contact with a flame but did not burst into flames. Secondly, there was no extra charge. Since no processes were involved it might be asked why a labelling scheme at all? The reason was that some makers-up might put on inflammable trimmings, appliqués and so on and use inflammable sewing threads. The greatest hazard, it was agreed, lay in below-the-elbow trimmings on sleeves and on the skirt. By imposing their conditions and tests the company could ensure that garments carrying their label would not flare up.

In 1963 Courtaulds Ltd. announced that the flameproof fibre on which they had been working for many years would be sold under the name 'Teklan'. Nightwear made of cloths from the fibre would be marketed at the end of that year. Courtaulds were also to promote extensively another fibre in the future, 'Celon' for children's non-flare nightwear.

Further efforts to bring home to the public its responsibilities were made in the same year when RoSPA with the support of the Parliamentary Home Safety Group, the BSI and other organisations, staged a two-day 'Buy for Safety' exhibition in the House of Commons. Following this, posters and leaflets on the theme were distributed to various bodies. Among the exhibits was a dressing-gown made from a cotton knitted fabric with a non-inflammable finish, the first breakthrough in a material of this kind, a cloth of immense importance for children's dressing-gowns. The aim of the show, it was said, was retail and consumer education. The former, however, had nothing to learn. Despite their endeavours to promote non-inflammable garments and cloths shops had irrefutable evidence in unsold stocks of consumer resistance to the processed materials. Nevertheless large multiple store groups refused to buy any children's night-dresses made from inflammable materials and some manufacturers stopped production. It was now up to the public but nothing it seemed would persuade it to buy the non-inflammable processed variety.

Shops were scathing about the processed materials, deeply critical of the patterns which were even described as 'hideous'. It appeared that once the non-inflammable process had been perfected it had been assumed that nothing else would matter. To the producers the patterns were a mere detail but they were not to mothers who refused to buy nightgowns printed with designs that offended them.

By 1964 it was evident that the prolonged campaign against inflammable nightwear, conducted with dramatic television coverage and sustained newspaper reports, had failed. The media tried to shock and frighten parents with harrowing stories and there would be a flurry of enquiries for a few days then these would die down and no appreciable increase in sales recorded. Always attention was focussed on the garments never on those careless enough to leave tiny children alone with unguarded fires *'for a few seconds'*. Among the public figures who pontificated on the subject were extremists who wanted a ban on everything, party dresses, home furnishings and so on, in case they should catch fire, but not one of them had the courage to stand up and tell the truth that less than 60 children died in one year from burning accidents *not necessarily due to their nightwear* but more than 800 boys and girls under 15 years of age were killed on the roads and the number was mounting. The same newspaper which initiated and plugged the 'ban on nightdresses' call put accounts of accidents to children through their clothes catching fire prominently on their front pages but buried the gruesome toll of the slaughter of the children at the back of the paper. Killing the children in their hundreds was an acceptable price to pay to keep motor cars rolling on their merry way—but nightdresses were to be banned. Banned, that is, except for one loophole which the agitators could not close. In the privacy of their homes mothers could make nightdresses from any material they wished, and they did, preferring the simplicity of the pattern to the extra work and skill entailed in pyjamas.

Responding to the clamour for action the Home Office proceeded to draw-up unique legislation. When draft regulations were circulated in April 1964 they caused a furore. What appeared to the layman to be a straightforward axeing of a product was going to have serious repercussions which must be prevented. The protests from trade bodies poured in, and at last received publicity, principally on two scores, (1) that nightgowns for new-born babies had been included and (2) no alternative supplies were available and could not be for some time. The inclusion of baby nightgowns in the ban unless they were of non-inflammable materials, had come as a shock. The authors of the proposed laws appeared to have lost all sense of proportion and failed to realise the importance of the information which experienced manufacturers and distributors of children's clothing had given them. Immobile, new-born babies did not require protection from fire hazards and there had never been any suggestion that babies up to 18 months were at risk. One reason advanced for the ban was that someone attending a committee meeting at the Home Office had said that a gown might catch fire when the mother was feeding her baby and smoking!

Trade representatives believed they had convinced the Home Office that it was neither necessary, nor desirable, that there should be any interference with nightgowns for babies up to 18 months. This was no biased objection based on self-preservation it was purely in the interests of the child. Chief protester was the National Children's Wear Association who immediately raised, in telling detail, the consequences which must follow. From their specialised knowledge the members of the Association asked whether any tests had been made of the effect on new-born babies of chemically treated fabrics. Whose responsibility would it be if any babies developed skin troubles as a result of the Government's decree? Only 12 washes were necessary to pass the test on which the draft Order was founded, a wholly inadequate number the NCWA insisted for babies' nightgowns especially for which daily washing was the rule rather than the exception. Would the chemical process withstand repeated washing through one child's requirements and on to the next when it was handed down? (It was estimated that a child's garment was washed at least 50 times during its life.) Behind this question was the fear that mothers might be lulled into a sense of false security and traders were only too familiar with the hasty carelessness with which much clothing was washed. If properly handled the processed cloths were recognised as satisfactory.

Another aspect which roused vehement protests was on the timing which revealed that the civil servants had not undertaken sufficient research into the availability of supplies: it was, after all, part of their job to ensure that the public would be able to obtain the articles which the Government was decreeing they should buy. The draft Order laid down that the ban on babies' and children's nightgowns, unless they were of non-inflammable material, would come into effect on September 1, 1964, at all stages of manufacture and distribution—to be replaced with what? At that moment except for one or two manufacturers who were experimenting with samples there were no alternative garments for babies. There were a few nightgowns in man-made fibre materials but these had not been found to be the answer for first sizes, for in mothers' estimation they were not warm enough, nor absorbent enough, for the early months. Aware of this, the fibre houses were launching a cloth with a better absorbent handle but this would not answer some mothers' aversion to putting synthetic materials next to a baby's skin. The amount of flame-resistant processed cloth coming through was a mere trickle compared with the country's requirements. The situation for the consumer was worsened by the predictable reaction of retailers who stopped buying babies' nightgowns immediately the Government's proposals were published.

It is to the credit of the officials at the Home Office that they accepted that the criticisms of their suggested legislation were justified. They must have regretted that they had paid more attention to the advice of laymen than they had to the trade's warnings of the repercussions which would result from the proposed measures. The next Draft removed gowns suitable for new-born babies from the restrictions but evaded the issue of defining the size which set off another controversy. At first sight it seemed that the top end of the scale covering girls' nightdresses would be clear-cut and a maximum length had been stipulated. This had led to an outcry from women's interests as it would take in most of the shortie nightdresses then in vogue. The second Draft had therefore reduced the length to 46ins. (116cms.) with a chest width of 38ins. (96cms.) but if the garment was small and could be shown to be unsuitable for a child then it would not be affected by the ban.

The further the authorities pursued the matter so the complications mounted: it was the old purchase tax story over again. There were second thoughts about labelling. Chemically processed materials had to be washed in detergent, soap or soap powders would cause deterioration in the flame resistance. It had been pointed out that mothers might not appreciate the significance of this proviso nor even be capable of distinguishing between detergent and soap powders. There was no onus on washing powder makers to state on their packets the nature of the contents, e.g. whether they contained soap or a bleaching agent. Evidently impressed by the force of this claim the Home Office solution was to decide that *all* children's nightdresses should carry a warning against the use of soap or soap powders. This upset the man-made fibre houses, they certainly did not want the public warned against washing their products in soap, or indeed warnings of any kind since flame-resistance was built-in to the fibre itself. The laundering provisions, including two that stated that nightdresses in chemically processed materials must not be boiled, nor bleached, could be on a removable ticket until a date to be announced later. This was regarded as a dangerous procedure. It was argued that tickets once taken off the garments would get lost and the instructions forgotten. The reason for the delay was to allow time for labels to be printed.

It was as well that the Draft proposals were circulated for comment prior to them coming before Parliament for when the Bill was presented alterations had been made which went some way to meet the critics. The ban was to come into operation one month later than originally intended, i.e. October 1, 1964: the clause covering labelling applied now only to chemically processed fabrics not to synthetic fibre cloths; after April 1, 1965, washing warning labels must be stitched into the nightdresses. Nightdresses for export were excluded from the regulations. Parliament passed the Bill, The Children's Nightdresses Regulations 1964, under the Consumer Protection Act, and it became an offence to sell or offer for sale children's nightdresses which failed to comply with prescribed low-flammability ratings. Penalties for any infringement of the Act were severe. It fell to the lot of the local authorities to enforce the legislation and only authorised laboratories would be permitted to carry out tests. The Home Secretary gave notice that it was only the limited production capacity of low flammability cloths which had confined the laws to nightdresses, it was his intention to consider applying them to other garments, but he reminded parents that fireguards were the best means of preventing burning accidents to children.

In the summer of 1966 it was announced that the Home Secretary had accepted the Recommendations of the Working Party set up in May 1965 to consider the possibility of extending the scope of The Children's Nightdresses Regulations 1964. Apart from decisions on women's nightdresses the Home Secretary announced that he had decided to restrict the exemption of infants' gowns to those with a chest measurement not exceeding 21ins. (53cms.). This would confine the exemption to nightgowns which could not be worn once the child was mobile. Two concessions had been made to the points put forward by the industry (1) it was admitted that there was no evidence to show that babies in the cot stage had been victims of burning accidents and (2) the reluctance of mothers to put newly-born babies into chemically-treated articles was acknowledged. It was proposed that garments made from fabrics subjected to a chemical process would have to bear a label warning against washing with soap or soap powder, boiling or bleaching. The revised law, The Nightdresses (Safety) Regulations 1967 came into operation on September 1, 1967 revoking and replacing the 1966 Act.

It was inevitable that the range of flame-resistant cloths would increase as research into man-made fibres and chemical processes achieved the qualities of softness and easy washing the public required. Dressing-gowns no less than nightdresses had been occupying the minds of manufacturers who had been searching for materials with the right qualities.

The most widely worn dressing-gown was still the cotton nap velour, a cosy inexpensive garment which provided warmth at the right price but after publicity in the national Press that it was not flare-free, shops started to take it out of stock. A natural reaction on the part of the retailers but fears were expressed that the impression would then be given, by implication, that other gowns were non-inflammable which was not the case. Responsible manufacturers began voluntarily to insert labels reminding the public that such garments should be kept away from fire although in not one case of death or injury had the cause been proved to be due to a dressing-gown catching fire.

Some unease was also felt that with quilted dressing-gowns there was a risk that separately the outer and lining materials might be flame-resistant but when assembled the fire hazard might be increased and any labelling in these circumstances might be misleading. The Working Party was to take action about this matter later. Enormous technical problems had to be overcome in perfecting a non-wool raised surface material which would possess the kind handle and warmth required for dressing-gowns of the non-quilted type, yet would not flare-up. After many years of research which included amongst the more weighty problems the ability to take dyes in acceptable colours, the outcome was a synthetic fibre which could be used for fabrics with a raised, brushed surface of the kind which would appeal to mothers and which passed the stringent tests of the British Standard for flameproof fabrics.

Although agreeing that dressing-gowns were not a frequent cause of burns the Working Party on Flammable Clothing nevertheless considered that steps should be taken to eliminate those gowns in quilted assemblies which, they considered, were beyond doubt excessively inflammable and at the end of 1968 decided to recommend that the voluntary co-operation of the trade should be sought to ensure that children's dressing-gowns of the more inflammable kinds were not made, imported or sold in the UK. Tests had confirmed that dressing-gowns made from certain quilted assemblies burnt so rapidly that they presented a very serious hazard if worn by children in '*households where common-sense precautions such as guarding open fires may not always be taken*'. Three different groups of fabrics or assemblies of fabrics covering a wide range of synthetics and untreated cotton were detailed as not suitable for use but it was emphasised that the Working Party was influenced by their burning behaviour solely as composite fabrics and not by the performance of any single fabric. Nor did their recommendations have any relevance to the use of individual component materials for clothing or for other purposes or in other combinations. Legislation was not sought to give the Recommendations the force of law, whether they were operated was the decision of individual manufacturers and distributors.

# Anoraks

Of the garments adapted for youngsters in the post-war period none was so universally accepted at every level of society as the anorak. Giving protection against wind and rain its basic design varied little over the years, merely passing through plain and patterned cloths as fashion dictated. It would have been difficult to find one family in the country which did not possess an anorak and it was a shocking blow when it transpired that this innocuous garment could present a danger to the wearer. Tragically it emerged that in one year, 1968, four children had died as a result of strangulation by the cords in the hoods of their anoraks. In three cases the cords, or the toggles on the ends, had become trapped in the slides on which the children were playing, in the fourth, the hood itself had caught on barbed wire on the top of a garden fence. Ironically it was because the cords used were so strong that the deaths had resulted, cheaper varieties would have snapped under strain.

The anorak makers and the Home Office were quick to act, the former by immediately altering the design of the hoods, eliminating cords and toggles and substituting elastic, and the Home Office by consulting trade associations and issuing recommendations:

1. draw cords should preferably not be used in anorak hoods and should be eliminated by the adoption of such devices as elasticated face-pieces or button-up type throat tabs

2. if cords *are* used, they should not have toggles or acorns on the ends and the breaking strain of the cords should not exceed 10 to 12lbs.

There were two snags in issuing recommendations of this kind, a tremendous number of anoraks were imported and might slip through the net and after the initial publicity the matter would be forgotten and/or newcomers might not be aware of the situation. This proved to be the case and the following year the Home Office felt it was necessary to issue a reminder and request that the recommendations should be observed. (Subsequently it was decided that the recommendations should have the force of law.)

# Riding Hats

That the perils of horse riding might be increased through unsatisfactory headwear led the British Standards Institution and the Pony Club to investigate the possibilities of ensuring that riding hats should give maximum protection.

In common with the post-war tendency to discard pre-war customs the rigid rules for the correct attire for riding were being broken, a movement helped by the influx of newcomers to this sport. Roll neck sweater and jeans were being substituted for hacking jacket and jodhpurs typifying to the traditionalists a horrifying 'cowboy' approach. To mothers, jeans were the perfect riding wear for girls and boys, impervious to rough handling and washable and as copies of the authentic cowboy's rig were manly enough to please the boys. Jodhpurs were not to disappear, they adapted: the bagginess was to decrease as the years went by and they fined down to long clean lines and figure hugging flattery.

Generally there was no frivolity about headgear for this sport. Sensible riders wore blocked jockey caps but there had been growing criticism that the button on top could be harmful in the event of a tumble. The best makers stitched in the button (it covered the ventilation hole) but others screwed it on to a circle of metal over the hole and this screw could be pushed into the head if the rider fell heaviliy. It was this aspect of the cap which alarmed the Pony Club and the BSI and at the end of 1963 a British Standard, Protective Hats for Horse and Pony Riders (BS3686), was published. This laid down the requirements for construction and strength which must be met, one of which was that there should be no screws, nor rigid projections which could injure the wearer's head in the event of a fall. All the conditions for qualifying for the 'Kite' mark were justifiably stringent and included the compulsory provision of a chin-strap.

# IV Government Investigation into Distributors' Margins

The cost of children's clothing has always been a bone of contention. Parents have an ingrained belief that it is somehow wrong to get a profit from making garments for children. The fact that the manufacturers and retailers have to meet similar overheads as adult clothing producers, plus the heavier charges for more skilled labour, is ignored. From time to time when the economy is bad and families are finding it difficult to manage, someone, usually an MP with an eye to the headlines, starts complaining about the price of children's clothing, quoting the amount of cloth required, the rate at which a garment leaves a factory and its price in the shops compared with men's and women's apparel. Such examples take no cognisance of the difference between gross and net margins which may vary between the type of retail outlet and service offered and rate of turnover and which on examination reveal that the actual margin between profit and loss is a fine one.

In 1968 when the Labour Government's Prices and Incomes Board was trying to peg prices, Barbara Castle, the then First Secretary of State for Employment and Productivity, announced that distributors' margins on children's clothing, among other things, were to be examined by the National Board for Prices and Incomes and sizes from infants to teens, boys' and girls', and all forms of distribution would be covered. It was one of the best things that could have happened. After a thorough investigation into the major forms of retailing, independent shops, smaller multiple stores, co-operative societies (4 per cent of sales), large national multiple stores (approximately 35 per cent) department stores (10 per cent), direct to the public (mail order firms 10 per cent) the Board's conclusion was that competitive forces were in general sufficient to preclude excessive margins and no recommendation with regard to margins was called for from the Board.

School uniforms had also received the attention of the Board due to reported dissatisfaction over their price, blamed on the excessive margins charged by shopkeepers. The Board's enquiries established that the complaints were not borne out. Far from the profits being excessive, retailers often regarded school business as unprofitable and the low stockturn a disadvantage.

The conclusions were a disappointment to the critics who had expected that investigations would disclose that parents were being held to ransom over tiny garments being sold at exorbitant prices, many times their value. That school uniforms should be considered as an unprofitable nuisance rather than a means of fleecing the public was even harder to bear.

# Index